MATERIAL TEXTS IN EARLY MODERN ENGLAND

What was a book in early modern England? By combining book history, bibliography and literary criticism, *Material Texts in Early Modern England* explores how sixteenth- and seventeenth-century books were stranger, richer things than scholars have imagined. Adam Smyth examines important aspects of bibliographical culture which have been under-examined by critics: the cutting up of books as a form of careful reading; book destruction and its relation to canon formation; the prevalence of printed errors and the literary richness of mistakes; and the recycling of older texts in the bodies of new books, as printed waste. How did authors, including Herbert, Jonson, Milton, Nashe and Cavendish, respond to this sense of the book as patched, transient, flawed and palimpsestic? *Material Texts in Early Modern England* recovers these traits and practices, and so crucially revises our sense of what a book was, and what a book might be.

ADAM SMYTH is Professor of English Literature and the History of the Book at Balliol College, the University of Oxford. He is the author of, among other things, *Autobiography in Early Modern England* (Cambridge 2010) and *Profit and Delight: Printed Miscellanies in England, 1640–82* (2004); the editor of *A History of English Autobiography* (Cambridge 2016); and the co-editor, with Gill Partington, of *Book Destruction from the Medieval to the Contemporary* (2014). He has published widely on the literary and bibliographical cultures of early modern England. He writes regularly for the *London Review of Books*.

MATERIAL TEXTS IN EARLY MODERN ENGLAND

ADAM SMYTH

Balliol College, Oxford

CAMBRIDGE
UNIVERSITY PRESS

University Printing House, Cambridge CB2 8BS, United Kingdom

One Liberty Plaza, 20th Floor, New York, NY 10006, USA

477 Williamstown Road, Port Melbourne, VIC 3207, Australia

314-321, 3rd Floor, Plot 3, Splendor Forum, Jasola District Centre, New Delhi - 110025, India

79 Anson Road, #06-04/06, Singapore 079906

Cambridge University Press is part of the University of Cambridge.

It furthers the University's mission by disseminating knowledge in the pursuit of education, learning and research at the highest international levels of excellence.

www.cambridge.org
Information on this title: www.cambridge.org/9781108421324
DOI: 10.1017/9781108367868

© Adam Smyth 2018

This publication is in copyright. Subject to statutory exception and to the provisions of relevant collective licensing agreements, no reproduction of any part may take place without the written permission of Cambridge University Press.

First published 2018

A catalogue record for this publication is available from the British Library

ISBN 978-1-108-42132-4 Hardback
ISBN 978-1-108-43177-4 Paperback

Cambridge University Press has no responsibility for the persistence or accuracy of URLs for external or third-party internet websites referred to in this publication, and does not guarantee that any content on such websites is, or will remain, accurate or appropriate.

for my mum

Contents

List of Figures	*page* viii
Acknowledgements	x
Introduction: 'the Case of Man'	1
1 Cutting Texts: 'Prune and Lop Away'	17
2 Burning Texts: 'His Studyeing Chaire ... Was of Strawe'	55
3 Errors and Corrections: 'My Galley Charged with Forgetfulness'	75
4 Printed Waste: 'Tatters Allegoricall'	137
Conclusion	175
Appendix: Sample Instances of Printed Waste	183
Bibliography	190
Index	206

Figures

1	Keith Douglas, 'Stars', lines 1–4 (author's photograph)	page 3
2	*The Protestatyon of Martin Marprelat* (1589), p. 4. By permission of St Catharine's College, Cambridge (D.11.77(5))	4
3	John Gibson's commonplace book. © British Library Board (BL Additional MS 37719, ff. 190 v)	27
4	John Gibson's commonplace book. © British Library Board (BL Additional MS 37719, f. 163)	28
5	Gospel Harmony (1635). © British Library Board (BL C.23.e.4, columns 37–38)	32
6	Gospel Harmony (1635). © British Library Board (BL C.23.e.4, column 38)	33
7	Christophe Leutbrewer, *Nouuelle methode pour se disposer aisément à vne bonne & entiere confession de plusieurs années* (1658). By permission of the Bodleian Library (Vet E3 f.506, p. 6)	42
8	*Recreation for Ingenious Head-peeces* (1663). © British Library Board (BL 11623aa33, sig. S3 v)	45
9	Gospel Harmony (1635). © British Library Board (BL C.23.e.4, column 462)	48
10	Matthew. © British Library Board (BL C.23.e.4)	52
11	Matthew (close-up of Figure 10). © British Library Board (BL C.23.e.4)	53
12	William Penn, *The Great Case of Liberty of Conscience Once More Briefly Debated & Defended* (1670), 'Errata'. By permission of The Huntington Library (8870)	86
13	Francis Wolferston, *The three books of Publius Ovidius Naso, De Arte Amandi* (1661). By permission of The Huntington Library (17112)	97
14	John Milton, *Areopagitica* (1644), p. 12. Beinecke Rare Book and Manuscript Library, Yale University (2111653)	111
15	Robert Barker's King James Bible (1611), Matthew 26.36 (R.1.1). Reproduced by kind permission of the President and Fellows of Queens' College, Cambridge	120

16 A present and absent slip-insertion, in *Englands Helicon* (1600), sig. H. By permission of the Bodleian Library (Crynes 920)   122

17 A present and absent slip-insertion, in *Englands Helicon* (1600), sig. H. By permission of the Bodleian Library (J-J Sidney 98)   123

18 Henry Constable, *Diana* (1592), sig. D3v. By permission of the President and Fellows of Corpus Christi College, Oxford (CCC Library Δ.22.9 (5))   124

19 Margaret Cavendish, *Plays Never Before Printed* (1668). By permission of the Folger Shakespeare Library (N867)   126

20 Printed waste from *Astrophel and Stella* (1591) facing the title page of Edward Lively's *A true chronologie of the times of the Persian monarchie* (1597). By permission of the Bodleian Library (J-J Sidney 173)   165

21 Sidney sonnet as waste, facing errata list in Lively, *A true chronologie*. By permission of the Bodleian Library (J-J Sidney 173)   166

22 Lively sig. Cc, with binding support from sonnet. By permission of the Bodleian Library (J-J Sidney 173)   167

23 Thomas Cooper, *The cry and reuenge of blood* (1620), as a box. By permission of the Bodleian Library (Vet. A2 f.405)   180

24 Thomas Cooper, *The cry and reuenge of blood* (1620), sig. E3. By permission of the Folger Shakespeare Library (N867)   181

Acknowledgements

I'd like to thank the many friends and colleagues who have helped this project along. In particular: Katherine Acheson, Anthony Bale, Kate Bennett, Giles Bergel, Karen Britland, Joe Brooker, Cedric Brown, Isabel Davis, James Daybell, Jerome De Groot, Dennis Duncan, Joshua Eckhardt, Andrew Gordon, Chloe Houston, Katherine Hunt, Miriam Jacobson, James Kidd, Zachary Lesser, Kirk Melnikoff, Lucy Munro, Molly Murray, Michelle O'Callaghan, Gill Partington, Jason Scott-Warren, Bill Sherman, Emma Smith, Tiffany Stern, Alan Stewart, Stephen Thomson, Dan Wakelin, Germaine Warkentin, Abby Williams, Sue Wiseman and Adam Zucker. In Oxford, Paul Nash and Will Poole have been extraordinarily generous with their expertise. Juliet Fleming continues to have a huge influence on my work. I talked about many aspects of this book with the late Stephen Colclough: I miss him greatly. Librarians at the Huntington, the Folger, the British Library, the Bodleian and at many Oxford colleges have been extremely helpful: particular thanks to Alan Coates, Alex Franklin, Francesca Galligan, Gaye Morgan, Anna Sanders, Naomi Tilley and Sarah Wheale. I wrote this book while teaching at Birkbeck, University of London, and at Balliol College, Oxford, and I owe a great deal to the exceptional students at both those institutions: my thanks to them for their questions, enthusiasms, humour, doubts and perspectives. Greatest thanks of all to those closest to me: to my brother Barnaby; to Eliane, Ezra and Anna; and to my mum, Gill, for her eternal support.

Shorter, somewhat different versions of Chapter 1 appeared in *English Literary Renaissance* 42(3), 452–481, and of Chapter 2 in *Book Destruction from the Medieval to the Contemporary*, edited by Adam Smyth and Gill Partington (Basingstoke: Palgrave, 2014), pp. 34–54.

Introduction: 'the Case of Man'

In December 2015, together with four friends, I bought an iron Model Number 4 printing press with three trays of type, two composing sticks, a chase, two galleys, furniture and quoins, ink and paper for £400. The press was extraordinarily heavy: Dennis and I just about managed to carry it the ten yards from the East Oxford print shop to my car, swearing as we lumbered, and the precarious two-mile drive felt like a mistake from the moment we pulled away. The boot of my Honda Civic might collapse on the road at any moment; the car's nose was always just about to lurch suddenly skywards. At home, we couldn't lift the press onto the desk, so parked it on the floor, where it remained, and remains to this day.

A week later our group of five spent a first day with the press. Several of us had spent time in supervised print rooms, setting type and wielding inking balls and delightedly holding up sheets wet with ink, but that was under the expert gaze of a professional: 'tighten this'; 'the ink's too thick'; 'slot another thin space in there'. Fumbling unguided towards some kind of knowledge of the Model Number 4 was a different proposition.

We decided to print the first four lines from 'Stars', a poem by Keith Douglas written in 1939:

> The stars still marching in extended order
> move out of nowhere into nowhere. Look, they are halted
> on a vast field tonight, true no man's land.
> Far down the sky with sword and belt must stand[1]

With the slowness of tortoises, we picked out slim pieces of lead alloy type, slotted them into the two composing sticks set to the same measure, transferred the four lines to the galley tray, bound the lines with string, and then – in the absence of an imposition stone – slid these lines on to a flat glass shelf plundered from my fridge. Around the metal text we set the

---

[1] Keith Douglas, *Complete Poems* (London: Faber and Faber, 2011), p. 29.

bottomless iron frame or chase, and with a satisfying sense of the *ad hoc*, of problem solving, built a web of furniture, lower than the height of the type, round the upside-down, inverted metal letters. We tightened the quoins until the whole locked into stability and we could lift the forme up – giddy at the danger – without the parts moving. What we had was a thick, heavy slice of something that seemed only dimly related to Douglas's poem. This was as material as a text could get.

We spread some ink on the disk or ink table: the ink was viscous and utterly black, and pulling the rollers back and forth produced a sticky gasp as ink was distributed across the disk. We slotted the chase vertically into the chase bed, and placed the paper on the tympan using four hairclips (unsurprisingly, I couldn't find any gauge pins in the house).

Gill pressed down on the handle, quickly, with a triumphant sense of a new chapter, and the iron parts moved. Immediately the bottom roller fell off and the paper wrapped round the upper roller like the thousand laser printer jams we have cursed. 'Disaster', Dennis said, as we circled round as if a child had fallen from his bike. The ink was too thick, and the absence of a frisket or frisket fingers meant the paper stuck to the forme instead of pulling away. We needed some tack reducer to make the ink less sticky, but we'd have to wait for that. Abby put another sheet of paper on the tympan and I wrapped an elastic band round the top and bottom, outside the image area. We repositioned the roller. Tentatively, Gill pulled on the handle. The platen pushed the paper to the forme – Gill kept it there for a second or two – and then it pulled away, as we'd hoped. There was a clunk as everything returned to a resting position, and a communal pause. 'Look!', said Gill, peering closer, pulling the paper out (Figure 1). 'It's actually worked.'

This was Douglas's four-line fragment, but not as Douglas had ever imagined it. The lines were littered with errors: not 'order', in line one, but 'orper'; not 'into' but 'iuto'; not 'tonight' but 'tonignt'; not 'land' but 'laud'; not 'down' but 'bown'. Six errors in four lines, plus some looming spaces and a left-hand margin that descended tipsily down the page. Our fragment reminded me of the first gathering of Martin Marprelate's final publication in 1589, produced by an amateur printer, probably on the run while fleeing the authorities, with an irregular left margin, eccentric spacing, and uneven inking: a *mise-en-page* that performed the dramatic contexts of its production.

For 'fleeing the authorities', read 'untrained on a Model Number 4'. Philip Gaskell's rather weary reminder came to mind: 'It may be as well to emphasize at this stage that real (as opposed to theoretical) printing was a

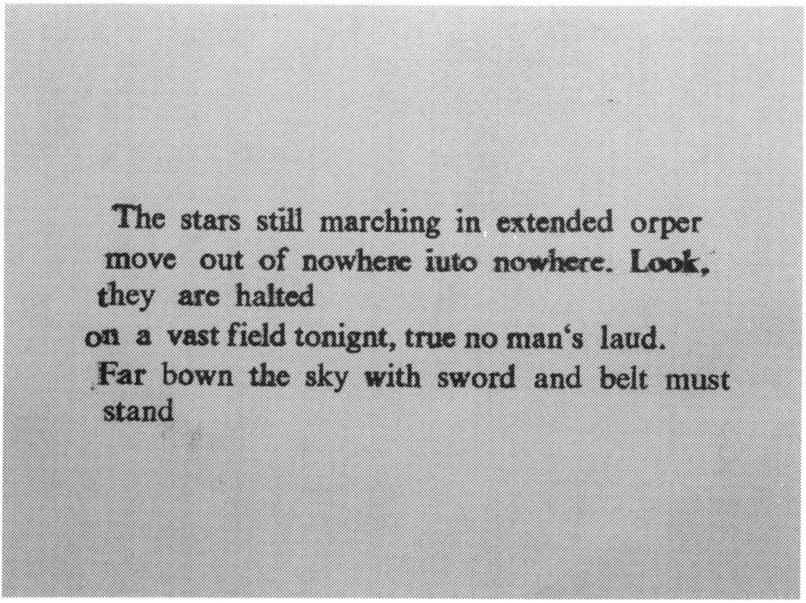

> The stars still marching in extended orper
> move out of nowhere iuto nowhere. Look,
> they are halted
> on a vast field tonignt, true no man's laud.
> Far bown the sky with sword and belt must
> stand

Figure 1 Keith Douglas, 'Stars', lines 1–4 (author's photograph)

complex craft carried out by fallible and inconsistent human beings of widely different capabilities.'[2] But even this first, flawed sheet taught us things, and as we continued to print, certain facts about the printing process emerged that struck a chord with features of the early modern book that I had been thinking about.

    Printing is a manual task, a labour, but a labour composed of distinct kinds of physical interaction. Picking type and placing it in a composing stick is delicate and exact, the work of fingertips and a deft sense of touch as one feels that the type's nick is facing up in the stick. Justifying lines needs an attention to detail that borders on the obsessive-compulsive: any wobble, however weak, needs eliminating through metal blanks, a change in orthography, or even the insertion of thin slips of paper. Pulling the handle is hard work but requires a carefully calibrated final push as the paper kisses the type: too brief and the print is weak, too strong and it's a fuzzy mess. Removing the paper from the tympan needs neatness and precision, otherwise inky fingers leave a trace.

---

[2] Philip Gaskell, *A New Introduction to Bibliography* (Oxford: Clarendon Press, 1972), p. 47.

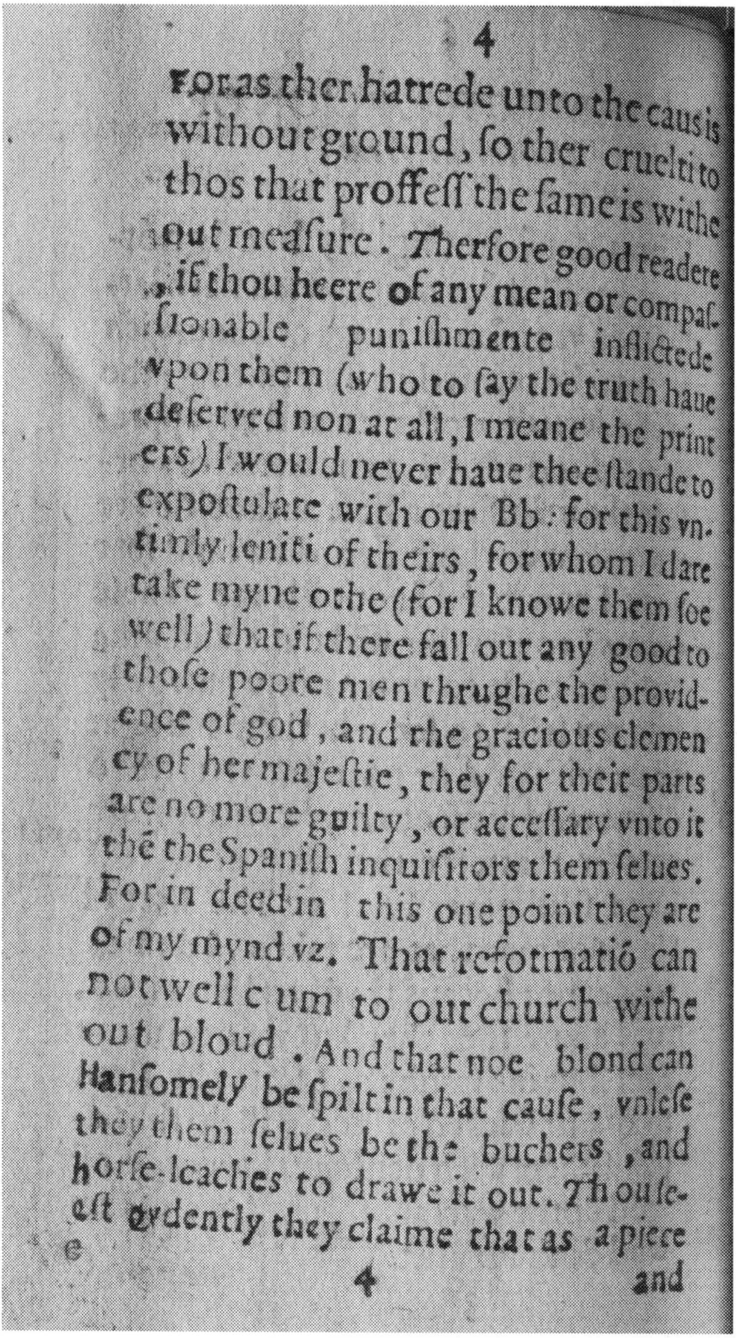

4

> for as ther hatrede unto the caus is without ground, so ther crueltito thos that proffeſſ the same is withe out meaſure. Therfore good readere if thou heere of any mean or compaſſionable puniſhmente inflictede vpon them (who to say the truth haue deſerued non at all, I meane the printers) I would never haue thee ſtande to expoſtulate with our Bb: for this vntimly leniti of theirs, for whom I dare take myne othe (for I knowe them ſoe well) that if there fall out any good to thoſe poore men thrughe the providence of god, and rhe gracious clemency of her majeſtie, they for their parts are no more guilty, or acceſſary vnto it thē the Spaniſh inquiſitors them ſelues. For in deed in this one point they are of my mynd vz. That refotmatiō can not well cum to our church withe out bloud. And that noe blond can hanſomely be ſpilt in that cauſe, vnleſe they them ſelues be the buchers, and horſe-leaches to drawe it out. Thou seeſt evydently they claime that as a piece

4 and

Figure 2 *The Protestatyon of Martin Marprelat* (1589), p. 4. By permission of St Catharine's College, Cambridge (D.II.77(5))

Introduction: 'the Case of Man' 5

Printing is a set of physical relationships between printer and type, and these physical relationships encourage in the printer a different imaginative relationship with language than a reader might experience, or a writer using other technologies to produce text (pen and paper; keyboard and screen) might enjoy. In the process of composing, imposing and printing, I came to think of the text less in terms of meaning and imagery – less in terms of the symbolism a literary critic mind find – and more as a problem or puzzle that occupies space, and that must be made to occupy a different space: from loose letters in a tray, to a composing stick, to a galley, to a locked-in chase, to a forme in the press, to marks of ink on a sheet, to a series of sheets needing folding and stitching. The process of printing was a series of interactions that, like a centripetal force, brought text into a more and more confined space. It's an oft-noted book historical corrective that what early modern print shops produced were not books, but sheets, unbound, unstitched, often unfolded, and this is true.[3] But it's a partial truth about the nature of text in the print shop, since that text passes through several stages of embodiment in order for sheets to be produced: the loose type, the set line, the tied-up galley, the boxed-in forme, the corrected proof, the sheet.

During this process, we were thinking about error all the time. We were obsessed with error. Printing brings errors into being with an astonishing frequency: it is difficult to appreciate how hard it is to set even the most unremarkable line of blank verse with any kind of accuracy until one tries. The processes of proofreading and correcting are efforts to confront this – in larger early modern print houses, the copy was read out loud while a corrector checked printed proofs, and we attempted to scan proofs carefully, using tweezers to pick out and replace or usually invert type in the forme. But it was difficult, and indeed for longer passages of text, almost impossible to eliminate error entirely. Certainly I came to think that the printer's calculation is not, *How can I make this book entirely free from all error?*, but rather, *How much error is tolerable for this book to be culturally acceptable, for this book to be legible as the book it claims to be?*[4]

---

[3] Peter Stallybrass, '"Little Jobs": Broadsides and the Printing Revolution', in *Agent of Change: Print Culture Studies after Elizabeth L. Eisenstein*, ed. Sabrina Alcorn Baron, Eric N. Lindquist and Eleanor F. Shevlin (Amherst: University of Massachusetts Press, 2007), pp. 315–341, p. 315 citing in particular Hugh Amory.

[4] David McKitterick has suggested that debates between printers and authors were less about absolute standardisation but rather 'what degree . . . [of] variation was acceptable'. David McKitterick, *Print, Manuscript and the Search for Order 1450–1830* (Cambridge, UK: Cambridge University Press, 2003), p. 111. See Chapter 3 for more on the inevitability of error.

Our printing frequently relied on acts of improvisation, or botching. Derrida described *bricolage* as the practice of re-using materials in order to solve new problems, of persisting with concepts that are broken but which are useful for the time being – 'the necessity of borrowing one's concepts from a text or heritage which is more or less coherent or ruined'.⁵ Printing is similarly indebted to the recycled, the leftover, the repurposed: to misprinted pages used as backing sheets between the platen and tympan; to tiny pieces of paper, narrower than the thinnest blank, squeezed between letters in the forme to tighten the text; to wood blocks of various sizes slotted in to patch together the forme; to the piece of bent wire used to keep the loose lower roller in place; to the inventive adjustment of orthography to alter a word and thus the line length in pursuit of a justified line; to creative inversions of type when supplies run low. This culture of reuse is encouraged by the fact that printing always produces an excess. However small the job, there are material leftovers, remnants: proof sheets that had been checked and so served their purpose; flawed sheets where the roller fell off or the over-inked type produced a thick blur instead of words. We could throw these away, but since one principle of printing is the extraction of maximal value from minimal resources, the leftovers can be fed back into the process of production: fed back imperfectly, but as best they can. Printing, then, seemed to be a profoundly analogue process: operating not within the 1/0 of a digital economy, but rather on a continuum of tending-towards-better-or-worse.

The process of printing suggests a combination of the permanent and the transient. Sheets are printed that will become pages that may live on in the form of a book. But even as it flings out these new products, the print shop returns to where it started from: the type is cleaned (we used white spirit; early moderns called their alkaline and water solution 'lye'); the formes are unlocked and the type is unpicked and returned to the cases' individual compartments – this 'dissing' or distributing, a process both arduous and tedious, the early modern equivalent of holding down delete and watching on-screen text disappear letter by letter, and (in the moments when type is replaced in the wrong compartment) the most common

---

⁵ Jacques Derrida, 'Structure, Sign, and Play in the Discourse of the Human Sciences', in *Writing and Difference* (1967; London: Routledge Classics, 2002), pp. 351–370. Derrida glosses Claude Lévi-Strauss, *The Savage Mind*, as follows: 'The *bricoleur*, says Lévi-Strauss, is someone who uses "the means at hand", that is, the instruments he finds at his disposition around him, those which are already there, which had not been especially conceived with an eye to the operation for which they are to be used and to which one tries by trial and error to adapt them, not hesitating to change them whenever it appears necessary, or to try several of them at once, even if their form and their origin are heterogenous' (p. 360).

source of later error. Moving repeatedly through this cycle of setting, printing and distributing, I came to think of words as impermanent gatherings of letters that could always be rescrambled, anagrammatised, turned into other words. The dissing has finished. The case is ready for the next book. Which book will it be this time?

***

The point of this account is not to make an argument about 'hard' practice and its superior relation to 'soft' theory: such a position is sometimes articulated in book historical circles, played like a trump card, but my experience of printing has suggested an interrelation between printing and reflection, and between printing and writing, that crumbles any binary, any sense of hierarchy. What I experienced was a cycle of ideas. I brought to printing certain questions and assumptions about the literary imagination and its relationship to the technologies of production (to give one specific example: a compositor who became an author had a particular relationship to language, prompted by the experience of print house composition, that informed his literary writing); the practical experience of setting type and printing became one way, among many, of thinking through these questions and, in the process, new or modified ideas emerged about the nature of the material text and the agencies that brought it into being (in this case, I came to wonder if the compositor engaged with text less in terms of semantic meaning and more as a spatial problem). I thus started to think and write about literature differently, working with these new or modified conceptions, and these new conceptions in turn became the questions I brought to printing, the questions that framed my engagement with the press.

If *Material Texts in Early Modern England* could be said to have at its heart a single question, that question would be: What was a book, and how does knowing more about the material book illuminate the study of literary culture? I can let a little air into that rather dense formulation and frame my book in terms of two ambitions. First, I want to examine features of early modern bibliographical culture that have been overlooked, misunderstood or underexamined by critics. Past critics have neglected certain crucial aspects of bibliographical culture because those critics have often been operating with an anachronistic idea of what a book was. Early modern books in many ways resist our commonsensical bibliographical assumptions, and I hope to explore the gap between what we might expect a book, and book use, to be, and how in fact these categories operated in early modern England. If early modern books seem stranger things at the end of this monograph than they did at the start, then I will have achieved one of my ambitions. Second, I want to think about the relationship between the materiality of the text (including the processes of book making) and the workings of the literary imagination. I will detail this latter ambition below, but for the moment it might be helpful to provide a brief overview of the chapters ahead.

Chapter 1, 'Cutting Texts', explores the rich culture of cutting up printed books in early modern England. At the centre of this chapter is the Anglican religious community of Little Gidding in the 1630s and 1640s, led by Nicholas Ferrar, who produced remarkable cut-and-paste gospels: Ferrar's nieces cut up and reordered, often on a word-by-word level, the printed text of Christ's life to create folio works of devotion, using knives, scissors and glue, that sought to resolve the contradictions between the accounts of Christ's life. These volumes are magnificently bound and formidably evocative of the skilled and time-consuming labour that produced them, but they resist or challenge many bibliographical and literary-critical variables of analysis. The books are printed, but they are also handmade, each one unique, bespoke: some libraries catalogue them as manuscripts; others class them as print. They are composed from printed texts, but those printed texts have been cut apart before being patched back together in a different order. How do these texts relate to a bibliographical language of, for example, edition (that is, all copies of a book printed from substantially the same setting of type)? They are literary works produced by knives and scissors, and so up-end most existing ideas of authorship, composition and writing. They are meticulous compositions whose production rests on a prior act of destruction, a cutting up of Bibles, and yet they instantiate the careful piety of the Little Gidding community. They are resistant texts even as they symbolise a Royalist Laudian orthodoxy. Little Gidding has previously been seen as an anomalous, even eccentric devotional experiment, but I hope to show how the cutting up of printed texts was widespread as a means of reading and of writing. I also show how cutting up texts was not necessarily an expression of hostility to a text but rather a form of careful and even pious reading. This new culture of cutting provides a vibrant context in which to read the poetry of George Herbert: Herbert's poems register, in ways not previously recognised, this practice of cutting. A new sense of the book, and of the bibliographical imagination, is thus opened up.

In Chapter 2, 'Burning Texts', I examine book destruction in order to explore the importance of transience to the culture of print. Scholars have often constructed a particular narrative about the capacity of print to fix and stablise texts – a narrative which usually focuses on particular landmark folio volumes, like Shakespeare's First Folio (1623) and Jonson's *Workes* (1616). But there is another story: a story of loss, destruction, and often-purposeful impermanence. This chapter ranges widely across early modern literary culture (Milton, Cervantes, Donne, Rabelais, John Leland, Matthew Parker, Robert Cotton), but focuses in particular on Ben Jonson. In 1623, Jonson's library, including several of his works in process, was lost in flames. Jonson responded with an angry, fascinating poem of loss, 'An Execration upon Vulcan', a poem that registers the injustice of his creative losses while noting the many books that deserve to burn. What emerges in Jonson's poem, and across early modern literary culture more generally, is an expectation that printed books would not endure, and a commitment to the value of literary destruction.

'God help the man so wrapt in Errours endlesse traine', laments Edmund Spenser's narrator in *The Faerie Queene*, and Chapter 3, 'Errors and Corrections', explores what we, as readers and critics, can do with errors in early modern printed books. This chapter suggests that the history of the early modern book is also a history of error, and proposes that we need to learn how to treat typographical slips seriously, or, at least, that we need to think more about their hermeneutical potential. In this chapter I explore four technologies of book correction – errata lists, handwritten corrections, paste-in slips, and cancel pages – and use this rich material to offer two broad lines of argument. First, I treat errors as moments when, in breaking down, the book briefly but vividly reveals the processes of its production. Errors thus grant us a rare glimpse inside the early modern print shop. Second, I consider the ways in which authors including Robert Herrick, Edmund Spenser, Margaret Cavendish and John Milton responded to bibliographical errors as sources of literary potential. Error thus emerges not as a problem to be erased but rather as a signature condition of the printed book, and as a presence that authors recognised and responded to with creativity.

Chapter 4 examines printed waste in books in order to explore the ghostly practice of lost books living on in new volumes. When John Aubrey wrote a sketch of his own life, he added the instruction that he wished his *Life* 'to be interponed [inserted] as a sheet of wast-paper only in the binding of a Booke.'[6] Aubrey's comment was in part an expression of his modesty: his role, and his life, was to serve other people's fame. But his

---

[6] John Aubrey, *Brief Lives with an Apparatus for the Lives of Our English Mathematical Writers*, ed. Kate Bennett (Oxford: Oxford University Press, 2015), 2 vols, vol. I, p. 429.

comment also alerts us to a wider culture of recycled books that has yet to receive sustained analysis: this chapter provides that first account. Early modern printed books frequently contained fragments of older texts in the boards, in the backing strips along the spine, in the hinges joining book to board, in pastedowns, or as flyleaves. The Bodleian Library's copy of Edward Lively's *A true chronologie of the times of the Persian monarchie, and after to the destruction of Ierusalem by the Romanes* (1597) carries fragments of Philip Sidney's *Astrophel and Stella* (1591) as end leaves: to read Lively means necessarily to turn the pages of Sidney's love poems. What did it mean to read a book that was haunted by parts of an older book? What, and how, did Sidney's poetry now signify? This chapter provides a meticulous account of the practice of using pieces of older books to compose new publications, and then tracks across a number of literary authors (including John Taylor, Henry Vaughan and John Dryden) to show how richly this feature of the early modern book resonated in the literary imagination.

Running through these chapters is an investment in the relationship between the material text and the literary imagination, and I want to pause here to spell out what I mean by this.[7] Scholarship on the materiality of texts has grown to be accomplished at noticing and thinking about material features (format, size, typography, binding and so on, and the practices of production they suggest) as signs that shape the meaning of a text, alongside the linguistic or literary content. In describing what he called the 'double helix of perceptual codes' that secure a literary work's effects, Jerome McGann makes the case for the symbolic power of the materiality of the text, arguing forcefully that 'every documentary or bibliographical aspect of a literary work is meaningful, and potentially significant'. McGann doesn't explain his apparently careful use of 'potentially', which suggests that materiality may be meaningful but not significant, but he does argue that works are enriched and made more substantial as a result of the interplay between content and form, and that a reading of a literary work is thus more attentive to the sum of a text's workings if it considers materiality:

> both linguistic and bibliographical texts are symbolic and signifying mechanisms. Each generates meaning, and while the bibliographical text

---

[7] For a rich discussion of this question, exploring commonalities of 'form' in both literary formalism and studies of material form, see András Kiséry and Allison Deutermann, 'The Matter of Form: Book History, Formalist Criticism, and Francis Bacon's Aphorisms', in *The Book in History, The Book as History: New Intersections of the Material Text. Essays in Honor of David Scott Kastan*, ed. Heidi Brayman, Jesse M. Lander and Zachary Lesser (New Haven and London: Yale University Press, 2016), pp. 29–63.

commonly functions in a subordinate relation to the linguistic text, 'meaning' in literary works results from the exchanges these two great semiotic mechanisms work with each other.[8]

Thus, McGann suggests, changes in the format of Dickens' novels due to serialisation, and the marginal glosses in 'The Rime of the Ancient Mariner' (1816), and the ink, typeface and paper used by William Morris in the first edition of his *The Story of the Glittering Plain* (1891) are all examples of bibliographical codes shaping interpretation. The neglect of materiality McGann sees in the ca. 1991 study of, for example, Emily Dickinson's poetry – 'her famous "fascicles", her scripts and their conventions of punctuation and page layout' – is, for McGann, expressive of 'a grave cultural ignorance' that is particularly damaging, given Dickinson's centrality to the literary canon of North America.[9] (McGann was writing 22 years before precisely this materiality was given meticulous display in *The Gorgeous Nothings: Emily Dickinson's Envelope Poems*.)[10]

McGann's notion that meaning is the product of 'exchanges' between linguistic and bibliographical 'semiotic mechanisms' – like D. F. McKenzie's pronouncement that forms 'effect' literary meaning – is surely right, but begs certain questions. What, exactly, is the nature of those 'exchanges', and of that process of 'effect'? In *How to Do Things with Books in Victorian Britain* (2012), Leah Price notes the catch-22 of many explorations of the relation between material form and literary meaning: if materiality enacts literary theme, then it is irrelevant, adding little or nothing to what we already think; and if materiality contradicts literary theme, then it is irrelevant, adding little or nothing to what we already think. One way forward might be to break out of a stark binary of enactment or subversion. Price suggests it 'may prove more productive to turn our attention to moments where these two strands of evidence pull apart, when (for example) ... an oath of revenge is sworn upon the same bible whose text preaches forgiveness.'[11] This is right, but it would be better still to avoid describing the relationship between the material and literary

---

[8] Jerome McGann, *The Textual Condition* (Princeton: Princeton University Press, 1991), p. 67. See also Matthew P. Brown, *The Pilgrim and the Bee: Reading Rituals and Book Culture in Early New England* (Philadelphia: University of Pennsylvania Press, 2007), pp. 21–67, which argues that 'pious reading [in early New England] gained from an appreciation of the qualitative differences of the material text, its look, feel and heft' (p. 67).
[9] McGann, *Textual Condition*, pp. 78, 57, 87.
[10] *The Gorgeous Nothings: Emily Dickinson's Envelope Poems*, ed. Marta Werner and Jen Bervin (New York: New Directions, 2013).
[11] Leah Price, *How to Do Things with Books in Victorian Britain* (Princeton: Princeton University Press, 2012), p. 36.

form of, say, John Donne's 1633 *Poems*, in homogenised terms (the material form suggests X; the literary content suggests Y; the relationship between X and Y is therefore either mutually enforcing or antagonistic). What can we do instead? We could note that multiple bibliographical codes co-exist in a book (something like X^1, X^2, X^3, X^4, ...), and we could consider an ongoing, sometimes fitful, back-and-forth flow of influence between these bibliographical codes and linguistic meaning (less X=Y, or X≠Y, but something like X/Y/X/Y/X/Y/X/Y) that functions differently at different points of the book and produces not an either/or of enforcement or subversion but something less resolved. In their discussion of medieval manuscript culture, Arthur Bahr and Alexandra Gillespie propose a wider range of terms to indicate a subtler, tenser sense of the ways in which material and literary form relate: form might not only 'effect' meaning, they suggest, but might also 'illuminate, defy, resist, augment, make, and unmake meaning as well.'[12] We could add other terms to the list ('amplify', 'invert', 'parody'?) and note that form might do all of this at different points in a single book.

Bahr and Gillespie offer us another helpful reminder. One bad model of scholarship misreads McGann's opposition and takes the physical form of the book as something self-evidently true – assuming a bibliographical facticity, 'projecting a determinism by matter', a sense that a book simply 'yield[s] up truth' which can act as a kind of anchor to the hermeneutical complexity of linguistic meaning.[13] But a book is no less ideological than a text, the network of signs that is its physical form, no less demanding of interpretation. So we should read material form rather as we read literary form: attentively and exactly, with an awareness of how bibliographical codes shift across a volume (we need to do more than note that a folio suggests cultural prestige, or that a duodecimo suggests portable use); with an awareness of the traditions and conventions underpinning the physical book, and the ways in which those traditions and conventions are sustained or resisted; with the knowledge that conventional bibliographical or literary critical terms and priorities might exclude or trivialise some material features; with a sense of the labour and the various agents behind the material object; with attention to what is being signified and by what means. Few literary critics would be content to reduce a poem, play or novel to a single pronouncement: '"The Canonization" is about love' is

---

[12] Arthur Bahr and Alexandra Gillespie, 'Medieval English Manuscripts: Form, Aesthetics, and the Literary Text', in *The Chaucer Review* 47.4 (2013), 346–360, 354.
[13] Bahr and Gillespie, 'Medieval English Manuscripts', 351 (quoting Frederic Jameson), 350.

true, but also virtually useless unless it is then nuanced and thickened, and we should approach materiality with a similar desire for precision, a similar sense that a book no less than a text is a dynamic form, teeming with bibliographical signifiers, and that things happen across it. As Price notes in a special edition of *PMLA* concerned with book history and the idea of literature, '[f]ar from replacing hermeneutics by pedantry, book history insists that every aspect of a literary work bears interpretation – even, or especially, those that look most contingent.'[14] Such an entwining of literary and material form can result, as András Kiséry and Allison Deutermann have recently written, in 'a critical practice that provides the analysis of literary form with material and historical specificity, and the analysis of material form with literary traction.'[15]

One implication of this inclusive approach to the book is that new agents of text-production become part of the critical discussion. Where once critics considered authors as the dominant variable of literary definition, McGann's notion of bibliographical codes introduces new figures into the book making process, since '"author's intentions" rarely control the state of the transmission of the text.'[16] Thus a reading of the *Pickwick Papers* would consider the 'mutual efforts of Dickens, two illustrators . . . and the production mechanisms set in motion by the publishers Chapman and Hall, all working together in cooperative consultation'[17] – although today's critics, writing 25 years after McGann, are more likely to emphasise tensions between agents rather than McGann's harmonious vignette. D. F. McKenzie's notion of the sociology of the texts suggests that the production of meaning is collaborative (with, for example, Congreve the author working closely with publisher Jacob Tonson and printer John Watts) and what is produced is a book that is 'a complex structure of meanings which embraces every detail of its formal and physical presentation in a specific historical context'. McKenzie is seeking to recover, through a reading that is attentive to 'the integrity of the text in all its details', the 'historical decisions made by authors, designers and craftsmen in deploying the many visual and even tactile languages of book form to help direct the readers' responses to the verbal language of the text.'[18] In this sense, both McGann

---

[14] Leah Price, 'Reading Matter', in *PMLA* 121.1, Special Topic: 'The History of the Book and the Idea of Literature' (January 2006), 9–16, 11.
[15] Kiséry and Deutermann, 'The Matter of Form', p. 41. [16] McGann, *Textual Condition*, p. 60.
[17] McGann, *Textual Condition*, pp. 78, 82.
[18] D. F. McKenzie, 'Typography and Meaning: The Case of William Congreve', in *Making Meaning: 'Printers of the Mind' and Other Essays*, ed. Peter D. McDonald and Michael F. Suarez, S. J. (Amherst: University of Massachusetts Press, 2002), pp. 198–236, p. 223.

and McKenzie are highly intentionalist critics, even as they disperse intention across a plethora of agents: McKenzie's sociology of texts can be understood as what McKenzie's editors nicely call a study of 'the intricacies of intention',[19] with the implication that we are to read bibliographic codes rather as we read linguistic codes, in pursuit of intended meanings, with the crucial emphasis that intention is spread across multiple sources: the nature of the hermeneutic act hasn't changed, although what we are reading (bibliographical as well as linguistic codes) and what we are pursuing (a dispersed rather than unitary intention) has. This in turn raises a question about the potential for anti-intentionalist readings of material form, and in particular in my discussion of printed waste in Chapter 4 I consider whether there is space for a reading of material form that looks for symbolic meanings that the agents (whether printers, binders, publishers or authors) never imagined: can we find hermeneutical life, for example, in the fragments of sonnets glimpsed in the endpapers of a volume of history, fragments that were not intended to be read as sonnets but are there to function as material supports to the physical book?

I want also to stress one other aspect of my consideration of the relationship between material form and meaning. While a reading of materiality as a shaping influence on the text is surely right, with the caveat of the complexity of that shaping dynamic, I want also to suggest that writers wrote with an often-acute sense of their intended medium – that an author's contingent, historically sensitive idea of what a book was influenced what he or she sought to achieve. On a local level, this opens up the potential for returning to particular moments in literary texts where bibliographical objects are invoked symbolically: a heightened sense of bibliographical forms can breathe new life into familiar similes and metaphors. A 'man's brow', says Northumberland in *Henry IV Part 2*, is 'like to a title-leaf, / Foretell[ing] the nature of a tragic volume'. 'Your face', says Lady Macbeth to her husband, is 'a book where men / May read strange matters'.[20] But what exactly was a title-leaf at this moment? How is a book a particular object in the early years of the seventeenth century, and how is Lady Macbeth's remark animated, made sharper, as a result? As Peter Stallybrass, Roger Chartier, John Franklin Mowery and Heather Wolfe have demonstrated, Hamlet's famous metaphor of tables for his memory ('from the Table of my Memory, / Ile wipe away all triuiall fond Records') becomes much more compelling when we have in mind a particular

---

[19] McKenzie, 'Typography and Meaning', pp. 206, 198.
[20] William Shakespeare, *Henry IV Part 2*, 1.1. *Macbeth* 1.5.

bibliographical form: that is, Robert Triplett's *Writing Tables with a Kalender for xxiii. Yeeres* (1604), a form associated not with textual permanence but rather – due to the gesso-treated pages, and the manner in which readers made notes with a stylus and then sponged them out – with writing and then deletion.[21] Hamlet's commitment to remembering looks more tentative as a result. More broadly, and beyond these local readings of symbolic books, a more finely calibrated sense of early modern print – in part the product of suspending modern bibliographical assumptions, and taking early modern texts on their own, strange terms – means we can read literary authors with a newly exact sense of their ambitions. Literary possibility is in part shaped (which means both 'enabled' and 'constrained') by the nature and conditions of its medium; if we know more about that medium, we can better understand the aesthetic effects writers pursued and created. So while we can think about the signifying potential of features of the material text (which is the traditional way for a literary critic to respond), we can also consider how writers wrote in the glow, or the shadow, of their chosen medium.

For some authors, this sensitivity to material form and to the mechanics of book production arose from first-hand experience of working in print shops, setting type, correcting proofs or more generally overseeing the production of works: a strikingly large number of literary authors (including Thomas Nashe, William Baldwin, Henry Chettle and Anthony Munday) spent a portion of their career employed in this way. But even authors who didn't work (or, in some cases, live) in 'chapels' had, like readers more generally, an awareness of materiality due to the unfinished state of books as they emerged into the early modern world. To give two examples: books were generally sold to readers unbound, so an early task for the reader was to organise binding, perhaps of a single text, perhaps of several that were in the eyes of the reader meaningfully linked into a sammelband; and lists of errata asked readers to intervene in the text before they began reading, correcting errors that escaped the print shop. In both instances, the reader was invited to serve a role that sustained the making of the text, functioning in effect as a supplementary print shop worker: even before reading began, the consumer encountered the book as a material object that needed reworking.

---

[21] Peter Stallybrass, Roger Chartier, John Franklin Mowery and Heather Wolfe, 'Hamlet's Tables and the Technologies of Writing in Renaissance England', in *Shakespeare Quarterly* 55.4 (Winter 2004), 379–419. See also Henry Woudhuysen, 'Writing-Tables and Table-Books', in *The Electronic British Library Journal* (2004), article 3.

When in 1644 the poet-priest William Strode sought ways of talking to his congregation about the resurrection, he turned at first to an analogy with music in order to think about the relationship between transience and living on. What happens to a melody after its performance?

> [W]hen a musicall Ayre hath been plaid, is it quite lost, never to be called for againe? or what is become of it? is it hid in the Bowells of the Instrument, in the prick'd or conceivd Copy, or in the hand and Power of the Musition? in all these?

After the last note has stopped, Strode wonders, what happens to an air? Does it cease to exist? Or is it – as Strode's argument suggests – somehow preserved and still latent across the means of its production: instrument, score, musician? Strode then drew on his knowledge of the world of printing to secure a second analogy to make a similar point:

> Againe, when a Printer dissolves his Impression, and casts it into the first Elements or Letters, is it quite lost, or what is become of it? is it hid in the Boxes which contain those Letters, or in the book out of which it was copied, or in the hand of the Printer that sets the Letters together? in all these?

This idea that a printed text exists after its material dissolution enables Strode to suggest, punning on 'case' as both condition and container of type, that

> such is the Case of Man: though all his quarters be divided into the quarters of the world, though his parts be distributed ... or digested into other bodies, or scattered into all Elements, they are still within Gods Boxes; though his Figure be Lost to the memory of men, it remaines fresh with Christ, and *in his Book are all our Members written.*[22]

For Strode's literary writing, printing has a potency of symbolic meaning: a symbolic value grounded in a familiarity with how printing worked – an awareness of the terminology of case and impression, of cast and set. In *Material Texts in Early Modern England*, I take my cue from Strode's sermon and explore the overlapping cultures of the bibliographical and the literary in the sixteenth and seventeenth centuries.

---

[22] William Strode, *Concerning death and the resurrection, preached in St. Maries, at Oxford* (1644), pp. 18–19.

CHAPTER I

Cutting Texts: 'Prune and Lop Away'

I must cut two testaments to make one good for my work of pasting . . .
I must take them to pieces.
–John Ferrar (1653)

This Man (says Dryden) Cuts us All Out, and the Ancients too.
– John Dryden's reported response on reading *Paradise Lost*[1]

I

In 'Paradise', George Herbert offers a sustained reflection on the relationship between cutting and spiritual virtue:

> I Bless thee, Lord, because I GROW
> Among thy trees, which in a ROW
> To thee both fruit and order OW.
>
> What open force, or hidden CHARM
> Can blast my fruit, or bring me HARM,
> While the inclosure is thine ARM?
>
> Inclose me still for fear I START.
> Be to me rather sharp and TART,
> Then let me want thy hand & ART.
>
> When thou dost greater judgments SPARE,
> And with thy knife but prune and PARE,
> Ev'n fruitfull trees more fruitful ARE.

---

[1] Letter from John Ferrar to Dr Basire, Durham, Dean and Chapter Library, MS Hunter, fol. 132 (Ferrar writes to request Eastern translations of the New Testament for a proposed polyglot Biblical Harmony in fifty languages); Jonathan Richardson *Explanatory notes and remarks on Milton's Paradise lost* (1734), pp. cxix–cxx. Thanks to Rhodri Lewis for the latter quote.

> Such sharpnes shows the sweetest FREND:
> Such cuttings rather heal then REND:
> And such beginnings touch their END.[2]

The narrator's happy spiritual condition – by no means a constant in Herbert's poetry – is ascribed to a process of spiritual direction likened at the outset to the regular planting of trees, row by row. Already enclosed, and so protected from harm, the narrator calls for still further encompassing, asking for God to be 'sharp', present and demanding. In the penultimate stanza, the sustained horticultural metaphor slides from enclosure to pruning, where pruning stands for an unspecified but nonetheless vivid act of discipline by God: the narrator's spiritual state is likened to a cut-back tree which becomes more fruitful as a result of this cutting, rather as *The Compleat Gardeners Practice* (1664) prescribes the cutting back of cowslips to produce growth: 'prune them handsomely, and setting of them at a distance atop of a border ... they will be rooted and come to perfection.'[3] In Herbert's poem, '[s]uch sharpnes', which might seem destructive, is the action of 'the sweetest FREND', and '[s]uch cuttings' heal the narrator and so prepare him for the 'greater' Last Judgement.

The narrator's description of a connection between pruning and salvation is enacted on a typographical level by the final words of each three-line stanza: as the first letter is clipped away, 'GROW' becomes 'ROW' which becomes 'OW'; 'CHARM' becomes 'HARM' and then 'ARM.' Thomas Buck's posthumous 1633 printed text deploys capitals to make clear this effect; in Bodleian MS Tanner 307 – a presentation copy of what Nicholas Ferrar (but not George Herbert) called *The Temple*, prepared at Little Gidding by Ferrar's nieces Anna and Mary Collett, aided perhaps by their mother, Susanna Collett, for the purposes of securing a license for printed publication – the final words are larger, but the word is not capitalised. Herbert thus performs a pruning of words, enacting the spirit of the poem at the level of composition. This act of cutting suggests a conception of words, or at least a conception of these words, as units that may be broken to reveal other words within. Reaching the end of line three, we read 'OW' as having emerged from 'ROW', and before this from 'GROW'. It is not quite true that the more words are cut back, the closer they come to truth.

---

[2] *The English Poems of George Herbert*, ed. Helen Wilcox (Cambridge, UK: Cambridge University Press, 2011), p. 464. Unless otherwise noted, all quotations from Herbert's poems come from Wilcox's edition.

[3] Stephen Blake, *The Compleat Gardeners Practice* (1664), p. 12.

But these words-within suggest not only thematic connections with their container words, but also collectively constitute a little narrative: 'FREND… REND… END'. These three-word narratives do not embody or epitomise the larger poem; rather they provide a looser series of connections. That the final, end word in the penultimate stanza refuses the rhyme we have come to expect – 'SPARE… PARE… ARE' – means that the poem relies on words as written and visual rather than spoken and performed for its fullest expression of meaning. It may be the case that the process of laying out these words in metal type would have granted the printer, Thomas Buck, or more exactly his compositors, a particular intimacy with this sense of words as loose moorings of letters which might be tugged away; copying the words by hand is a less vivid way of experiencing a verse composition that proceeds by reducing words, letter by letter.

The seeming paradox – that cutting heals; that destruction yields growth; that snipping away letters produces meaning – registers a broader preoccupation with cutting and creativity that runs across much of Herbert's poetry, and across early modern literary culture more generally. Poems in *The Temple* invoke a variety of instruments that cut: 'piercer'; 'sithe'; 'hatchet'; 'spear'; 'pruning-knife'. Herbert is careful to distinguish between different kinds of blade, and different kinds of cutting. In 'Time', Herbert's narrator renounces any fear of time, and of death, by looking forward to the afterlife ('Christs coming hath made man thy debter, / Since by thy cutting he grows better'). The poem's wit depends upon the narrator distinguishing between varieties of blade and sharpness. Time's 'sithe' is found by some to be too blunt ('where one man would have me grind it'), while others 'too sharp do finde it'. To those who fear Time, his 'sithe' appears a 'hatchet': a threatening axe. But in an argument which pairs this poem with 'Paradise', the narrator finds Time's blade to be only 'a pruning-knife': that is, an instrument whose cutting leads to the happy prospect of the afterlife, which 'convey[s] our souls / Beyond the utmost starres and poles'. As a result, and shifting between two different kinds of cutting, the personified Time is no longer an 'executioner', but 'a gard'ner now, and more'.

Why might Herbert have been preoccupied with cutting? Pruning as spiritual welfare was a well-established biblical trope, and Herbert certainly would have been aware of John 15.1–6, where Jesus is 'the true vine', and God 'the husbandman': 'Every branch in me that beareth not fruit he taketh away: and every branch that beareth fruit, he purgeth it, that it may bring forth more fruit.' There are two kinds of cutting here: unproductive branches are discarded ('he taketh away'), while promising branches are pruned ('he purgeth it') to yield more fruit.⁴ Such biblical sources inform numerous seventeenth-century sermons, including Daniel Price's *The Spring* (1609): '*God* our father is the husbandman, *Wee* are his husbandry, the *Soule* is the ground, the *Seede* is the word.'⁵ The influence of more literal horticultural writing provides another context: there is extensive commentary on the merits and methods of pruning, and on the relationship between cutting and growth, and indeed such was pruning's importance that one horticultural author 'could scarcely resolve with my self how to teach this art of *pruning*: since it would merit an express Discourse to instruct you perfectly.'⁶ This vibrant discourse often acquires allegorical significance in literary works, from the pruning gardener in Shakespeare's *Richard II*, to Andrew Marvell's mowers, to Adriana in *A Comedy of Errors* when she describes rival claims on her husband as 'Usurping ivy ... Who, all for want of pruning, with intrusion / Infect thy sap'. The horticultural pruning tradition migrates also into discussions of what we would call textual editing: Abraham Cowley laments the fact that '*Poets*, whose *Works* (commonly printed after their deaths) we find stuffed out ... [by stationers who are] like *Vinters* with sophisticate mixtures, [who] spoil the whole vessel of wine, to make it yield more *profit*.' Cowley sees such a stuffing in the printed poems of '*Shakespear, Fletcher, Johnson* and many others', and suggests 'I should take the boldness to prune and lop away [parts of the collections], if the care of replanting them in print did belong to me.'⁷ Anatomy and dissection is another cultural sphere in which cutting was prominent, and metaphorical applications of this kind of cutting were common, as in Robert Burton's *The Anatomy of Melancholy* (1621), in which melancholy is '*Philosophically, Medicinally, Historically, Opened and Cut Up*'⁸.

But while Herbert's poetry might be responsive to all these contexts, it also registers a sense of cutting that is both more quotidian and, for modern scholarship, less visible: the cutting of scissors through paper. As a way of sustaining and amplifying Juliet Fleming's recent call for scholars to

---

⁴ Random Cloud [sic] explores the connections between biblical passages about grafting and pruning, and George Herbert's use of a metaphor of imping ('if I imp my wing on thine'), in 'Easter Wings'. See Cloud, 'FIAT fLUX', in *Crisis in Editing: Texts of the English Renaissance*, ed. Randall M. Leod (New York: AMS, 1994), pp. 61–172, p. 132.

⁵ Daniel Price, *The Spring* (1609), sig. B1, in Stanley Stewart, *The Enclosed Garden: The Tradition and the Image in Seventeenth-Century Poetry* (Madison: University of Wisconsin Press, 1966), p. 58.

⁶ Nicolas de Bonnefons, *The French Gardiner Instructing How to Cultivate All Sorts of Fruit-trees and Herbs for the Garden* (1658), p. 29.

⁷ Cowley, *Poems*, sigs Av–A2, cited and discussed in Arthur Marotti, *Manuscript, Print and English Renaissance Lyric* (Ithaca: Cornell University Press, 1995), pp. 263–264.

⁸ Robert Burton, *The Anatomy of Melancholy* (1621), title page.

recognise and reflect on the fact that early modern readers 'cut their books... in ways that were free of the modern inhibitions that make such a thing seem scandalous to us',[9] I want to suggest that Herbert's writing took place within, and found some of its bearings from, a reading culture in which the consumption of texts was regularly accompanied by the cutting up of printed and manuscript pages.

II

Scholars of eighteenth- and nineteenth-century literature have analysed the practice of 'Grangerising' – that is, of augmenting or illustrating a text by inserting prints cut from other books, a practice encouraged by James Granger's *Bibliographical History of England* (1769).[10] Ellen Gruber Garvey has lovingly described nineteenth- and early twentieth-century American scrapbooks,[11] and Anke te Hesson has considered newspaper clipping agencies in ca. 1920 Berlin and, fascinatingly, their relationship to Alfred Döblin's *Berlin Alexanderplatz* (1929), written with extensive use of clippings pasted by Döblin into his manuscript.[12] But early modern scholars have not until very recently been attentive to related bibliographical impulses. The first sustained attempt to recognise and theorise this practice came in 2015.[13]

How, then, might we think about cutting and early modern literature? Scholarship has in the past understood cutting primarily as a metaphor for something like quotation: an act of transcription; a copying out, from source to text. But what if we treat cutting as something literal, an excising enacted not with pen and ink but with scissors, knives and penknives?[14]

---

[9] Juliet Fleming, 'Afterword', *Huntington Library Quarterly* 73 (2010), 543–552, 550.
[10] Lucy Peltz, 'Facing the Text: The Amateur and Commercial Histories of Extra-Illustration, c. 1770–1840', in *Owners, Annotators and the Signs of Reading*, eds Robin Myers, Michael Harris and Giles Mandelbrote (New Castle, DE: Oak Knoll, 2005), pp. 91–135; Robert A. Shaddy, 'Grangerizing: "One of the Unfortunate Stages of Bibliomania"', *The Book Collector*, vol. 49, no. 4 (Winter 2000), 535–546; Erin C. Blake and Stuart Sillars (eds), *Extending the Book: The Art of Extra-Illustration* (Seattle: University of Washington Press, 2010); Luisa Calè, 'Dickens Extra-Illustrated: Heads and Scenes in Monthly Parts (The Case of Nicholas Nickleby)', *The Yearbook of English Studies*, 40 (2010), 8–32.
[11] Ellen Gruber Garvey, *Writing with Scissors: American Scrapbooks from the Civil War to the Harlem Renaissance* (Oxford: Oxford University Press, 2013).
[12] Anke te Hesseon, 'News, Paper, Scissors: Clippings in the Sciences and Arts around 1920', in *Things That Talk: Object Lessons from Art and Science*, ed. Lorraine Daston (New York: Zone Books, 2008), pp. 297–327.
[13] *The Journal of Medieval and Early Modern Studies* 45.3 (September 2015), special edition on 'Renaissance Collage: Towards a New History of Reading', ed. Juliet Fleming, William Sherman and Adam Smyth. See in particular Juliet Fleming, 'The Renaissance Collage: Signcutting and Signsewing', 443–456.
[14] Fleming, 'Afterword', 545.

What happens to our sense of early modern textual production if we accept Thomas Dekker's description of *The Wonderfull Yeare* (1603) – 'At the ende of all (like a mery epilogue to a dull play) [are] certaine tales... *cut out in sundry fashions*' – as a literal account of his compositional process, and not merely a metaphor? Or John Taylor's report that *Mad verse, sad verse, glad verse and bad verse* (1644) was made of pieces of text '*cut out, and slenderly sticht together*'? Or barber-surgeon Richard Lichfield's admission, in *The Trimming of Thomas Nashe* (1597), that since 'Wheras thou commendst thy Epistle to me as a garment for a foole, and therefore that it should bee long: I (as is thy desire) haue cut it with my scissers'?[15]

There are institutional reasons why cut-up texts are less visible now than they were in early modern England: libraries have, unsurprisingly, preferred to acquire texts in as pristine condition as possible (a preference that has until very recently led to volumes with handwritten annotations being under-represented in collections, too); information about cutting is rarely noted in records; and catalogues generally do not allow for searches that will locate cut texts.[16] As is often the case, the modern terms and variables around which archival work is organised – from the framing of questions, to the entering of online search terms – work to occlude pre-modern forms of textuality.[17] In some instances, traces of cuts even seem to have been edited out of the Photostat reproductions on which *Early English Books Online* is based: this appears to be the case, for example, for the *EEBO* facsimile of Thomas Heywood's *The fayre mayde of the Exchange* (1607), which shows none of the title page excisions that the Huntington Library original retains.[18]

Nonetheless, and allowing for a certain amount of archival serendipity, evidence of cutting texts is not uncommon, both in the instructions books provided for their consumption and in the tattered remains left by obliging

---

[15] Thomas Dekker, *The Wonderfull Yeare* (1603), title page (my italics); John Taylor, *Mad verse, sad verse, glad verse and bad verse* (1644), title page; Richard Lichfield, *The Trimming of Thomas Nashe* (1597), sig. G2. Andrew Boorde, *The First Book of the Introduction of Knowledge* (1562), sig. A2v, presents a woodcut of a largely naked Englishman (Boorde himself?) holding tailor's shears, attempting to decide which new fashion to follow. The target here is the fashion-hungry youth cutting his cloth to suit the times, but the image perhaps also nods at the author as snipper of texts.

[16] Private correspondence with the curators of British Printed Collections 1501–1800, and Manuscripts Collections, at the British Library. The Folger Shakespeare Library's Hamnet catalogue is a rare exception: thanks to Steven K. Galbraith, Andrew W. Mellon Curator of Books at the Folger, for advice on this.

[17] For the gap between early modern and post-nineteenth-century bibliographical categories, see Jeffrey Todd Knight, *Bound to Read: Compilations, Collections, and the Making of Renaissance Literature* (Philadelphia: University of Pennsylvania Press, 2013), pp. 21–53.

[18] Huntington 61412. My thanks to Stephen Tabor for this point. That these title page excisions – possibly attempts to remove manuscripts notes – perhaps came after the early modern period does not alter the point about *EEBO*'s failure to register this text's materiality.

readers. John White's *Briefe and easie almanack for this yeare* (1650) instructs readers to snip out 'the whole kalender' for 1650 for use elsewhere: 'which being cut out, is fit to be placed into any book of accompts, table book, or other.'[19] An enactment of this prescription survives in the Folger: White's 1650 almanac, along with another from 1656, have been excised and glued into a manuscript notebook, which in turn contains within it *A manual for A justice of peace his Vade-mecum* (1641).[20] This composite illustrates the material complexity of many early modern material texts, which were often produced by combining different forms, both manuscript and print: a complexity obscured through a modern conception of the book as autonomous, whole, singular, a work in one medium.

There are prescriptions for readers to cut in Thomas Tusser's *A hundreth good pointes of husbandry, lately maried unto a hundreth good poynts of huswifery* (1570). Tusser offers patterns for short verses that might be displayed on the walls of the reader's house: 'Posies for [that is, to be written on] the hall'; 'Posies for the Parler'; and 'Posies for thine own bed Chamber'. These texts might be copied out, but they might also have been cut out and pinned or glued to the walls.[21] In a comic dialogue in *The Academy of Pleasure* (1656) that plays upon the relative class pretensions of shopkeeper and scholar, a shopkeeper affects the behaviour of a scholar by saying, 'I am of late become a great lover of sacke, and can make shift now and then to cut out a Copie of Verses'.[22] (There may have been particular comedy in the shopkeeper's 'Copie' if the word carried pedagogical connotations of 'a short composition in verse: now chiefly applied to such a composition (*esp*. Greek or Latin verses) as a school or college exercise' (*OED*, 'copy', 7.)) Such an action is being offered as something ridiculous, particularly since to cut a copy is to enact a double transfer and therefore to display a double dependency; but the joke depends upon a recognised cultural possibility.

Material enactments of these representations and endorsements include the title page of a copy of *A sermon preached at the funeral of Mr. John Bigg* (1691), which has been cut down – the opening 'A', and the 'MDCXCI' of the colophon are no longer visible – with an ornamental border, cut from another book, added. The final page of the text ('His EPITAPH') has also been cut out and pasted on the reverse of the title page, and – to mark the revised end of the volume – a new 'FINIS' has

---

[19] John White, *Briefe and easie almanack for this yeare* (1650), title page. [20] Folger V.a. 395.
[21] Juliet Fleming, *Graffiti and the Writing Arts of Early Modern England* (London: Reaktion, 2001), pp. 29, 43.
[22] *The Academy of Pleasure* (1656), sig. D1.

been cut from another book and glued in.[23] William Sherman has analysed a 1560s manuscript copy of the Book of Common Prayer and Psalter which includes illuminated letters cut from late medieval manuscripts, and Stella Panayotova has discussed a fifteenth-century Wycliffite Bible which contains, in the Psalter section, pasted-in historiated initials cut from a copy of Peter Lombard's *Magna Glossatura* on the psalms (ca. 1160).[24] The manuscript commonplace book of one Thomas Jackson has cut-out printed pages glued on the inside front and back covers: 'How the Sunne cometh to be eclipsed'; 'The Dominion of the Moon In Mans Body'; 'A note of the time forbidding marriage'.[25] A copy of Edward Pond's *An almanack for the Year of our Lord God 1696* includes not only copious manuscript notes, but also stubs indicating cut-out pages: usually whole pages have been cut out, but sometimes only the top third.[26] More strikingly still, the owner of a 1710 copy of *Parker's ephemeris* has sewn into the back of his almanac a paper wheel, made from cut up printed pages, that can be rotated to reveal the astrological alignment of the present moment, and whether the 'Conjunction [is] good . . . indifferent good . . . very Good . . . very bad . . . most excellent . . . bad . . . [or] worst of All.'[27] Such cutting should not be seen as necessarily scandalous or destructive but rather as a potentially quotidian mode of textual consumption. As Juliet Fleming and Ann Blair have demonstrated, there are many motives behind cutting, including a desire to avoid laborious hand-copying; to cope, by excising and compressing, with that flood of print which Burton called 'the vast *Chaos* and confusion of bookes';[28] to expand or reformat texts; to create space for marginal commentaries; to

---

[23] *A sermon preached at the funeral of Mr. John Bigg* (1691), Huntington 448742.
[24] See William H. Sherman, *Used Books: Marking Readers in Renaissance England* (Philadelphia: University of Pennsylvania Press, 2007), pp. 87–109; and Stella Panayotova, 'Cuttings from an Unknown Copy of the *Magna Glossatura* in a Wycliffite Bible (British Library, Arundel MS. 104),' *British Library Journal* 25 (1999), 85–100.
[25] Folger V.a. 391.
[26] Edward Pond, *An almanack for the Year of our Lord God 1696* (Cambridge, 1696), Folger V.a. 515. For more stubs and cut pages, see Cardanus Rider, *British Merlin* (1680), Folger A2254.5, and George Wharton, *Calendarium Carolinum* (1664), Folger A2655.
[27] George Parker, *Parker's ephemeris for the year of our Lord 1710* (1710), Folger 182–194q. The cited annotations appear on blanks before and after the printed almanac.
[28] Burton, pp. 8–9. For more on information management and strategies for dealing with multiple books, see John Considine, 'Cutting and Pasting Slips: Early Modern Compilation and Information Management', in *JMEMS* 'Renaissance Collage', 487–504; Ann Blair, 'Reading Strategies for Coping with Information Overload ca. 1550–1700', *Journal of History of Ideas* 64 (2003), 11–28; Ann Blair, *Too Much to Know: Managing Scholarly Information Before the Modern Age* (New Haven: Yale University Press, 2010), ch. 4, 'Compilers, Their Motivations and Methods'. Garvey, *Writing with Scissors*, suggests nineteenth- and early twentieth-century American scrapbooking was to a large degree an attempt to deal with information overload, although the practice of clipping and

remove censored material, particularly prayer book references to the Pope, Thomas Becket, indulgences and purgatory in response to legislation under Henry VIII and Edward VI;[29] to correct or delete contentious, mistaken or knowingly false title page claims (as was perhaps the case with at least two copies of *Aphorismes, or, Certaine Selected Points of the Doctrine of the Jesuits* (1609), both of which have the colophon's 'LONDON' removed);[30] or to illustrate manuscripts with cut-out printed images to produce presentation volumes, as John Harington used cut-out printed images to create the manuscript from which Richard Field printed *Orlando Furioso* (1591).[31] Cutting might also produce fragments to embellish texts: Mary Erler has described 'a substantial tradition' in the late fifteenth and early sixteenth centuries of pasting cut-out printed woodcut roundels, initials and images into devotional texts such as psalters and primers. She also notes that the manuscript of London alderman Robert Fabyan's *Great Chronicle of London* (ca. 1504) is 'adorned with ... pasted-in printed paper cut-outs.' While such examples are 'relatively scarce' in English books, Erler suggests 'it may be misleading to regard those few survivals as idiosyncratic.' Erler connects inserted cut-outs with the early years of the printed book, 'when we might expect a degree of exchange between [the cultures of] manuscript [and] ... printed book',[32] and certainly Julia Boffey locates Fabyan's use of cut-out printed initials, roundels and engravings in his *New Chronicles* and *Great Chronicle* within the overlapping cultures of manuscript and print in London ca. 1475–1530. Fabyan's mixed-media productions, Boffey suggests, are best understood as the product of 'a genuinely innovative impulse to meld different processes of book production', but the work of Erler and others suggests the impulse was not unique.[33]

---

organising excerpts from newspapers and other sources might also enable the marginalised user to resist or rework dominant narratives. For a contemporary instance of cutting as a means to excise and organise parts from printed papers, see Keith Thomas, 'Diary', in *London Review of Books* 32.11 (10 June 2010), 36–37, where Thomas describes his working methods and how '[a]t breakfast, I often take a pair of scissors to the *LRB*, the *TLS* or the *New York Review of Books*.'

[29] Dunstan Roberts, 'The Expurgation of Traditional Prayer Books (c. 1535–1600),' *Reformation* 15 (2010), 23–49. Roberts focuses on instances of prayer book censorship by crossing out with ink or scratching away with a knife, but cutting might be another method of excision.

[30] Huntington 53907; British Library T.785(2). *Marre Mar-Martin: or Marre-Martins medling, in a manner misliked* (1589), Lambeth Palace Library Main Collection, [ZZ]1589.18.06, has the words '*with Authoritie*' cut out after the imprint reads '*Printed*'.

[31] Fleming, 'Afterword,' 543–552. As Fleming notes, the Harington case is detailed in Simon Cauchi, 'The "Setting Foorth" of Harington's Ariosto', *Studies in Bibliography* 36 (1983), 137–168.

[32] Mary C. Erler, 'Pasted-in Embellishments in English Manuscripts and Printed Books, c. 1480–1533', *The Library*, 6th series, 14.3 (1992), 186, 201–202, 205–206.

[33] Julia Boffey, *Manuscript and Print in London c. 1475–1530* (London: British Library, 2012), pp. 162–204, 171.

Nor was this 'kind of hybrid or crossover volume'[34] particular to the early years of printing – an argument that assumes the early years of printing were a kind of stumbling improvisation that later gave way to a more stable sense of medium: similar practices persisted into the seventeenth century, and beyond. Royalist Sir John Gibson produced a commonplace book while imprisoned in Durham Castle in the 1650s, hoping that the text would serve and aid his son as a 'companion some times to looke upon, in this Vale of teares'.[35] The volume features several pages cut from printed volumes and glued into the pages of the manuscript, to which Gibson has added his own handwritten notes (Figures 3 and 4).[36]

Such ease with cutting was in part a consequence of the purposeful nature of Renaissance reading: a reflection of that early modern pursuit of commonplaces and aphorisms, and the excising of sententious remarks. As one printed verse miscellany advises: 'Like chesse-nuts sweet, take ... the kernell out.'[37] Since a text was often imagined as an assemblage of pieces, which might be crumbled, or shredded, into its constituent parts, the act of cutting was always at least implicit. This willingness to cut also reflects the fact that the coherent, bound, unannotated, 'complete' printed book, with which modern bibliographical culture has been fixated, was not yet the dominant medium for conveying text. The establishment of the book through iconic publications like Jonson's and Shakespeare's Folios is of course one of the dominant narratives of seventeenth-century literary culture; but through much of the early modern period, that modern assumption that 'the work is coterminous with the book' was not yet axiomatic.[38] Thus Henry Briggs' *Tabulæ logarithmicæ, or Two tables of logarithms* (1663) includes a table 'For the speedy reduction of centesmes or decimall minutes to sexagenary minutes, *& contra*', with the instruction to the binder that this table should be inserted in such a way as to exceed or surpass the edges of the book: 'Place this Table at the end of the Booke, in such sort that it being unfolded may appear quite without the leaues of the booke, when the rest of the booke is shut.'[39]

---

[34] Boffey, *Manuscript and Print*, pp. 171–172.
[35] British Library Additional Manuscript 37719, fol. 5v. Adam Smyth, '"Rend and teare in peeces": Textual Fragmentation in Seventeenth-Century England', *The Seventeenth Century* 19 (2004), 36–52.
[36] For another later example, from a manuscript produced between the later sixteenth and mid-seventeenth century, see BL Add. MS 4900, featuring handwritten notes from almanacs with cut-out printed capital letters and small figures glued in.
[37] *Wits Recreations* (1640), p. 3, 'To a verse reader'.   [38] Fleming, 'Afterword', 548.
[39] Henry Briggs, *Tabulæ logarithmicæ, or Two tables of logarithms* (1663), sig. Dd. In the Bodleian's copy, Savile H. 19, this table has indeed been bound in this way.

Cutting Texts: 'Prune and Lop Away'

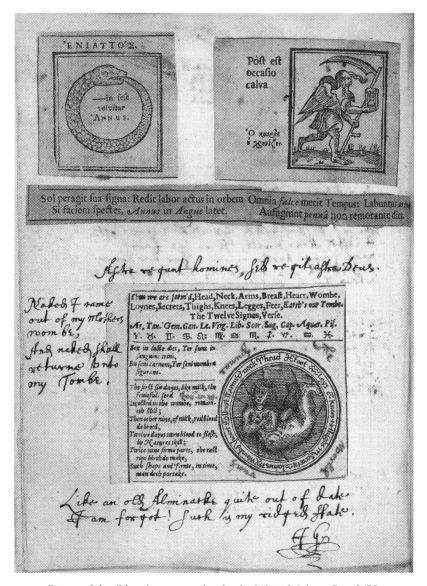

Figure 3 John Gibson's commonplace book. © British Library Board (BL Additional MS 37719, ff. 190 v)

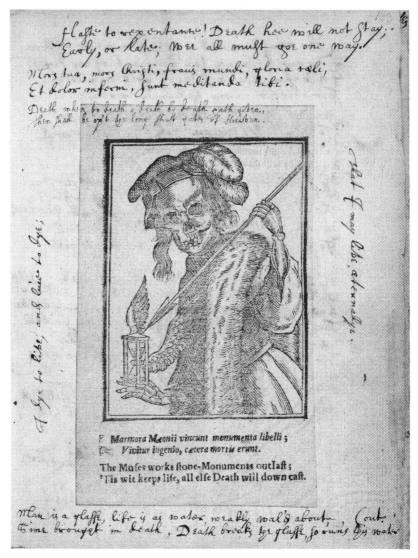

Figure 4 John Gibson's commonplace book. © British Library Board (BL Additional MS 37719, f. 163)

III

Herbert's interest in cutting might then plausibly be read as a register of this broader early modern culture of reading with blades to hand; but it also expresses more local concerns. Herbert's links with Nicholas Ferrar's Little Gidding are well known. Long before T. S. Eliot made Little Gidding famous as the fourth of his *Four Quartets* (1944), Little Gidding established a seventeenth-century reputation as an Anglican religious community, made up of Nicholas Ferrar and his extended family: 'like a little college', Isaak Walton wrote, 'and about thirty in number.'[40] Their fame rested in part on a series of what look to modern readers like radical interventions in what is now called the history of the book. Ferrar and his family made at least fifteen Biblical Harmonies. The majority of these books were Gospel Harmonies: that is, lavish folio books constructed by selecting printed texts of the four Gospels; cutting up these printed texts, often on a word-by-word level; reorganising the text, and distributing and gluing the new order under 150 chapters, describing Christ's life. To this cut-up text, images were often added: images cut out from source texts, and often trimmed and reworked and conflated to produce something that would later be called collage.[41] The point of these complicated textual shufflings was to build a text that revealed but then reconciled 'agreements & differences' (as one title page put it) between gospel accounts, and offered a coherent, harmonised narrative, 'Digested into order'.[42]

George Herbert was familiar with the community at Little Gidding and with the cut-up Biblical Harmonies that they produced. John Ferrar's 'Life' of his brother stresses the great friendship between Herbert and

---

[40] Izaak Walton, *The Lives of Dr. John Donne, Sir Henry Wotton, Mr. Richard Hooker, Mr. George Herbert* (1670), p. 69.

[41] Joyce Ransome, 'Monotessaron: The Harmonies of Little Gidding', *The Seventeenth Century* 20 (2005), 22–52, and 'George Herbert, Nicholas Ferrar, and the "Pious Works" of Little Gidding,' *George Herbert Journal*, 31 (2007–2008), 1–19; Paul Dyck, '"A New Kind of Printing": Cutting and Pasting a Book for a King at Little Gidding', *The Library*, 7th series, 9.3 (2008), 306–333, and '"So Rare A Use": Hands and Minds on the Gospels at Little Gidding', *George Herbert Journal* 27 (2006), 67–81. For the use of images, see George Henderson, 'Bible Illustration in the Age of Laud', *Transactions of the Cambridge Bibliographical Society* 8 (1982), 173–204.

[42] *The Actions & Doctrine & Other Passages touching Our Lord & Sauior Jesus Christ* (1635), BL C.23.e.4, title page. Fifteen Biblical concordances survive; eight are gospel harmonies; two are drafts. Two lost harmonies were made for George Herbert and Thomas Jackson, President of Corpus Christi College, Oxford. The eight gospel harmonies are at Harvard (1631); the Bodleian (1631); the British Library ('King's Book') (1635); Cotsen Library, Princeton (1635); British Library (1637); Hatfield House, Hertfordshire (1637); Ickworth House, Suffolk (1640); and one (1640) that belonged to a nineteenth-century Miss Heming but is now in private hands. The polyglot gospel made for Prince Charles by young Nicholas Ferrar (the elder Nicholas' nephew) in 1640 is owned by Lord Normanton, Somerley. In addition to the gospels, there are also the following extant harmonies: British Library (Acts and Revelation) (1635); British Library (Kings and Chronicles) (1637); St John's College, Oxford (Pentateuch made for Archbishop Laud) (1640); Royal Library, Windsor Royal (Pentateuch made for Prince Charles) (1642). The two drafts are at Magdalene College, Cambridge: FP 1057 (a draft for British Library (1637)) and 1892a (perhaps a draft of St John's College, Oxford (1640)).

Nicholas Ferrar: each styled the other 'most entire friend and brother', and although their relationship was primarily epistolary, 'their very souls cleaved together most intimately.'[43] In 1626, Herbert was installed as canon of Lincoln Cathedral and prebendary of Leighton Ecclesia, and Ferrar supported Herbert in his costly repairs of the church at Leighton Bromswold, just five miles from Little Gidding. On his death Herbert entrusted his poetry to Nicholas Ferrar. As John Ferrar reports,

> when Mr Herbert dy'd, he recommended... his Divine Poems, & willed it to be delivered into the hands of his Brother N.F. appointing him to be the Midwife, to bring that piece into the World, If he so thought good of it... The wch when N.F. had many & many a time read over, & embraced & kissed again & again, he sayd, he could not sufficiently admire it, as a rich Jewell, & most worthy to be in ye hands & hearts of all true Christians, that feared God, & loved the Church of England.[44]

Perhaps most significantly of all for the purposes of Herbert's interest in cutting, the scissors and knives of Little Gidding constructed a Biblical Harmony for Herbert. The book is now lost, or perhaps sleeping in some aristocrat's attic, but records of Herbert's ownership survive. A letter written by Ferrar's cousin Arthur Wodenoth on 13 October 1631, after his visit to Herbert, records Herbert's 'esteme of my Cosens Concordance' and his 'high prizing of it & thank full acknowledgmt for it.'[45] Since many of Herbert's poems were written after 1625, after the founding of Nicholas Ferrar's community, the bibliographical commitments of Little Gidding provide a reasonably sturdy contextual framework for reading Herbert's verse.[46]

---

[43] *Materials for the Life of Nicholas Ferrar*, ed. Lynette R. Muir and John A. White (Leeds, 1996), pp. 92, 93. It is remarkable that no letters between Herbert and Ferrar survive, particularly given the very many letters extant in the Ferrar Papers at Magdalene College, Cambridge. The closest we have is the one document in the Ferrar Papers in Herbert's hand: a piece of advice, dated 4 or 5 October, 1631, directed at Ferrar's cousin, Arthur Wodenoth, concerning Wodenoth's dilemma about whether to pursue a career in the church (FP 814). The letter is transcribed in *The Works of George Herbert*, ed. F. E. Hutchinson (Oxford, 1941), pp. 380–381. As Amy Charles noted, this absence may reflect the particular value of these letters: they were perhaps removed from other documents after Herbert and Ferrar's deaths, and being separate, were lost. See 'Herbert and the Ferrars: Spiritual Edification', in *Like Season'd Timber: New Essays on George Herbert*, ed. Edmund Miller and Robert DiYanni (New York, 1987), p. 12.

[44] *Materials for the Life*, p. 94.   [45] FP 815.

[46] The chronology of Herbert's poetry is only tentatively established. While Herbert's earliest sonnets date from 1610, and while the poems in MS Jones B62 at Dr Williams' Library, London, perhaps date from 1615–1625, the poems in Bodleian MS Tanner 307 (copied at Little Gidding after Herbert's death) which are not also in MS Jones B62 probably date from 1625–1633. See Wilcox, *Poems*, p. xxxvii.

Stanley Stewart and Paul Dyck have explored some connections between Herbert and Little Gidding. In *A Priest to the Temple*, Herbert prescribes 'a diligent Collation of Scripture with Scripture', and Stewart demonstrated the overlaps between this mode of reading – in which sections were compared, in an often non-linear fashion – and the process of making and reading Harmonies: 'For all Truth being consonant to it self, and all being penn'd by one and the self-same Spirit, it cannot be, but that an industrious, and judicious comparing of place with place must be a singular help for the right understanding of the Scriptures.'[47] This way of reading Scripture finds expression in Herbert's poetry. 'The H. Scriptures II' provides a description of active, devotional reading that resonates with the non-linear structures that the Harmonies encourage: 'This verse marks that, and both do make a motion / Unto a third, that ten leaves off doth lie.' Dyck has more recently provided an important exploration of connections between Herbert's conception of the Bible in *The Country Parson* as a 'storehouse' of commonplaces providing precepts for life, and the Harmony-making of Little Gidding.[48]

But it is also worth exploring the rather simpler shared interest between Herbert and Little Gidding in cutting text: in a sense of cutting as productive. Figure 5 shows a page from a Little Gidding Harmony made for King Charles I in 1635, now in the British Library: an imposing volume, almost immovably large and heavy. In the thirteenth of 150 chapters, titled 'JOHNS Baptisme, Preaching, Foode, & Rayment', the text presents a description of John the Baptist's preaching; his disputes with the Pharisees; and the moment when he predicts (according to Luke) that 'one mightier then I commeth, the latchet of whose shoes I am not worthy to unloose.' To produce this chapter, the Harmony-makers at Little Gidding selected the Gospel texts that narrate this moment: Matthew 3.1–12; Mark 1.1–8; and Luke 3.1–18. Through meticulous scissor work, these three accounts were cut out and then presented in three formats. In 'The Comparison', the three columns of text were aligned to produce a parallel edition: Matthew, Mark and Luke. In 'The Composition', all the words from the three different Gospel accounts of this description of John the Baptist were interlaced to create a single piece of continuous prose. Figure 6, a closer image of 'The Composition', shows clearly the level of detail involved in the production of this conflated account: the cutting up is sometimes at the level of the individual word.

---

[47] *Priest*, p. 229; Stewart, *Garden*, p. 6.
[48] Paul Dyck, '"So rare a use": Scissors, Reading, and Devotion at Little Gidding', *George Herbert Journal*, 27 (2003–2004), 67–81, esp. 75–78.

32 Material Texts in Early Modern England

Figure 5 Gospel Harmony (1635). © British Library Board (BL C.23.e.4, columns 37–38)

Figure 6 Gospel Harmony (1635). © British Library Board (BL C.23.e.4, column 38).

The superscript 'Mr' at the start indicates the ensuing text comes from Mark; the 'L', a couple of lines on, indicates Luke – although there is just one word, 'Now', from Luke, before the text switches to Matthew, for 'In those dayes'. The third method of presentation was 'The Collection', which presents a brief overview in large black letter and then, beneath, in a smaller roman font, what was called the supplement: details, repetitions and elaborations.

In his unfinished biography of Nicholas Ferrar, Nicholas' brother John offers a description of the mechanics of cutting and pasting that lay behind these Harmonies. Ferrar describes how the Harmonies were assembled in the Concordance room at Little Gidding on large tables, the room hung with passages from Scripture pinned up on the walls:

> with their scissors they... cut out [of] each Evangelist such and such verses and thus and thus lay them together to make and perfect such and such a head or chapter. Which when they had first roughly done, then with their knives and scissors they neatly fitted each verse so cut out to be pasted down on sheets of paper. And so artificially they performed this new-found-out-way, as it were a new kind of printing, for all that saw the books when they were done took them to be printed the ordinary way.[49]

John Ferrar's description expresses a sense of both the novelty and the technical sophistication of the process of harmony production: 'this new-found-out way'. (That phrase might also carry an echo of the Ferrar's commitment to exploration in the New World.) It also catches a sense of mild unease in the first readers of these texts, their sense of being disorientated by these books: 'all that saw the books... took them to be printed the ordinary way.' What, exactly, are we reading?

For book historians accustomed to narratives linking print with fixity and the establishment of a stable literary canon, these cut-and-paste Gospels convey the very opposite: a willingness to dismantle and reorder printed Bibles. The Harmonies are a response to the culture and technology of the printing press by skilled amateur book makers who converted printed books back into unique texts. To read these Harmonies today is to experience a kind of twin-pull: a sense of the intricacy and completeness of these volumes, but also an awareness of the cutting and pulling apart that lies behind the assembling. The Harmonies are poised awkwardly on the border of destruction and creation, and the creativity at work at Little Gidding rests on a prior act of cutting apart. In a similar way, Little Gidding has endured conflicting charges of elevating the image too much, and of not elevating the image enough. Before the loose, often-altered prints now held at Magdalen were identified as Little Gidding's, they were described in the *Catalogue of the Pepys Library* (1980) as having 'been deliberately defaced by an iconoclast',[50] and, more recently, they featured in Tate Britain's 2013 exhibition 'Art

---

[49] *Materials for the Life*, p. 76.
[50] *Catalogue of the Pepys Library at Magdalene College, Cambridge,* gen. ed. Robert Latham, vol. III 'Prints and Drawings', part I 'General', compiled by A.W. Aspital (Cambridge: D.S. Brewer, 1980), 289.

Under Attack: Histories of British Iconoclasm'.[51] Recent studies of early modern iconoclasm have emphasised the purposeful, often precise nature of acts of image destruction: the removal of particular figures or parts from stained glass windows, for example, rather than a cruder wholesale demolition (which did of course also occur).[52] One consequence is that depleted stained glass windows look uncannily like the carefully altered prints of Little Gidding: the scene of *The Presentation in the Temple* in Canterbury Cathedral, for example, had the figures of the Virgin and St Simeon, and the head of Christ, neatly removed.[53] Given that the Little Gidding community was attacked for perceived links with Laudianism and thus implicitly for a celebration of the visual – in the words of a 1641 pamphlet, Little Gidding was 'The Arminian Nunnery', a 'late erected Monasticall Place' filled with 'a fond and fantasticall *Family of Farrars*'[54] – it is ironic that these loose prints create the impression of iconoclasm. Cut pictures, then, suggest both the denigration and the elevation of the image.

Herbert prized the Little Gidding Harmony he was sent 'most highly as a rich jewel worthy to be worn in the heart of all Christians', and expressed delight 'to see women's scissors brought to so rare a use as to serve at God's altar.'[55] If *The Temple* is preoccupied with the unquantifiable and ineffable nature of sin, love and faith, it is also an exploration of alternative modes of conveying meaning, whether by shaping text into spatialised expressions ('Easter wings'; 'The Altar'); scratching text into windows ('The Posie'); or offering 'precepts' which are 'sprinkled' ('Superliminare'), as holy water might be dispersed by a 'Perirrhanterium'. Cutting represents one of these alternative modes.

IV

What does it mean to imagine literary composition as a process of cutting? If cutting occurred in both the production and reception of printed texts, what difference does this make to our reading? What happens to a word when it is treated as a physical object? What happens to one's relationship

---

[51] Tabitha Barber and Stacy Boldrick (eds), *Art Under Attack: Histories of British Iconoclasm* (London: Tate Publishing, 2013), 82–83.
[52] Julie Spraggon, *Puritan Iconoclasm during the English Civil War* (Woodbridge: Boydell and Brewer, 2003).
[53] Barber and Boldrick, *Art Under Attack*, 88.
[54] *The Arminian Nunnery* (London, 1641), title page, 9. This text is the product of a tendentious reading of a 1633–1634 letter by Edward Lenton who investigated 'the Reputed (at least reported) Nunnery at Gidding'. For Lenton's letter, see FP 939, and BL Harley 4845.
[55] *Materials for the Life*, p. 76.

with a piece of text when it is cut out, held, turned around and glued back down in a new position? How is our relationship to letters and words and literature different if cut-up text is the medium in which we encounter them? These are large questions with many possible answers, but the following points, which draw on Herbert, Little Gidding and early modern culture more generally suggest some tendencies for this culture of scissors and knives.

i Cutting up Texts Is Not Destruction

In a twenty-first century in which the destruction of religious books is a powerful cultural taboo, cutting up printed Gospels seems a surprising pursuit for a religious community, and a paradoxical way of registering piety. And certainly, within many early modern contexts, the notion of cutting scripture was indeed seen as transgressive: in an attempt to prevent the clipping of coins, Henry VII introduced a statute declaring that all gold coins 'shall have the hole scripture about ev[er]y pece of the same gold w'out takking any p[ar]te therof, to thentent that his subjettis hereaft[er] may have p[er]fite Knowledge by that ... scripture when the same Coines be clipped or appaired.'[56] It is not clear whether the scriptural text is deployed because it is simply well known and therefore would reveal any clippings more clearly or whether the Biblical subject matter made the cutting particularly transgressive, and therefore less likely. But the statute nonetheless imagines scripture as a foil for cutting: something to blunt the blade. Later cultures also often link Bible cutting with transgression: both *Treasure Island* ('Where might you have got the paper? Why, hillo! Look here, now; this ain't lucky! You've gone and cut this out of a Bible. What fool's cut a Bible?') and *Jude the Obscure* register a practice with a sense of taboo. When, in the latter novel, Sue describes making a 'NEW New Testament' by 'cutting up all the Epistles and Gospels into separate *brochures* [from the French, literally "a stitched work"], and rearranging them in chronological order as written' – 'I know that reading it afterwards made it twice as interesting as before, and twice as understandable' – Jude's response is the reaction we might expect from culture at large: '"H'm!" said Jude, with a sense of sacrilege.'[57]

---

[56] The statute is 19 Henry VII c.5. Stephen Deng, *Coinage and State Formation in Early Modern English Literature* (Basingstoke: Palgrave, 2011), p. 113. Thanks for Jason Scott-Warren for this reference.
[57] Robert Louis Stevenson, *Treasure Island*, ed. Wendy Roberta Katz (Edinburgh: Edinburgh University Press, 1998), p. 175; Thomas Hardy, *Jude the Obscure* (London: Random House, 2008), pp. 183–184. Thanks to Jason Scott-Warren and Simon Gatrell for these references.

Cutting Texts: 'Prune and Lop Away'   37

But when members of the Little Gidding community took scissors to printed copies of the Gospel, their cutting was a register of piety. Lisa Jardine, drawing on the work of Helen I. Roberts, notes that the representations of scissors on the desks of Carpaccio's Augustine and Metsys' Erasmus suggest not only a practical candle trimmer but also the symbolism 'of the interpretation of the Scriptures by the Doctors of the Church'. 'Trimming the wick of scriptures', as Jardine puts it, 'so that their light shines out strongly and brightly', recalls Erasmus's editorial and exegetical labours in the *Novum Instrumentum*, the *Letters* of Jerome and the first of the *Paraphrases*.[58] More generally, if Protestantism encouraged believers to reflect carefully on every word, scissors and knives helped the Ferrars and Colletts do this. Cutting up Gospels was a way of caring about the Word, rather as, in similar theological contexts, descriptions of devotional writing might portray a hyper-embodied relation between author or reader and text. Describing the murky textual history behind Lancelot Andrewes' posthumous *A manual of private devotion*, Richard Drake linked devotional authorship with staining and marking a text:

> *Had you seen the* Original Manuscript, *happie in the glorious deformitie thereof, being slubber'd with His pious hands, and water'd with His penitential tears, you would have been forced to confess* That Book belonged to no other then pure and Primitive Devotion.[59]

A relatively relaxed or, we might say, more productive attitude to cutting was also encouraged by the practice of commonplacing, in which short excerpts or aphorisms were transcribed into commonplace-books. Cutting texts is on one level a literalisation of this mode. More generally, the early modern printed book was not treated with the reverence with which later cultures approached it. The book was not yet the exclusive or perhaps even dominant medium for carrying text (there were manuscripts, walls, endless single sheets), and it was a material form that might easily be reworked. Books were sold unbound; several volumes might be bound together at a later date to create new composite wholes; readers might request that blanks be added to receive their handwritten annotations (as was the case with almanacs, for example). Amid this culture, the printed book was a

---

[58] Lisa Jardine, *Erasmus, Man of Letters: The Construction of Charisma in Print*, revised edition (Princeton: Princeton University Press, 2015), p. 75, drawing on Helen I. Roberts, 'St Augustine in "St. Jerome's Study": Carpaccio's Painting and Its Legendary Source', in *The Art Bulletin*, 41.4 (December 1959), 283–297, 295. Thanks to Jason Scott-Warren for this reference.

[59] *A manual of the private devotions and meditations of The Right Reverend Father in God Lancelot Andrewes* (1648), sig. A8v–A9. My thanks to Michael Lam for drawing this text to my attention.

tentative mode of embodying text, a negotiable material form, and cutting devotional pages was not necessarily the transgressive act that later periods took it to be: '[i]t being the peculiar happiness of *Sacred Commodities*, to be made *better by their using*.'[60]

ii Cutting Is a Form of Writing

It is tempting to regard cutting and writing as two fundamentally different acts, and to view the latter as more sophisticated (because more mobile and precise) than the often-infantilised former. But every written word, and therefore every written sentence and written text, can only come into being through a process of selection: a process of eliminating or cutting out other possible words, letting them fall to the floor, and of grasping the word intended. Whether writing proceeds through pen, pencil, stylus, knife, scissors, typewriter, word processor or any other local technology is of course a significant material difference with consequences for our relationship to language; but on a more fundamental level, all these technologies are involved with the seizing, ordering and deploying of letters, a process of snipping out, of writing *qua* cutting. Such a reframing is important because critics have often trivialised cutting as a kind of non-writing: in discussing the contribution of John Ferrar's daughter Virginia to a 1640 Harmony, David Ransome writes, 'but the writing is all his [John's]; seemingly she merely pasted in the cuttings.'[61] If cutting and pasting is thought of as writing, such clouding judgements spring less readily to mind. Certainly poets of the time tended to resist such patronising judgments and saw cutting as both like and in some ways superior to writing, as that term is normally understood. Edmund Waller's 'Of a Tree cut in Paper' celebrates an unstained form of textual production:

> Fair hand! that can on virgin paper write,
> Yet from the stain of ink preserve it white;
> Whose travel o'er that silver field does show
> Like track of leverets in morning snow.
> Love's image thus in purest minds is wrought,
> Without a spot or blemish to the thought.
> Strange, that your fingers should the pencil foil,
> Without the help of colours or of oil!
> For though a painter boughs and leaves can make,

---

[60] *A manual of the private devotions*, sig. A6.
[61] David R. Ransome, 'Ferrar, John (c.1588–1657)', *ODNB* (2004), www.oxforddnb.com/view/article/60958.

>'Tis you alone can make them bend and shake;
> Whose breath salutes your new-created grove,
> Like southern winds, and makes it gently move.
> Orpheus could make the forest dance; but you
> Can make the motion and the forest too.[62]

This is writing without the staining of ink: a better, purer writing, performed with blades, not ink, white to ink's corrupting black, a mode more suitable for meditations on love and for women authors. Strikingly, too, cutting outdoes the pencil or brush by producing a text that has life: the static trees that a painter might create have, when produced by cutting with scissors, the power to 'bend and shake'. Like a second, better Orpheus, the cutter's breath brings the forest they made to life.

iii Cutting and the Pursuit of Slowness

While previous discussions of cutting from printed and manuscript texts have seen the practice as a time-saving way of dealing with what Ann Blair calls 'information overload', to produce Biblical Harmonies by snipping individual words and sometimes letters was a tremendously slow process.[63] In terms of hours of work, the amount of printed books required and the leftover texts produced, this kind of cutting was the opposite of efficient. Why did members of the Little Gidding community choose this laborious process of cutting up, reordering and gluing printed text, rather than copying words out by hand? Centuries of monastic manuscript production offered a convenient model for the Ferrars and Colletts to follow, and the careful handwritten title pages and prefaces to their Harmonies indicate their calligraphy was up to the job. We might answer that by changing the question and instead asking why have we assumed that temporal economy was always a priority? The attraction of cutting for the Ferrars was, precisely, its time-consuming nature: the hours and days it consumed. The printing press's capacity quickly to produce Bibles and Harmonies was in many ways a great opportunity for Protestantism in terms of dissemination; but the careful, word-by-word reflection that devotional reading encouraged was also surely threatened by this culture of speed. Cutting up text was a way of slowing things down, and therefore a way of thinking patiently about the word.

---

[62] *The Poems of Edmund Waller*, ed. George Thorn-Drury (London: Routledge, 1893), 2 vols, vol. II, 68. See Kate Bennett, 'John Aubrey and the Circulation of Edmund Waller's "Of a Tree Cut in Paper"' in *Notes and Queries* 49 (2002), 344–345.
[63] See Blair, 'Reading Strategies', and Blair, *Too Much to Know*, ch. 4.

40   Material Texts in Early Modern England

iv Cutting and Ideology

Does the act of cutting up text carry particular political or religious significances? Individual, sometimes spectacular, case studies certainly suggest that this was the case. John Gibson's commonplace book, for example, compiled while the Royalist Gibson was a prisoner in Durham Castle in the 1650s, is defiantly Royalist in all ways: a celebration and lament for the King, and a defence of Gibson's own political decisions. The cutting here does become a mechanism for articulating a Royalist position, and in particular for assembling a counter-narrative of mid-seventeenth-century political history. For Gibson, cutting is a revisionist technology. But cutting need not always be Royalist: Parliamentarian and non-political snippings are perfectly possible. Similarly, while the cutting at Little Gidding might seem to register a Protestant idea of reading as an active, solitary wrestling with the text, there are numerous European Catholic manuscripts with cut-out, printed pages glued in.[64] One of the more striking manifestations of this European tradition of cut books is the genre of the Catholic confessions book, or the confession coupée, in which sins are listed on printed pages cut into narrow horizontal strips: using a stylus or needle, the sinner can unpick the particular sin from the margin and fold it back to serve as a reminder of their transgression (transgressions like 'De n'avoir pas aimé Dieu de tout mon coeur, de toute mon ame, & de toutes mes forces de n'avoir pas dirigé mes actions à sa gloire', or 'de n'avoir pas dirigé mes actions à sa gloire').[65] Then, crucially, after confession, the user can return the strip to its original, unfolded (and unfallen) position, ready for the next cycle of sin-book marking-confession. The form seems to have been invented by Christophe Leutbrewer, whose *Nouuelle methode pour se disposer aisément à vne bonne & entiere confession de plusieurs années, en moins de deux heures* (Paris, 1658) was a bestseller.[66] One user of a copy now in the Bodleian (Figure 7) was evidently a fairly diligent confessor, and the curled slips reveal sins that have been folded back and then returned to their starting, non-sinful position, including, on

---

[64] Feike Dietz has examined a seventeenth-century illustrated Catholic manuscript based on the popular emblem book *Pia desideria* (1624), showing how fragments from different printed sources were cut out and combined to produce a new text. See 'Gedrukte boeken, met de pen gelezen. Sporen van leesinterpretaties in de religieuze manuscriptcultuur', *De Zeventiende Eeuw*, 2 (2010), 152–171.

[65] Christophe Leutbrewer, *Excellente et Facile Méthode Pour se préparer à une Confession générale de toute sa vie* (Brussels, 1721), n.p. My thanks to Francesca Galligan for introducing me to this book.

[66] Texts weren't confined to France, but were published in Brussels and Mexico, among other places. For the latter, see *El pecador arrepentido. O methodo facil para disponerse a una buena Confession General, o particular. Discurrido en Frances ... traducio en Espanol ... por Juan Bautista Joseph de Barry* (Mexico, 1716).

page 6, 'Auoir esté trop impatient'; 'Auoir maudit sa Naissance'; and 'Auoir differé de bien faire'. On page 10, the whole page of ten sins has been, and remains, folded back: as complete a confession as the page will allow.[67]

Here, the cut book works in the service of the Catholic Church, but such is the range of instances of cutting that it is more useful to think of cutting as a bibliographical practice, a way of reading and writing that could, in particular moments and contexts, speak to and enact particular religious or political positions – the Protestantism of Little Gidding in 1635; the Royalism of Sir John Gibson in the 1650s; a Catholic culture of confession – but that in the first instance need not be coded in those ways.

v Cutting and Inventio

Producing a text by cutting up and reordering existing texts places less stress on the creation of new words, and more on the reordering of the already present. Cutting thus recalls that understanding of invention, or *inventio*, within Renaissance rhetoric, from the Latin *invenire*, meaning to come upon, discover or find, rather than to invent *ex nihilo*, in a more modern sense. Many of Herbert's poems are preoccupied with the recycling of biblical scripts, and in particular with the degree to which an appropriated script becomes the speaker's own voice. In 'Coloss: 3.3', Herbert threads a reworked version of a passage of text taken from St Paul's letter to the Colossians ('Our life is hid with Christ in God') through his verse:

> *Our life is hid with Christ in God.*
>
> *My* words & thoughts do both express this notion,
> That *Life* hath with the sun a double motion.
> The first *Is* straight, and our diurnal friend,
> The other *Hid*, and doth obliquely bend.
> One life is wrapped *In* flesh, and tends to earth.
> The other winds towards *Him*, whose happie birth
> Taught me to live here so, *That* still one eye
> Should aim and shoot at that which *Is* on high:
> Quitting with daily labour all *My* pleasure,
> To gain at harvest an eternal *Treasure*.[68]

---

[67] Christophe Leutbrewer, *Nouuelle methode pour se disposer aisément à vne bonne & entiere confession de plusieurs années, en moins de deux heures; & rendre vn compte exact de toutes les fautes que l'on peut auoir commises, mesme durant toute sa vie, pourueû que l'on obserue soigneusement ce qui y est prescript* (Paris, 1658), Bod Vet E3f.506.
[68] *The Temple* (1633), p. 77.

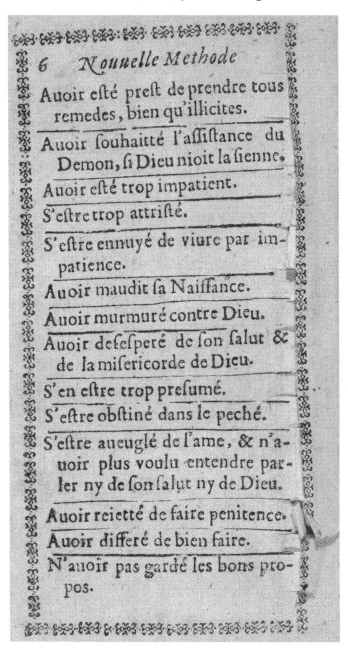

Figure 7 Christophe Leutbrewer, *Nouuelle methode pour se disposer aisément à vne bonne & entiere confession de plusieurs années* (1658). By permission of the Bodleian Library (Vet E3 f.506, p. 6)

Just as Herbert's narrator describes his life as both a straight, earthly journey, and God-facing travel that 'doth obliquely bend', so the diagonal biblical text tracks this second path, from 'My' to 'Treasure'. Stanley Fish's claim that the speaker 'loses himself' amid an inherited script, and that the poem consequently charts a process of 'self-abnegation', is surely wrong.[69] Herbert's verse asks its readers rather to observe how a biblical passage may simultaneously remain a biblical passage, but also lie at the centre of an individual's voice. The speaker's voice is composed through a process of taking on a block, or a sequence of smaller blocks, of existing text, although the point is not the seamless integration of text and voice: we note the source, the voice, and toggle between the two.

Something related but different happens in 'The Forerunners', Herbert's celebrated poem on growing old, and the fear that 'dulnesse [will] turn me to a clod.' Old age threatens a loss of 'sparkling notions', and the poem sketches a shift from an earlier poetic style of 'sweet phrases, lovely metaphors' towards plainer verse. This loss of 'sparkling notions' is not a principled reorientation of style (it is wrong to read the poem as the narrator *rejecting* embellishment), but rather the consequence of waning powers: it is not the narrator who is leaving poetic ornament, but poetic ornament that is departing the narrator ('[b]ut will you leave me thus?'). The spirit of abandonment that in Petrarchan poetry describes the loss in love, and that in much of Herbert's poetry conveys a too-distant God, here defines the relationship between poet and metaphor. The poem is compelling in part because it contains the embellished language it describes as fled – 'Louely enchanting language, sugar-cane, / Hony of roses, whither wilt thou flie?' – and, as a consequence, recalls a capacity that has not yet passed; the verse is poised on the edge of change, and plain style is a prospect, not yet a present medium.

What is left behind after 'sparkling notions' have departed the narrator's brain are, in his heart, five stark words repeated three times in the poem: 'Thou art still my God.' This quintet anticipates and contains within itself everything that 'lovely metaphors' can ever say: 'For, *Thou art still my God*, is all that ye / Perhaps with more embellishment can say.' That 'perhaps' admits a note of concession: a sense of the power of embellished language, which implies a narrator less than triumphant, and perhaps not entirely convinced of his thesis. Nonetheless, these clinching lines suggest five lean words containing all other metaphors and phrases. As so often in Herbert's poetry, the image is of a dense compression of the vast into a small space,

---

[69] Stanley Fish, *Self-Consuming Artifacts: The Experience of Seventeenth-Century Literature* (Berkeley: University of California Press, 1972), p. 205; noted in Wilcox, *Poems*, p. 303.

like Barabas' 'Infinite riches in a little room'. The italicised '*Thou art still my God*' is not primarily a description of a relationship. Its significance in the poem is as a phrase, a *unit* of five words, a little script or 'dittie' that, by being italicised and repeated three times across the poem, moves around the verse and has the quality of a catchphrase or a slogan. It is a small archive: all that remains, but capacious, despite its brevity. In place of his earlier 'sweet phrases,' the narrator has this chunk of text. The repeated deployment of this phrase is informed by a culture of cutting out lines of text, moving passages around on a page: the kind of process that went on daily in the Concordance Room of Little Gidding. Because the passage is repeated, we become conscious of this phrase as a mobile block of text, shunted around the space of the poem: we become conscious that words might be treated as a material block, like a strip cut from a Bible, glued down onto blank pages.

The poem thus charts not only a shift in age and poetic style, but also, more fundamentally, a transition in compositional methods. From poetry written in 'enchanting language', the narrator at the end of the poem is composing by moving around a strip of text. Herbert's poem thus mimics the effect of cutting out, and his verse might be read as an homage not only to God, but also to the textual aesthetics associated with Little Gidding.

vi Cutting and Spatialised Poems

Later editions of *Wits Recreations* – a playful verse miscellany containing short poems and riddles, later retitled *Recreation for Ingenious Head-peeces* ('A pleasant grove for their wits to walk in') – include several examples of what might be called 'spatialized poems'. Among these are verses that are printed in such a way that they appear as text on a narrow strip of paper, folded and manipulated: thus the verse beginning 'This is love and worth commending' (Figure 8), in which the twisting form, its final words returning the reader to the start, enacts the ensnaring, never-ending nature of love. The poem is presented as the product of scissors and knives: the text is striking because it appears to exist on a narrow, winding strip of paper, snipped dexterously from a regular sheet.[70] Print culture asserts not its stability and permanence, but rather the possibility of blades reworking a page. Readers of mid-seventeenth-century printed miscellanies evidently

---

[70] *Recreation for Ingenious Head-peeces* (1663), sig. P11v. See also 'True love is a pretious pleasure', which is similarly constructed (sig. Q2).

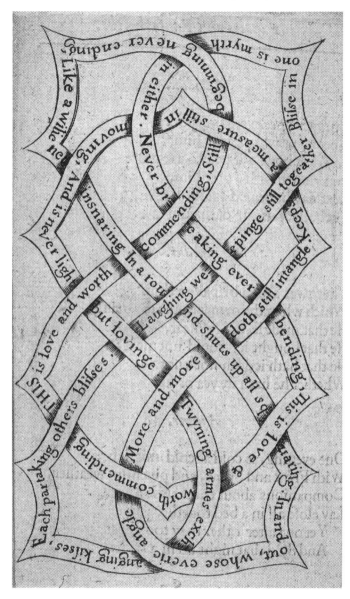

Figure 8 *Recreation for Ingenious Head-peeces* (1663). © British Library Board (BL 11623aa33, sig. S3 v)

enjoyed this kind of ludic spatialisation. *The Card of Courtship* (1653) – a miscellany of verse conveying 'The language of love fitted to the humours of all degrees, sexes, and conditions' – offers a section of what it calls 'Emblematical Fantasticks': poems that make playful use of layout. The lines of 'Round about all in a Ring' coil in on themselves, and strips of text in 'Ever in a wand'ring Maze' are laid out as a series of misdirected movements.[71]

In part, these verses engage with that Renaissance conception of language, informed by neoplatonism and cabalistic concerns, as 'material things that belong to the same network of resemblances that endows natural objects with allegorical meaning.'[72] Just as the shape of Egyptian hieroglyphs and Hebrew text had a deep symbolic meaning, so the physical form of English letters yielded a spiritual significance. This is certainly a helpful intellectual framework for reading Herbert's famous pattern poems such as 'The Altar' and 'Easter wings'. But the manner in which these strips of text invite readers to imagine the cutting that produced them also very vividly conjures a culture of scissors and knives.

vii   Words as Things That Can Be Broken Apart and Remade

Composing text through cutting makes us aware that phrases and words might not only be made, but also unmade: pulled apart, pared down. Through a process of rearrangement, words might be made to say more than they presently do. Just as Little Gidding's scissors snipped away at the printed Gospel text as a prelude to remaking, so Herbert's poetry imagines embodied words being broken or crumbled into letters, before a process of reassembling reveals a greater truth. In 'JESU', the speaker's heart, 'deeply carved' with his saviours 'sacred name', is shattered 'all to pieces' in a moment of affliction. The narrator gathers each piece or 'parcel', engraved with a letter of the name – 'And first I found the corner, where was J, / After, where ES, and next where U was graved' – until, piecing them together and spelling them out, he finds that they reveal the sentence 'I ease you.' Text, then, is first materialised, as something 'deeply carved', and is then fragmented, then gathered and reread. As a result, a new meaning is revealed which, while new ('I ease you'), was also already contained in the earlier text ('Jesu').

---

[71] *The Card of Courtship* (1653), pp. 126–127.
[72] Martin Elsky, 'George Herbert's Hieroglyphic Poems and the Materiality of Language: A New Approach to Renaissance Hieroglyphics', *ELH* 50 (1983), 245–260, 258.

In 'The Flower', Herbert's narrator compares God's returning gifts, and his consequent recovering heart, to re-emerging 'flowers in spring'. 'Thy word is all', the speaker concludes, 'if we could spell.' That Herbertian 'spell' is significant: as the *OED* observes, 'spell' can mean both to read letter by letter (breaking up text into parts) and to 'discover or find out ... by close study or observation.' Something is revealed through a process of breaking apart. God's word becomes comprehensible through a process of breaking up text.

Previous criticism has productively located these poems within the discourse of Holy Communion. As Helen Wilcox notes, this 'process of breaking down words' to yield 'true meaning has sacramental overtones.'[73] As the sacrament by which Christ became present to the participant through the process of consuming bread and wine, the Holy Communion takes its precedent from Christ's Last Supper, and, in particular, from that moment when Christ breaks the bread. Matthew 26.26–28 renders it thus: 'And as they were eating, Jesus took bread, and blessed it, and brake it, and gave it to the disciples, and said, Take, eat; this is my body. And he took the cup, and gave thanks, and gave it to them, saying, Drink ye all of it; For this is my blood of the new testament, which is shed for many for the remission of sins.'

Figure 9 shows the 'Collection' to chapter CXXXI of the Harmony made for King Charles I (1635), in which the text from the three Gospel accounts of this moment (Matthew 26.26–28; Mark 14.22–24; Luke 22.19–20) has been cut up and reordered. The Holy Communion provides one context for reading Herbert's preoccupation with crumbled, shattered or atomised language. As Heather Asals suggests, Herbert's language is 'broken eucharistically'.[74] But the culture of cutting up text which I have outlined – an interest in unmooring or snipping letters from words as a prelude to remaking – is another important context.

viii Book Not as Surface but Space

An investment in a culture of cutting also enables us to rethink the book as a site for meaning. More particularly, to produce a Biblical Harmony through cutting, or to write a devotional poem conceiving of text as something that might be cut and moved around, suggests that the book is less a surface for inscription, as it is usually imagined in the moment of writing, and more a space onto which strips or blocks of texts are placed, glued or pinned, as pictures are placed on a gallery wall. Conceiving of a

---

[73] Wilcox, *Poems*, p. xliv.
[74] Heather Asals, *Equivocal Predication: George Herbert's Way to God* (Buffalo: University of Toronto Press, 1981), p. 27.

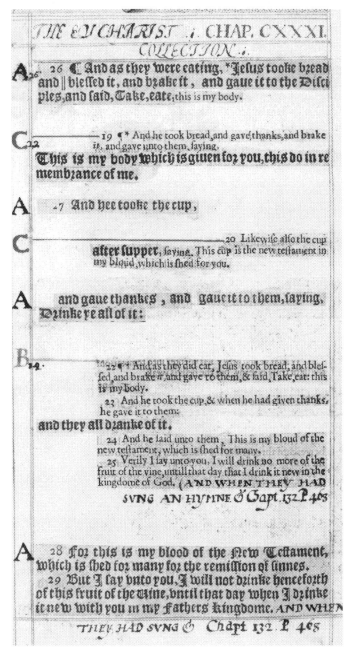

Figure 9 Gospel Harmony (1635). © British Library Board (BL C.23.e.4, column 462)

book as an architectural space was evidently important to Herbert.[75] The opening poems of *The Temple* are built around the idea of the book as architecture, and of reading as a movement through space, from 'The Church Porch', to 'Superliminare', to 'Altar'. The reader who is about to read is asked to 'approach' ('Superliminare'). In the words of Random Cloud, Herbert's metaphor here is 'Reading into a Book as Entry into a Building'[76] – a metaphor amplified in later editions, which feature engravings of a church porch, door ajar, and which reverse the order of the two stanzas under 'Superliminare' to invite readers to read the stanza printed lower on the page first, then the higher, as one would move through the entrance to the church. We are directed 'to take the quatrains in the order we would walk over them.'[77] Herbert also reversed the equivalence, imagining rooms as kinds of book, advising country parsons that 'the wals [of their house] are not idle, but something is written, or painted there, which may excite the reader to a thought of piety.'[78] In a similar fashion, the workers in the Little Gidding Concordance room hung scriptural texts from the walls; also 'in their great parlour' a large 'inscription, hung up in a large table, written in a fair legible hand' that warned off troublesome guests – a text that was erected '[c]hiefly upon the invitation of his [Nicholas'] dear friend, Mr. George Herbert.'[79] Lady Anne Clifford ordered her maids to adorn 'her Walls, her Bed, her Hangings, and Furniture' with 'Sentences, or Sayings of remark' that Clifford 'had read or learned out of Authors... that she, or they, might remember, and make their descants on them.'[80]

If rooms were imagined as books – Clifford's chamber has been called a 'commonplace-book bedroom'[81] – then Herbert was turning his book into

---

[75] See Anne M. Myers, 'Restoring "The Church-porch": George Herbert's Architectural Style', *English Literary Renaissance*, 40 (2010), 427–457.
[76] Random Cloud, 'Enter Reader', in *The Editorial Gaze: Mediating Texts in Literature and the Arts*, ed. Paul Eggert and Margaret Sankey (New York, 1998), pp. 3–50, p. 4.
[77] Cloud, 'Enter Reader', p. 39. As Cloud notes, pp. 23–25, Richard Crashaw's *Steps to the Temple, Sacred Poems* (1646), a response and homage to Herbert's collection, features, in later editions, frontispieces depicting figures climbing steps to enter a church or temple.
[78] George Herbert, *Herbert's Remains, or sundry pieces of that Sweet Singer, Mr. George Herbert, containing A Priest to the Temple, or the countrey parson, Jacula Prudentum, &c.* (1652), ch. 10.
[79] *Materials for the Life*, p. 88.
[80] Edward Rainbowe, *A Sermon Preached at the Funeral of the Right Honorable Anne, Countess of Pembroke, Dorset, and Montgomery* (1677), pp. 39–40. For writing on walls in early modern England, see Fleming, *Graffiti*, pp. 9–72; for handwritten annotations in books considered as a kind of graffiti, see Jason Scott-Warren, 'Reading Graffiti in the Early Modern Book', *Huntington Library Quarterly* 73 (2010), 363–381.
[81] Heidi Brayman Hackel, *Reading Material in Early Modern England: Print, Gender and Literacy* (Cambridge, UK: Cambridge University Press, 2005), p. 231.

a space, an attitude encouraged by cutting and pasting. In 'Good Friday', Herbert takes the familiar metaphor of the heart as a surface on which to write, and replaces it with a much more complicated description:

> Since bloud is fittest, Lord, to write
> Thy sorrows in, and bloudie fight;
> My heart hath store, write there, where in
> One box doth lie both ink and sinne:
>
> That when sinne spies so many foes,
> Thy whips, thy nails, thy wounds, thy woes,
> All come to lodge there, sinne may say,
> *No room for me*, and flie away.
>
> Sinne being gone, oh fill the place,
> And keep possession with thy grace;
> Lest sinne take courage and return,
> And all the writings blot or burn.

In these lines the heart is the surface on which God might write ('write there'), but it is also immediately turned into a space: a desk, containing a supply of ink, 'where in / One box doth lie both ink and sinne'. It is also the location in which that writing can take place: a cabinet or office. The heart is a text, but a text that is also a space, in which, as a result of the crowded presence of God's 'whips', 'nails', 'wounds' and 'woes', sin finds itself pushed out: 'sinne may say, / *No room for me*, and flie away.' The poem's description of a movement between a writing surface and a writing space is also apparent in Herbert's 'Confession', in which his heart is revealed to be full of 'Closets; and in them many a chest; / And like a master in my trade / In those chests, boxes; and in each box, a till.' The inexorable presence of sin in the narrator's sense of self is described not as a writing on a surface – a metaphor that we might expect in Shakespeare's sonnets, or in Philip Sidney's – but rather as an extraordinarily embodied process of entry: 'No scrue, no pierecer can / Into a piece of timberwork and winde, / As God's afflictions into man.'

The status of cutting as a form of textual production has often been low. In a remarkably dismissive analysis of false attributions of Little Gidding bindings, Geoffrey Hobson described the 'pious tedium of life at Little Gidding', and took aim at the cut-and-paste Harmonies: 'dreadful monuments of misdirected labour', and, at best, 'an admirable diversion for a rather backward child of eight.'[82] This wrongly dismisses the labour

---

[82] Geoffrey Hobson, *Bindings in Cambridge Libraries* (Cambridge, UK: Cambridge University Press, 1929), p. 122.

involved in the production of the famous books made at Little Gidding, books which Charles I praised for their 'singular composition' and 'exquisite workmanship... [not] paralleled... by any man.'[83] Herbert evidently thought carefully about the relationship between knives and poetry: *The Temple* is in part about the potency of cutting as a mechanism for making meaning. A criticism that seeks to recover the historicised modes of textual production now needs to think much harder about scissors and knives and the things that they can do. Such criticism also needs to consider how writing works when it proceeds through cutting. Such a process of assessment can help to overturn the centuries-long trivialisation of the labour of Anna and Mary Collett at Little Gidding – artists hitherto seen as little more than mute enactors of their uncle's great vision – and, more broadly, to bring to critical prominence a culture of cutting that seems to have been part of the reading and writing experience of early modern England.

The Harmony makers at Little Gidding can provide us with one more instance to encourage us to take seriously cutting as a form of textual production. Figure 10 and its close up in Figure 11 come from the final chapter of *The Actions & Doctrine & Other Passages touching Our Lord and Saviour Jesus Christ*, the gospel harmony made for Charles I in 1635 from cut-up editions of the English Bible and a wide range of Antwerp devotional prints. The image shows the Apostle Matthew writing his gospel, turning to face a beckoning angel, while, in the foreground, a desk bears the props of writing: an hourglass, a book clasped shut, a quill in an inkpot, and an open book bearing text which seems to be both on the page and floating above it: 'And loe / I am / with you al / way Euen unto / the End of the World / Amen' – the closing lines of Matthew chapter 28, that moment when the risen Jesus tells the disciples to 'teach all nations' and disseminate the word.

This image of Matthew is built around a print designed by Peter de Jode, engraved by Egbert van Panderen and published by Theodore Galle. Early modern representations of Matthew writing his gospel were common: Caravaggio's first version, *Saint Matthew and the Angel* (1602) – destroyed by the burning of the Kaiser Friedrich Museum in Berlin in 1945, but known today through reproductions – showed a thick-set Matthew, with crossed lumbering legs and eyes staring over the book in apparent bafflement. This hyper-embodied Matthew failed to impress Caravaggio's patrons at the church of San Luigi dei Francesi, Rome, and his second,

---

[83] *Materials for the Life*, pp. 77–79.

Figure 10 Matthew. © British Library Board (BL C.23.e.4)

more refined representation, *The Inspiration of St Matthew* (1602), hangs in the chapel today.

How are we to read Figure 10? The most striking feature is that the English letters, which appear to flow from the apostle's quill, take the form of printed text produced by type, oriented for us, the readers: text which has been cut up,

Figure 11 Matthew (close-up of Figure 10). © British Library Board (BL C.23.e.4)

rearranged, and glued down. The words also appear to float above the surface of the book, lending the text (as a result of the cut-and-paste material practice) a numinous quality. Matthew seems to be both turning to face the angel for inspiration – suggesting a text in process – and presenting to us a finished narrative: a text complete. Most visual representations of Matthew writing show the opening words ('Liber generationis', or – as the King James Version has it – 'The book of the generation of Jesus Christ'); Caravaggio's depiction offers these words in Hebrew, and then shows Matthew writing the start of the next verse, 'Abraham begat'.[84] The Little Gidding representation displays the closing words of the closing chapter: that is, verse 20 of chapter 28.

The Little Gidding community seized on this iconic moment of the word made flesh to offer a representation of writing as the product of scissors and glue, reconceiving a founding moment in the history of text as a scene of cutting and pasting. According to Jerome and others, Matthew wrote his gospel in his own hand: in Matthew's biography in Jacobus of Voragine's thirteenth-century collection of saints' lives,

---

[84] Irving Lavin, 'Divine Inspiration in Caravaggio's Two St. Matthews', in *The Art Bulletin* 56.1 (March 1974), 59–81, 65.

Matthew derives etymologically from 'manus' and 'theos', the hand of God.[85] Little Gidding thus reformulates writing by hand as the work not of pen and ink but of knives and scissors. Given the significance of Matthew's gospel as the earliest Christian text, Little Gidding's reworking suggests that collage precedes inscription as Christianity's written mode. 'In the beginning was the cut.'[86]

[85] Lavin, 'Divine Inspiration', 62. [86] Fleming, 'Renaissance Collage', 445.

CHAPTER 2

Burning Texts: 'His Studyeing Chaire ... Was of Strawe'

'publish it not, but yet burn it not; and between those, do what you will with it.'
— John Donne (1619)[1]

'I am a scribbled form, drawn with a pen / Upon a parchment, and against this fire / Do I shrink up.'
— Shakespeare, *King John*, 5.7

'What is the material history of books with names but no bodies?'
— Anne Lake Prescott (1998)[2]

'This Booke,' wrote Leonard Digges in a preface to Shakespeare's First Folio, 'When Brasse and Marble fade, shall make thee looke / Fresh to all Ages.'[3] If we chose the First Folio of Shakespeare (1623) and Ben Jonson's *Workes* (1616) as our bibliographical landmarks, then the history of early modern print is likely to look like a journey towards material permanence: towards the production of books and therefore authors that had the power to endure through time. 'Thou ... art alive still,' wrote Jonson to the dead Shakespeare in a characteristically conditional statement of praise, 'while thy Booke doth live'.[4]

But this is only part of the story. The history of the early modern book is also a history of loss and destruction: of print as impermanent; of literature as something that needs to be forgotten; of books that burn; of reading as an act of throwing away. Most printed texts lived very briefly, and then

---

[1] John Donne on *Biathanatos*, letter to Robert Ker, April 1619, in *Complete Poetry and Selected Prose*, ed. John Hayward (New York: Nonesuch Press, 1929), p. 470.
[2] Anne Lake Prescott, *Imagining Rabelais in Renaissance England* (New Haven: Yale University Press, 1998), p. 175.
[3] Leonard Digges, 'To the Memorie of the deceased Author Maister W. Shakespeare', in *Shakespeare's Comedies, Histories, & Tragedies* (1623), sig. A7r.
[4] Ben Jonson, 'To the memory of my beloved, The Author, Mr. William Shakespeare', in *Comedies, Histories, & Tragedies*, sig. A4.

were gone, forever. About 1 in 10,000 sixteenth-century broadside ballads survives today.[5] Where did printed pages go to die? Some were used for lining pie dishes; for lighting tobacco; for wrapping vegetables at Bucklersbury Market. 'Great *Iulius* Commentaries lies and rots,' rhymed poet and waterman John Taylor, 'As good for nothing but stoppe mustard pots.'[6] Taylor probably wants us to hear the echo of Hamlet, also on Caesar: 'Imperious Caesar, dead and turn'd to clay, / Might stop a hole to keep the wind away.' [7] Sir William Cornwallis kept what he called 'pamphlets and lying-stories and two-penny poets' in his privy, and many texts were 'pressed into general service', as Margaret Spufford put it, as toilet paper.[8] As Chapter 4 explores, books were pulled apart to serve in the binding and endpapers of later books: the pages of an unwanted Bible perhaps padding the spine of an unholy prose romance. A *Booke of Common Prayer* (1549) in Lambeth Palace Library has endpapers made from a broadside almanac from 1548;[9] the Folger Shakespeare Library copy of *The Tunnyng of Elynour Rummyng* (1521) – John Skelton's great poem of drunkenness – only survives because it was used as waste paper for the binding of another book.[10] New books were often pulled apart and reconstituted old books, and while literary criticism has imagined creativity as a process of patching together existing forms, this happened on a material level, too. In such instances, to read an early modern book meant confronting the broken, recycled material remains of former texts, and the effect is of a kind of memory or haunting: of a book remembering its origins. As Leah Price has recently described, we can do many things to books apart from read them.[11] Many books were simply read to pieces: the more popular the text (almanacs, ballads), the greater the chance of

---

[5] Tessa Watt, *Cheap Print and Popular Piety, 1550–1640* (Cambridge, UK: Cambridge University Press, 1994), p. 141.
[6] John Taylor, 'Laugh, and be Fat', in *All the workes* (1630), p. 72.
[7] William Shakespeare, *Hamlet*, 5.1.211–212, in *Arden Shakespeare Complete Works*, ed. Ann Thompson, David Scott Kastan, Richard Proudfoot (London: Bloomsbury Publishing, 2014), p. 326.
[8] Margaret Spufford, *Small Books and Pleasant Histories: Popular Fiction and Its Readership in Seventeenth-Century England* (Cambridge, UK: Cambridge University Press, 1981), p. 48.
[9] *The Booke of The Common Prayer* (1549), Lambeth Palace Library H5145.A2 (1549), with endpapers from *An Almanack and Pronosticacion* [sic] *for the yeare of oure Lorde M.D. and xlviii* (1548). F. H. Stubbings, 'A Cambridge Pocket-Diary, 1587–92', *Transactions of the Cambridge Bibliographical Society*, v (1971), 191–202, 192, notes that fragments of Gabriel Frende's *Almanacke and Prognostication* (1591) survive 'in the binding of a book at Shrewsbury School'.
[10] Folger Shakespeare Library STC 22611.8. See also Strickland Gibson, 'Old Bindings as Literary Hunting-Grounds', in *The Academy* 1748 (4 November 1905), Illustrated Supplement, 1–4.
[11] Leah Price, *How to Do Things with Books in Victorian Britain* (Princeton: Princeton University Press, 2012).

destruction, with the paradoxical consequence that archival absence in the twenty-first century might be a marker of extensive early modern presence. (This can lead to certain paradoxes: if numerous extant copies indicates popularity, while no extant copies also indicates popularity, how is a lack of popularity conveyed?)[12] As one book historian mournfully notes, 'the entire productions of many of the [almanac] authors of this period have disappeared ... we know of such authors as George Williams ... Barnabe Gaynsforth ... [and] Thomas Stephens, Gent, ... [only] by their names appearing among the licenses.'[13]

Such a culture upsets any direct coupling of print with textual permanence. Famous literary celebrations of the capacity of writing to endure – like Shakespeare's 'Yet, do thy worst, old Time: despite thy wrong, / My love shall in my verse ever live young'[14] – might thus be read not as descriptions of bibliographical norms, but rather as counter-voices whose wit and urgency derived from their inversion of a prevailing culture of textual transience. Such a culture might be one surprising point of contact or empathy between twenty-first-century scholars, and the early modern period which they study. If the constant doubting hum that accompanies scholarly writing is that sense of how much from the past has been lost, then early modern writers wrote, and early modern readers read, with a related expectation of quotidian loss.[15]

Alongside everyday transience, there was also destruction of a more spectacular kind.[16] The link between early modern book destruction, and in particular burning, and censorship or punishment, has been described.[17] Religious discord in the form of the Reformation catalysed an emerging English tradition of burning prohibited books: while in China, a lengthy tradition of book burning extended back to the third century BCE, it was only in the 1520s that (in Brian Cummings' words) book burning became 'a

---

[12] For early modern print popularity, see Andy Kesson and Emma Smith (eds), *The Elizabethan Top Ten: Defining Print Popularity in Early Modern England* (Farnham: Ashgate, 2013).
[13] Eustace F. Bosanquet, *English Printed Almanacks and Prognostications: A Bibliographical History to the year 1600* (Chiswick Press: London, 1917), p. 42.
[14] William Shakespeare, *Sonnets*, ed. Katherine Duncan-Jones (London: Arden, 2010), no. 19, p. 149. See also sonnets 54, 71 and 81.
[15] For more on the experience of researching while recognising how much of the past does not survive, see Thomas Fulton, *Historical Milton: Manuscript, Print and Political Culture in Revolutionary England* (Amherst: University of Massachussetts Press, 2010), chapter 1, esp. pp. 15–16 and 21–22.
[16] For a hugely entertaining survey of forms of destruction – including fire, water, the bookworm, 'other vermin' and 'servants and children' – see William Blades, *The Enemies of Books* (Cambridge, UK: Cambridge University Press, 1888, 2015).
[17] David Cressy, 'Book Burning in Tudor and Stuart England', in *The Sixteenth Century Journal* 36.2 (Summer 2005), 359–374; Ariel Hessayon, 'Incendiary texts: book burning in England, c.1640 – c.1660', in *Cromohs*, 12 (2007): 1–25, www.cromohs.unifi.it/12_2007/hessayon_incendtexts.html.

major European sport'.[18] Martin Luther's books were burnt in May 1521 in the churchyard of St Paul's cathedral, as Cardinal Wolsey and the papal ambassadors watched on: the books, here, a surrogate for their author. William Tyndale's English translation of the New Testament was burned at Cheapside Cross on 19 November 1530. In February 1557, and with, to modern eyes, a slippage between corpus as body (the early modern sense) and corpus as a collection of writing (an eighteenth-century connotation), the remains of the buried Martin Bucer and Paul Fagius were dug up and burnt at Cambridge along with their books: an event remembered and illustrated in John Foxe's *Actes and Monuments*, and also in Henry Machyn's 'Book of Remembrance'.[19] Religious discord might also catalyse provincial, *ad hominem* instances of book destruction. Quarter session records record that in September 1641, a weaver of Earls Colne, Essex, named Thomas Harvy, was so angered by the preaching of Ralph Josselin – known now, but not then, as the diarist – that he returned to the church later in the day and 'tooke the Common prayer booke and threw it into a pond thereby, & the next day in the morning he went to the pond & tooke out the sayd booke [and] Cutt it in pieces: p[ar]te thereof he did burne, some he threw away & some he kept in his pocket.'[20] This remarkable instance of book destruction across three forms (cutting, burning, drowning), suggests that different modes of destruction carried different connotations. How was burning a book different from drowning or 'Cutt[ing] it in pieces'?

Other burnings were not explicitly religious in motivation, but rather expressed a jumpy royal authority. The so-called 'Bishops Ban' of 1599 ordered 9 books of epigrams and satires to be burned outside Stationer's Hall: the texts seen as politically subversive by a teetering and paranoid Elizabethan regime. At the same time, some 1,500 copies of the second edition of John Hayward's *The First Part of the Life and Raigne of King Henrie IIII* (1599) – a text understood by Queen Elizabeth as a catalyst for the Earl of Essex's ambitions – were burned at the Bishop of London's residence at Fulham Palace. James I ordered books to be burnt at Paul's Cross, including, in February 1625, 800 copies of Edward Elton's *God's*

---

[18] Brian Cummings, 'Iconoclasm and Bibliophobia in the English Reformations, 1521–1558', in *Images, Idolatry, and Iconoclasm in Late Medieval England: Textuality and the Visual Image*, ed. Jeremy Dimmick, James Simpson and Nicholette Zeeman (Oxford: Oxford University Press, 2002), pp. 185–206, p. 200.
[19] Andrew Gordon, *Writing Early Modern London* (Basingstoke: Palgrave, 2013), p. 22.
[20] Alan Macfarlane, *The Family Life of Ralph Josselin: A Seventeenth-Century Clergyman* (Cambridge, UK: Cambridge University Press, 1970), p. 26.

Holy Mind; and in 1634, William Prynne's anti-theatrical tirade, *Histrio-Mastix* (1634), which seemed to criticise Queen Henrietta Maria directly, was condemned to a kind of over-determined destruction: burnt by the hangman in, ironically, as theatrical a manner as possible. Eye witness reports described the watching Prynne choking from the smoke.

Such performances of judicial coercion were one very public way in which books were destroyed. Powerful as a symbol, or as a moment of theatre, such burnings were inefficient as mechanisms of censorship, since the flames could never consume all copies: 'at least one example survives of every book, pamphlet, broadsheet and newsbook ordered to be burned in England between 1640 and 1660.'[21] In Jonson's *Sejanus His Fall* (1603), the historian Cordus's writing seems – like John Hayward's *Life and Raigne of King Henrie IIII* – to draw parallels, and find an application, between history, in the form of Julius Caesar's assassination, and the contemporary ruler, Tiberius. As a result, the writings are condemned to 'be burnt. / All sought, and burnt, today.' But this tool of punishment appears inept and absurd, at least to Arruntius:

> Let 'em be burnt! Oh, how ridiculous
> Appears the *Senate's* brainless diligence,
> Who think they can, with present power, extinguish
> The memory of all succeeding times!

What Sabinus calls 'this rage of burning' lends 'to the writers an eternal name.'[22] And if the material inefficacy of burning was apparent – destruction defeated, according to Arruntius, by the immateriality of memory – then the theatre of such punishments might also be subverted, or parodied, as David Cressy has argued. London merchant Thomas Sommers, guilty of possessing the Gospels in English, was forced to 'ryde from the Tower into Cheapeside ... behanged with bookes rounde about him'. But Sommers adopted the costume with exaggerated, parodic exuberance: 'I haue always loued to goe hansomly in my apparell,' he declared, '& takyng the bookes and openyng them, he bound them together by the stringes and cast them about his necke (the leaues beyng all open) like a coller, & beyng on horse backe, rode foremost thorow the streetes'.[23] (The resistance was temporary: Sommers died in the Tower in 1541.)

---

[21] Hessayon, 'Incendiary texts', 23. See also Cummings, 'Iconoclasm and Bibliophobia', pp. 200–202.
[22] *Sejanus His Fall*, in Jonson, *Works*, vol. 2, 3.469, 471–474, 478, 480. Discussed in Ian Donaldson, *Ben Jonson: A Life* (Oxford: Oxford University Press, 2011), pp. 188–189.
[23] 'A note of one Thomas sommers prisoned for the Gospell', in John Foxe, *Acts and Monuments*. See also Cummings, 'Iconoclasm and Bibliophobia', pp. 202–203.

If book destruction as censorship and punishment is one noisy tradition, then accidental book loss was another refrain throughout the early modern period. 1623 saw the publication of Shakespeare's First Folio – a crucial moment in the history of the book, and in the establishment of categories like 'authorship', 'print' and 'literature'; but it was also the year in which a fire destroyed some – or much – or all – (we don't exactly know) – of Ben Jonson's library. What happens to an author's writings when his library goes up in smoke? What kind of transformation occurs when the books he's bought and borrowed, and his own creative work, unpublished, mid-composition, are devoured by flames? Is a library fire a story of loss, or is it something else, too?[24]

John Aubrey gives a vignette of Jonson's disciplined but reckless working habits:

> he would many times exceed in drinke: Canarie was his beloved liquor: then he would tumble home to bed; and when he had thoroughly perspried then to studie. I have seen his studyeing chaire, which was of Strawe, such as old woemen used; and as Aulus Gellius is drawen in.[25]

References to Jonson's fondness for alcohol are frequent: William Drummond described drink as 'one of the elements in which … [Jonson] liveth', and a verse remembering Jonson after his death noted that 'Sack was the Morning, Evening of thy name'.[26] From March 1630, King Charles granted Jonson a tierce of canary on top of his annual salary of £100: that is, a sixth of a tun (252 wine gallons), or 42 gallons.[27] Amid such enthusiastic consumption, it is not hard to imagine – as Jonson's most recent biographer, Ian Donaldson, does – a candle knocked over, and then Jonson's works-in-progress, and his treasured library, including books

---

[24] For a modern analogue, see accounts of the fire that destroyed the library of the author Francis Wheen in April 2012. While Jonson's response to his fire was to write an angry poem, Wheen said he would simply 'sit in the lotus position and contemplate the four noble truths'. www.independent.co.uk/arts-entertainment/books/news/bonfire-of-the-first-editions-author-loses-lifes-work-in-garden-shed-fire-7646612.html.

[25] Aubrey, *Brief Lives*, vol. I, p. 363. For more on Jonson's creative practices, see Adam Smyth and Michelle O'Callaghan, 'Tavern and Library: Working with Ben Jonson', in Ceri Sullivan and Graeme Harper (eds), *Authors at Work: the Creative Environment* (Suffolk: Boydell and Brewer, 2009), pp. 155–171.

[26] 'Conversations with William Drummond (1619)', in *Jonson*, ed. Parfitt; 'Verses written over the Chair of Ben: Johnson, now remaining at Robert Wilsons, at the signe of Johnson's head in the Strand', in *Wit and Drollery* (1656), pp. 79–80.

[27] David Riggs, *Ben Jonson: A Life* (Cambridge, MA: Harvard University Press, 1989), p. 319.

leant by friends, quickly destroyed.[28] The image we have of Jonson's working environment is of something like a tinderbox: 'no dramatist of the period', Joseph Loewenstein writes, 'so needed to surround himself with piles of books and papers.'[29]

The archival traces of Jonson's book fire are scant, as the paradoxical archive of lost things must be. Jonson's copy of the works of Catullus (1608) has damage from damp which may suggest the volume was saved from the fire,[30] and Jonson's *The Works of Claudian* (1585) in the Bodleian Library, carries, alongside the usual Jonsonian annotations (the underlinings, the symbols of flowers) and the marks of its later owner, John Selden, evidence of fire damage – perhaps, but not definitively, from 1623.[31] The fire's more visible imprint lies in Jonson's furious, riveting poem of loss, 'An Execration upon Vulcan'.[32] Across 216 lines, during which Jonson shifts from a position of bafflement ('And why to me this, thou lame lord of fire?' (1)) to angry accusation and insult ('Thy wife's pox on thee' (216)), Jonson defends his writing against charges that it deserved destruction (no 'treason' in there, Jonson claims, a bit touchily, scorched, presumably, by memories of imprisonment after *The Isle of Dogs* (1597), *Sejanus* (1603) and *Eastward Ho* (1605); no 'heresy'; no 'witchcraft'); describes the kinds of

---

[28] Donaldson, *Jonson*, p. 367. The extent of this fire is disputed: Mark Bland, 'Ben Jonson and the Legacies of the Past', in *Huntington Library Quarterly* 67 (2004), 371–400, says Jonson's reference to his 'desk' (l. 85) suggests a small fire (392), and argues that the 'escalation of the fire among Jonson's papers to a conflagration of his library' can be traced to W. Gifford's 1816 edition of *The Works of Ben Jonson* (391, fn. 91). For counter views suggesting a large fire, see Ian Donaldson, 'Jonson, Shakespeare, and the Destruction of the Book', in *Jonson's Magic Houses: Essays in Interpretation* (Oxford: Clarendon Press, 1997), pp. 198–216; and Marcus Nevitt, 'Ben Jonson and the Serial Publication of News', in *Media History* 11 (2005), 53–68, which describes the 'catastrophic' event of 'the wholesale destruction of Ben Jonson's library' (53). As Donaldson sensibly concludes, '[i]t is impossible to know how trivial or serious an event the fire of 1623 actually was' (*Life*, p. 368). Jonson was the victim of a later fire, too: neighbour and literary son James Howell wrote, perhaps unreliably, of rescuing him from a similar blaze some years later, 'this being the second time that Vulcan hath threatened you': see Howell, *Epistolae Ho-Elianae* (1645), section 5, xvii, 22–3. Noted in Donaldson, *Life*, p. 368.
[29] Joseph Loewenstein, 'Personal Material: Jonson and book burning', in Martin Butler (ed.), *Representing Ben Jonson: Text, History, Performance* (Basingstoke: Macmillan, 1999), pp. 93–113, p. 99.
[30] *C. Val. Catulli, Albii Tibulli, Sex. Aur. Propertii, opera omnia quae extant. cum variorum doctorum virorum commentariis, notis, etc.* (Paris, 1608), now Huntington 613589. David McPherson, 'Ben Jonson's Library and Marginalia: An Annotated Catalogue', in *Studies in Philology* Vol. 71, No. 5, Texts and Studies (December 1974).
[31] *Cl. Clavdianvs, Theod. Pvlmanni Cranebvrgii diligentia, & fide summa, e vetustis codicibus restitutus* (1685), Bod. 80 C. 90 Art. Seld.
[32] 'An Execration upon Vulcan', in *The Underwood*, no. 43, in *The Cambridge Edition of the Works of Ben Jonson*, general editors David Bevington, Martin Butler and Ian Donaldson (Cambridge, UK: Cambridge University Press, 2012), 7 vols, vol. 7, ed. by Colin Burrow, pp. 94–108. I have found Burrow's notes extremely helpful in the writing of this chapter. The poem was first published by John Benson in 1640.

books that might usefully be burnt (of which more later); lists his lost writing; surveys other fires (the Globe; St Paul's; Ephesus; the library of Alexandria); before concluding by scattering abuse in Vulcan's direction: 'Pox on Your Flameship ... if it be [/] To all as fatal as't hath been to me.'

How 'fatal' was this fire? One way to read Jonson's poem is as an attack on, or a lament about, book destruction, *per se*. In this sense, the poem could sit neatly within a liberal humanist narrative of the horrors of bibliographical loss: a narrative that often equates book destruction with the violation of 'civilization itself', and which describes (and in describing also often enacts) a sense of 'deep emotion ... sadness and fear'.[33] But a more careful reading of Jonson's poem reveals a text invested in discriminating between forms of destruction: some are deplorable (like the flames that engulfed Jonson's own books); others are more productive.[34] Seen in this light, Jonson's poem becomes, at least in part, a meditation on the uses of destruction, and a consideration of the necessary role of burning books.

At the heart of the poem is Jonson's meticulous list of his works that, mid-composition, were lost in the flames.

> All the old Venusine in poetry,
> And lighted by the Stagirite, could spy
> Was there made English, with a Grammar too,
> To teach some that their nurses could not do,
> The purity of language. And, among
>   The rest, my journey into Scotland sung,
> With all th'adventures; three books not afraid
> To speak the fate of the Sicilian maid
> To our own ladies, and in story there
> Of our fifth Henry, eight of his nine year;
> Wherein was oil, beside the succour spent
> Which noble Carew, Cotton, Selden lent:
> And twice-twelve years' stored up humanity,
> With humble gleanings in divinity
> After the fathers, and those wiser guides
> Whom faction had not drawn to study sides.[35]

---

[33] Rebecca Knuth, *Libricide: The Regime-Sponsored Destruction of Books and Libraries in the Twentieth Century* (Westport, CT: Praeger, 2003), p. 1.

[34] In this sense I am disagreeing with Ian Donaldson's argument that '"An Execration upon Vulcan" marks Jonson's attempt to assert, through the printed word, his capacity for survival when faced with the ultimate test, the destruction of his writings'. Ian Donaldson, 'Jonson, Shakespeare, and the Destruction of the Book', in *Jonson's Magic Houses: Essays in Interpretation* (Oxford: Clarendon Press, 1997), pp. 198–216, 214.

[35] 'Execration', lines 89–104.

These lines – a kind of annotated bibliography of lost works – seem to refer to (i) a commentary on the *Ars Poetica* by Horace (born in Venusia), with a preface drawing on the *Poetics* of Aristotle (born in Stagira); (ii) an English Grammar; (iii) a song describing Jonson's 1618 walk to Scotland; (iv) a translation of three books of John Barclay's popular Latin prose romance *Argenis*; (v) a history, of some kind, of Henry V, in part based on books leant by antiquarian friends Richard Carew, Sir Robert Cotton and Sir John Selden; and (vi) a commonplace book, 'twice-twelve years' stored up humanity, / With humble gleanings in divinity'. Apart from a mention of 'parcels of a Play' and '[a]dulterate masquings' (line 43), this list suggests Jonson the serious scholar – recipient of an honorary Master of Arts from Oxford University in 1619 – much more than Jonson the popular playwright.[36]

How might we respond to this list of apparently lost works? One way is with a kind of bibliographical literalism: to ask whether these books ever actually existed. This is an alluring method, especially since such 'gaps in the literary record tantalise all the more for being so clearly labelled'.[37] Some references can be linked with later publications, or works Jonson elsewhere suggested he was writing. Two different versions of Jonson's translation of Horace's *Ars Poetica* were published after his death, in 1640 and 1641;[38] Jonson later published an *English Grammar*; three books of his translation of *Argenis* were included in the Stationer's Register on 2 October 1623, although it seems after the fire, Jonson (in Ian Donaldson's words) 'could not bring himself to begin the translation all over again', and the commission passed to Kingsmill Long, whose translation was printed in 1625;[39] and 'parcels of a Play' may refer to an early draft of *The Staple of News* (1626).[40] That leaves some unknowns: the commonplace book; the history of Henry V; the song about Jonson's walk to Scotland. Jonson did tell Drummond that he wanted 'to write his foot pilgrimage hither, and to call it A Discovery', and there might be further recent evidence: in 2009 James Loxley discovered a 7,500-word prose account of Jonson's journey, written by an unknown companion, and titled 'My Gossip Joh[n]son / his foot voyage / and myne / into Scotland'.

---

[36] Donaldson, *Life*, p. 369.
[37] James Loxley, 'My Gossip's Foot Voyage: A recently discovered manuscript sheds new light on Ben Jonson's walk to Edinburgh', in *Times Literary Supplement*, no. 5554, (11 September 2009), 13–15, 13.
[38] For these identifications, see Burrow, *The Underwood*, pp. 100–101.
[39] Donaldson, *Jonson*, p. 369.
[40] G. B. Johnston, 'Notes on Jonson's Execration Upon Vulcan', in *MLN* 46.3 (1931), 150–153, makes this suggestion by noting that lines 79–84 of 'Execration' reference several subjects discussed satirically in the play.

The text was found among the Aldersey family papers in the Chester Archives, and an edition appeared in 2015.[41]

Jonson's former friend George Chapman – stung by Jonson's critical annotations in his copy of Chapman's *The Whole Works of Homer, Prince of Poets* (1616) – had his doubts about all of these claims: he wrote his 'Invective written against Mr. Ben Jonson' to question those works in progress obliterated in what Chapman sarcastically calls 'your sacred deske / (The wooden fountayne of the Mughtye Muses)'. Did Jonson, Chapman suggests, invent these lost works to placate King James ('criing fire out In a dreame to kinges') after Jonson's honorary degree?[42] Was Jonson rather nervously showing James he was worth it?

But do Jonson's books need to exist? How material does a book need to be for it to be recorded as a book? With Chapman's qualifications ringing in our ears, any search for actual books needs to be qualified by the fact that Jonson may have been writing, at least partly, within the minor but established literary tradition of the imagined or fictitious library catalogue. The best known English example is perhaps John Donne's *Catalogus librorum aulicorum incomparabilium et non vendibilium*, or *The Courtier's Library of Rare Books Not for Sale*, unpublished until 1650 but written between about 1603 and 1611, and popular in manuscript with Donne's coterie readers.[43] It is a parody of guides to courtly behaviour – a sort of turning-on-its-head of Castiglione's *Il Cortegiano* (1528), and it lists 34 imaginary books from which (the joke runs) aspiring courtiers ('elite fops and layabouts', in Anne Lake Prescott's words)[44] may derive a kind of parody of wisdom: 'with these books at your elbow', Donne suggests, 'you may in almost every branch of knowledge suddenly emerge as an authority'. Among Donne's titles are *Edward Hoby's Afternoon Belchings*; Martin Luther's *On shortening the Lord's Prayer*; and *The Art of copying out within the compass of a Penny all the truthful statements made to that end by John Foxe*.[45] Donne was perhaps inspired by Rabelais's satirical description of

---

[41] *Informations*, 406–408, 644–645. James Loxley, Anna Groundwater and Julie Sanders (eds.), *Ben Jonson's Walk to Scotland: An Annotated Edition of the 'Foot Voyage'* (Cambridge, UK: Cambridge University Press, 2015).

[42] George Chapman, 'Invective written against Mr. Ben Jonson', in *The Poems of George Chapman*, ed. Phyllis Brooks Bartlett (Oxford: Oxford University Press, 1941), pp. 374–378. Chapman's poem is in Bod MS Ashmole 38.

[43] Piers Brown, '"Hac ex consilio meo via progredieris": Courtly Reading and Secretarial Mediation in Donne's *The Courtier's Library*', in *Renaissance Quarterly* 61.3 (Fall 2008), 833–866, 833.

[44] Prescott, *Imagining Rabelais*, p. 175.

[45] John Donne, *The Courtier's Library, or Catalogus Librorum Aulicorum incomparabilium et non vendibilium*, ed. and translated by Evelyn Mary Simpson (London: Nonesuch Press, 1930), pp. 42, 50, 46, 44, 43.

Burning Texts: 'His Studyeing Chaire ... Was of Strawe' 65

the imaginary Library of St Victor in Paris – Europe's 'first imaginary library'[46] – in the seventh chapter of *Pantagruel*: while Donne's target is the would-be courtier, Rabelais' satirical net is wider as he mocks popular supersitition, lawyers, the Sorbonne and – in particular – the hair-splitting of scholasticism. 'Collectively', writes Anne Lake Prescott, Rabelais' books 'exact a humanist and evangelical revenge on enemies of the new learning.'[47] Among the volumes Pantagruel finds are *The Codpiece of the Law; The Testes of Theology; On the Art of Discreetly Farting in Company; Martingale Breeches with Back-flaps for Turd-droppers*; and *The Elbow-rest of Old Age*.[48]

Jonson's literary intimacy with Donne ('Who shall doubt, Donne, where I a poet bee, / When I dare send my Epigrammes to thee?')[49] and perhaps Rabelais suggests Jonson would have known of this mock catalogue tradition, and this complicates a desire to read Jonson's book list at face value: the verse bibliography is a verse before it is a bibliography. Prescott calls Rabelais' fictive titles 'nonbooks' or 'promises of books' – '[o]scillating between being and nonbeing, they are ... the librarian's equivalent of negative wonder'[50] – and this latter sense of intended or desired texts may catch something of Jonson's verse: this is perhaps bibliography as a to-do list, the titles not quite fictions, but hopes, things somewhere in the pipeline. 'I dare not say a body', Jonson confesses before itemising his lost works, 'but some parts / There were of search and mastery in the arts' (87–88).

Whether or not some, or all, of Jonson's listed lost works actually sat expectantly in his library on the day of the fire, they certainly all acquire a

---

[46] Prescott, *Imagining Rabelais*, p. 168. [47] Prescott, *Imagining Rabelais*, p. 168.
[48] François Rabelais, *Gargantua and Pantagruel*, ed. and translated by M. A. Screech (London: Penguin, 2006), pp. 39–44. Rabelais' list of books inspired the inclusion of similar nonbooks in the margins of John Healey's *Discovery of a New World* (ca. 1609), a translation of Joseph Hall's *Mundus alter et idem*. Prescott, *Imagining Rabelais*, pp. 170–173. Note also Thomas Browne's 'Musœum Clausum, or Bibliotheca Abscondita: containing some remarkable Books, Antiquities, Pictures and Rarities of several kinds, scarce or never seen by any man now living', in *Certain Miscellany Tracts* (1683), tract 13. As noted by Simpson, *Courtier's Library*, p. 54, in the mid-seventeenth century, imagined library catalogues became a means to articulate political satire: see, for instance, *Bibliotheca Fanatica* (1660) and *A Catalogue of Books, of the newest Fashion, To be sold by Auction at the Whig's Coffee-House at the Sign of the Jackanapes in Prating Alley* (1693). This tradition of writing about imaginary books is alive and well in the twentieth and twenty-first centuries: see, for instance, Jorge Luis Borges, Italo Calvino, Douglas Adams, Roberto Bolaño and Mark Z. Danielewski, among many others. For a brief survey, see Adam Smyth, 'Not to Be Read without Shuddering', in *London Review of Books* 36.4 (20 February 2014), 31–32.
[49] Ben Jonson, 'To John Donne', in *Epigrammes*, no. 96, in *Cambridge Edition*, vol. 5, ed. Colin Burrow, p. 163.
[50] Prescott, *Imagining Rabelais*, p. 167, 168.

life within the poem: we can be certain of this form of existence. For while Jonson laments that he's left with 'ruins', the fact of the fire creates a kind of utopian space within the poem, in which Jonson can deny bad texts which he had in fact written (like the acrostics he scorns at line 39,[51] or the works deemed sufficiently seditious to land him in prison), and imagine other texts that perhaps he had not. And while Chapman's 'Invective' perhaps, in David Riggs' words, 'reeks of envy', it neatly captures the creative logic in Jonson's poem: 'Burne things vnborne,' Chapman complains, 'and that way generate things?' Jonson himself notes that cities might flourish after the flames: 'For they were burnt but to be better built' (166).[52]

This says something rather important about poetry: about its capaciousness, its ability to hold within its 216 lines not only Jonson's fire, but seven other historic fires, from Troy to the Fortune Theatre in 1621.[53] On a formal level, then, Jonson's poem pens in Vulcan's destruction, even as it describes an uncontrollable appetite. There is a relationship between material and literary form, as the loss of physical books prompts into being Jonson's long but meticulously controlled poem whose formal exactness also stands in contrast to Vulcan's unpoliced flames. Jonson defeats Vulcan, too, by turning his poem into, in part, a kind of library: an alternative space in which his works can live.

Part of the point of so carefully naming his writings is to show Jonson engaged in careful acts of bibliographical discrimination.[54] What Jonson objects to is not destruction, but hasty, indiscriminate loss. Indeed, certain kinds of books could be justifiably burnt. Had Jonson written riddles, 'curious palindromes' (34), anagrams, shape poems or acrostics, or had he 'compiled from' romances such as *Amadis de Gaul* or those in 'The learned library of Don Quixote', Vulcan's burning would have been justified, or at least less unjustified: 'Thou then hadst had some colour for thy flames' (40).[55] Jonson also introduces a second category of books that, while not necessarily deserving the flames, might have stood as tolerable substitutes for Jonson's own texts had he known Vulcan was in the book-burning

---

[51] See, for example, Jonson's 'On Margaret Ratcliffe', in *Epigrams* XL.
[52] David Riggs, *Ben Jonson: A Life* (Cambridge, MA: Harvard University Press, 1989), p. 289.
[53] Fires referenced, in chronological order, are Troy (ca. 1260–1240BCE); Ephesus (356 BCE); Alexandria (640 CE); St Paul's Steeple (1561); the Globe Theatre (1613); Whitehall Banqueting House (1619); the archives at Chancery (1621); and the Fortune Theatre (1621).
[54] Loewenstein notes that Jonson 'sets up a contrast between Vulcan's indiscriminate *consumption* and his own discriminating literary *taste*'. Loewenstein, 'Personal Material', p. 100.
[55] '[C]ompiled from' suggests merely reorganised ('assembled', in Burrow's words) existing parts in a version of authorship, Jonson implies, common to romance writers.

mood: 'many a ream / To redeem mine I had sent in' (62–63). Thus: the Koran; the collection of Saints' lives known as the *Legenda Aurea*; prose romances ('the whole sum of errant knighthood, with their dames and dwarves'); Arthurian legends; the stories of 'the mad Rowland and sweet Oliveers' (that is, probably, the *Chanson de Roland*, and Ariosto's *Orlando Furioso*); pamphlets promising alchemical magic, like (the imaginary) *The Art of Kindling True Coal* (76); satirical texts, such as Nicholas Breton's, adopting the voice of Pasquil; fashionably difficult writing ('strong lines' (78)); newsbooks; prophetic texts by fanatical puritan preachers. All of these Vulcan might have burnt – or 'lick[ed] up' (84) – in preference to Jonson's texts, undeserving of destruction.

Jonson's preoccupation with romances as books that might tolerably be burnt echoes, and might have been directly informed by, Cervantes' *Don Quixote*, Part I, Chapter 6, available in Thomas Shelton's English translation since 1612.[56] Here the priest, barber, housekeeper and niece burn most of the works on chivalry that have pushed Don Quixote into a world of fantasy. Like Jonson's narrator, Cervantes' priest carefully distinguishes between the savable (*The Four Books of Amadis of Gaul*) and the damned (*The Exploits of Esplandian*), with a further pending category for books whose status is as yet uncertain (*Galatea*, by Miguel de Cervantes). The offending books are condemned primarily for the damaging delusions they convey (what the niece calls the 'chivalry illness'), but also because of literary failings ('*Florismarte of Hyrcania* ... [is] soon going to end up in the yard [on the fire] ... given the clumsiness and dullness of his style') – rather as, in Jonson's *Every Man in His Humour*, Justice Clement calls for the burning of the bad, plagiarised verses of the pot-poet Matheo.[57] The priest burns poetry, too, despite some initial doubts ('these are books for the intellect, and do nobody any harm'): one of the few things worse than a deluded knight-errant is a deluded poet ('a catching and incurable disease').[58] This connection with *Don Quixote* is a reminder that Jonson's poem is not simply, or only, a catalogue of real books, but rather a literary work operating in a tradition of what we might call ludic bibliography: as much Jorge Luis Borges as Donald Goddard Wing.

Jonson's poem is not a condemnation of book destruction *per se*, but rather a call for certain kinds of books (namely, his own) to be preserved. To formulate that rather more sharply: Jonson's poem is a call for certain

---

[56] Loewenstein, 'Personal Material', pp. 100–102.
[57] Discussed in Donaldson, 'Jonson, Shakespeare', pp. 202–203.
[58] Miguel de Cervantes Saavedra, *The Ingenious Hidalgo Don Quixote de la Mancha*, trans. by John Rutherford (London: Penguin, 2000), pp. 54, 56.

kinds of books (like romances) to be burnt instead of his own; and, more broadly, for destruction to play a trimming, quasi-editorial role in the construction of the aesthetic and bibliographical category we call 'literature'. The 'Execration' might thus be read as a meditation on the uses of destruction for the process of canon formation and the preservation of books.

This notion of justifiable book burning has a long history. It receives scriptural sanction in the Acts of Apostles, 19: 19–20, where Paul's presence in Ephesus causes sorcerers to burn their books. Indeed, the Biblical text describes a causal link between this purposeful (but, as John Milton notes in *Areopagitica*, crucially *voluntary*, and so not magistrate-imposed)[59] book burning and the spread of Christianity: 'Many of them also which used curious arts brought their books together, and burned them before all men . . . So mightily grew the word of God and prevailed'.[60] In Marlowe's *Doctor Faustus*, Faustus' desperate final-minute appeal to the Devils who have come to take his life – 'Ugly hell, gape not! Come not, Lucifer! / I'll burn my books! Ah, Mephistopheles!' – looks like a last-ditch attempt to appease this fate by destroying his books in this tradition of virtuous bibliocide.[61] But Faustus is too late, and the final scene of the 1616 B-text (but not the 1604 A-text) follows this prospect of the potentially ameliorating destruction of a necromantic corpus with the actual destruction of Faustus' 'mangled' corpse: 'See, here are Faustus' limbs / All torn asunder by the hand of death.'[62] While early modern culture repeatedly imagined, prescribed, doubted and worried about the relationship between body and book, particularly in moments of crisis – Foxe's *Book of Martyrs*, for example, is a book of burning bodies which often hold books and out of whose mouths scrolls of text unfold – Faustus' attempt to substitute his books for his body fails: body and text are almost, but not quite equivalent, rather as Milton's famous 'as good almost kill a man as kill a good book' nearly but doesn't exactly make the two terms fungible.[63]

---

[59] John Milton, *Areopagitica*, in *The Major Works*, ed. Stephen Orgel and Jonathan Goldberg (Oxford: Oxford University Press, 2008), p. 247.
[60] Kings James Bible. Noted and discussed in James Kearney, *The Incarnate Text: Imagining the Book in Reformation England* (Philadelphia: University of Pennsylvania, 2009), p. 177.
[61] Christopher Marlowe, *Doctor Faustus*, ed. David Scott Kastan (New York and London: W.W. Norton and Company, 2005), 5.2.115–6. Kearney, *Incarnate Text*, p. 177 argues that Faustus' burning is not a simple renunciation, but is also in part a kind of sacrifice, and so a celebration of the power of necromantic books. Faustus' final offer of burning is thus unstable in terms of its signification.
[62] Marlowe, *Faustus*, 5.3.17, 6–7. [63] Milton, *Areopagitica*, p. 240.

Jonson's particular objection is to Vulcan's indiscriminate consumption. There is a problem of speed.[64] In Chapter 1, I detailed how the Little Gidding community used scissors to slow down the pace of devotional textual production. In Jonson's poem, speed is also a source of anxiety: Vulcan's 'greedy flame' burns everything 'in an hour', without stopping to think, and is the bad other to the First Folio's careful reader, who will (in words Jonson himself may have written) 'Reade him, therefore; and againe, and againe'.[65] Jonson's creativity is proudly sluggish: these texts were '[s]o many my years' labours', and their volume is measured in time. By inverting that Renaissance commonplace that figured good reading as moderate digestion – in *Poetaster*, Virgil instructs Crispinus to 'take / Each Morning of old Cato's Principles . . . / Till it be well digested: Then come home, / And taste a piece of Terence'[66] – Jonson describes Vulcan as a kind of aberrant, gorging, eroticised appetite, 'ravenous and vast', compelled to persecute writers due to his disappointed hopes of marrying Minerva. Books become 'a meal for Vulcan to lick up', 'a feast . . . Especially in paper' (60–61), 'ravished all hence in a minute's rage'.

The link between time and creativity – and, more particularly, between slowness and creativity – preoccupied Jonson. His rather tetchy assertion in *Volpone* that 'five weeks fully penn'd it, / From his own hand', sounds like an answer to a prior charge of tardiness, and Thomas Dekker's *Satiromastix* (1602) presents Horace, a thinly disguised Jonson, composing verse with a costive difficulty: Horace is 'sitting in a study behind a Curtaine, a candle by him burning, bookes lying confusedly', as he battles to find rhymes for 'an *Epithalamium* for Sir *Walter Terrels* wedding' ('Immortall name, game, dame, tame, lame, lame, lame . . . ').[67] Elsewhere Jonson seems committed to writing as a measured labour that shouldn't flow too fast: writing as the necessary difficulty that eventually produces what Joseph Loewenstein calls the 'rambling ease' of Jonson's finished work.[68] In his poem on Shakespeare in the First Folio, Jonson describes the process of writing poetry in terms of craft and work: he

> Who casts to write a living line, must sweat,
> (Such as thine are) and strike the second heat

---

[64] Nevitt, 'Serial Publication', 54–55.
[65] For Jonson as the potential author of parts of 'To the Great Variety of Readers' in the First Folio, see Donaldson, *Life*, pp. 371–374.
[66] Ben Jonson, *Poetaster*, in *Works of Ben Jonson*, vol. 2, 5.3.473–7.
[67] Thomas Dekker, *Satiromastix*, in *The Dramatic Works of Thomas Dekker*, 4 vols, vol. I, ed. Fredson Bowers (Cambridge, UK: Cambridge University Press, 1953), I.2, p. 316.
[68] Loewenstein, 'Personal Material', p. 99.

> Upon the muses' anvil: turn the same,
> (And himself with it) that he thinks to frame;
> Or for the laurel, he may gain a scorn,
> For a good poet's made, as well as born.
> And such wert thou.[69]

This is the Jonson who 'wrought sometime', according to Aubrey, 'with his father-in-lawe [a bricklayer], and particularly on the Garden-wall of Lincoln's-Inn next to Chancery-lane'.[70] His discourse of creativity is powerfully shaped by a language of slow, meticulous production. Pot poets write quickly ('common rhymers pour forth verses'), but slow labour is a mark of good work: 'if it comes in a year or two, it is well ... things wrote with labour deserve to be so read.' A poet does not 'leap forth suddenly ... by dreaming he hath ... washed his lips ... in Helicon.'[71]

Slowness, then; and a commitment also to a kind of anti-fluency, to creative set-backs: if writing is a struggle, Jonson advised, 'cast not away the quills yet, nor scratch the wainscot, beat not the poor desk, but bring all to the forge and file again; turn it anew.' We see this coupling of literary quality with things struck out in Jonson's complicated assessment of his great other, Shakespeare. 'I remember the players have often mentioned it as an honor to Shakespeare,' Jonson wrote,

> that in his writing, whatsoever he penned, he never blotted out a line. My answer hath been, 'Would he had blotted a thousand,' which they thought a malevolent speech ... [But] I loved the man, and do honor his memory on this side [of] idolatry as much as any. He was, indeed, honest, and of an open and free nature; had an excellent fancy, brave notions, and gentle expressions, wherein he flowed with that facility that sometime it was necessary he should be stopped. 'Sufflaminandus erat,' ['he should have been clogged'] as Augustus said of Haterius.[72]

We might imagine that blotting and burning exist on a continuum: they are both ways of deleting to write; the necessary acts of destruction or forgetting that lie within literary productivity. Shakespeare would have been so much better had he written less: at least according to Jonson's account. And it's true that Shakespeare's most celebrated mid-career plays (*Hamlet; Lear; Macbeth*) are marked by the absence, the cutting away, of explanation, motive, dialogue: an aesthetic of unknowns and gaps and

---

[69] Ben Jonson, 'To the Memory of My Beloved, The Author Master William Shakespeare And What He Hath Left Us', in *Cambridge Edition*, vol. 5, ed. Colin Burrow, pp. 638–642, p. 641.
[70] Aubrey, *Brief Lives*, p. 171.   [71] Jonson, *Discoveries*.   [72] Ben Jonson, *Discoveries* (468–476).

things – not burnt away – but perhaps, as Jonson would have said, blotted out.

If Jonson's poem establishes a relationship between loss and creativity, then a similar dynamic of necessary destruction – of a kind of discriminating forgetfulness – often characterises acts of book collecting, and library building, in Reformation England. Jonson was catching something circulating more broadly in his culture, and of the culture of previous generations. When John Leland described *The Laborious Journey and Serche ... for Englandes Antiquitees* under Henry VIII, he and his editor, John Bale, found themselves in an awkward moral position: applauding the monarch for dissolving the monasteries – Leland called them 'sodometrouse Abbeyes & Fryeryes' – but lamenting that 'lytle respecte was had to theyr lybraryes'.[73] Leland lingers, painfully, over the fate of books once in monastery libraries:

> some [are used by the plunderers] to serue theyr iakes, some to scoure theyr candelstyckes, & some to rubbe their bootes. Some they solde to the grossers and sope sellers, + some they sent ouer see to ye bokebynders, not in small nombre, but at tymes whole shyppes full, to the wonderynge of the foren nacyons ... I knowe of a merchaunt man, whych shall at thys tyme be namelesse, that broughte the contentes of two noble lybraryes for xl shyllynges pryce, a shame it is to be spoken. Thys stuffe hath he occupied in the stede of graye paper by the space of more than these x yeares, + yet he hath store ynough for as many yeares to come.[74]

What should a protestant bibliophile do with books and manuscripts from 'sodometrouse ... Fryeryes'? Bale responds with a rhetoric, and a methodology, of weeding out: he 'wyshed (and I scarsely utter it wythout teares) that the profytable corne had not so unaduysedly and ungodly peryshed wyth the unprofytable chaffe.'[75] The process of collecting was, Leland wrote, a process of 'casting awaye trifles, cutting off olde wiues tales, and superfluous fables' from those texts one should 'reade, scanne upon, and preserve in memorie'.[76]

As Jennifer Summit has argued in *Memory's Library*, Reformation-era library building was about constructing a particular version of a national past that required the throwing out of many texts. Libraries were concerned,

---

[73] *The Laborious Journey and Serche of Johan Leylande, for Englandes Antiquitees, geuen of hym as a newe yeares gyfte to Kynge Henry the viii in the xxxvii yeare of his Reygne, with declaracyons enlarged: by John Bale* (1549), sigs A2v, A7v.
[74] *Laborious Journey*, sig. B1r-v. [75] *Laborious Journey*, sig A7v.
[76] Quoted in Jennifer Summit, *Memory's Library: Medieval Books in Early Modern England* (University of Chicago Press: Chicago and London, 2008), p. 129.

in Summit's terms, with making memory, not preserving it, rather as Matthew Parker (1504–1575), Archbishop of Canterbury, altered the structure of printed books and manuscripts now in Corpus Christi College, Cambridge (removing one book's leaves to decorate another; supplying missing text; reordering sammelbände), often (but not always) enacting the political and religious agenda of his office;[77] and rather as Robert Cotton (1586–1631) unbound, reordered, and cut apart gathered manuscripts in pursuit of a particular version of English history: signs not of a curatorial slackness or indifference but rather of a working library, and of the ideological currents that necessarily subtend collection and curatorship.[78] (Ironically, fire did later consume parts of Cotton's library at Ashburnham House on 23 October 1731: about a quarter of the holdings were lost or damaged.[79]) But in this form of destruction Summit suggests we see this sense of a 'perenially fragmentary, incomplete ... post-Reformation archive' playing out in a literary aesthetic of 'silences and gaps over comprehensiveness and totality'.[80] Thus in Book 2 of Spenser's *Faerie Queene*, in a description of memory's library, Arthur reads a history of Britain but finds the final page torn out (something which generates in Arthur a sense of 'secret pleasure'), and Guyon turns the leaves of a history of faeire land but the volume has no end.[81]

***

Despite the fact that the Earl of Pembroke gave Jonson £20 each new year to buy books, William Drummond reported that 'Sundry tymes [he] [Jonson] heth devoured his books': by which he meant 'sold th[em] all for Necessity'.[82] That is why lots of Jonson-owned books also have other signatures on them, like John Selden's: Jonson sold them on to pay the rent, or the bar tab. Drummond's use of 'devour' – 'Sundry tymes [he] heth *devoured* his books' – reminds us of that overlap, in early modern discourse, between eating, reading and destroying. Devour means all these things. It's also the verb Jonson uses to describe Vulcan's rampage through his library ('thy greedy flame thus to

---

[77] Knight, *Bound to Read*, pp. 40–53, pp. 42, 46.
[78] Kevin Sharpe, *Sir Robert Cotton, 1586–1631: History and Politics in Early Modern England* (Oxford: Oxford University Press, 1979), p. 68.
[79] For images of leaves of Henry Machyn's 'Chronicle' (1550–1563), scarred by the Cotton fire, see http://quod.lib.umich.edu/m/machyn.
[80] Summit, *Memory's Library*, p. 127.
[81] Edmund Spenser, *The Faerie Queene*, ed. A. C. Hamilton (Harlow: Pearson, 2007), Book II, canto X, stanzas 68, 70, pp. 258–259. Summit, *Memory's Library*, p. 127.
[82] *Conversations with Drummond*, 312–313, 328–329. Discussed in Donaldson, 'Jonson, Shakespeare', pp. 199–200.

devour / So many my years' labours in an hour?'). To read passionately and intensely was perilously close to an act of destruction.

But perhaps 'perilously' is a wrong and anachronistic term. Today we're inclined to see the loss of old books as unfortunate, or even tragic, but early modern bibliophiles were quite happy for most texts to go the way of the pie dish, or the privy, or the vegetable market. Thomas Bodley was careful to exclude 'idle books, & riffe raffes', including plays, from his library, and many commentators felt there were simply too many titles in the world – 'a vast *Chaos* and confusion of bookes', according to Robert Burton, for which 'the longest life of a man', lamented John Cotgrave, 'is not sufficient to explore so much as the substance of them, which (in many) is but slender'.[83] We see a similar sense of exhaustion, and lament, voiced by Memoria ('An old decrepit man, in a black Velvet Cassock') in Thomas Tomkis' *Lingua: or, The combate of the tongue, and the fiue sences for superioritie* (1607).[84] Able to recall watching Socrates being 'abused most greatly' at 'a Comedy of *Aristophanes making*' ('It is now, let me see, about 1800 years ago'), Memoria is absent-minded in the present: 'I forgot my spectacles, I left them in the 349. *page* of *Hall's* Chronicles, where he tells a great wonder of a multitude of Mice'.[85] Memoria voices despair that contemporary texts are charged with remembering too much.

> I remember in the age of *Assaracus* and *Ninus*, and about the warres of *Thebes*, and the siege of *Troy*, there were few things committed to my charge, but those that were well-worthy the preserving, but now euery trifle must be wrapt up in the volume of Eternity. A rich pudding-wife, or a Cobler cannot die but I must immortalize his Name with an Epitaph: A dog cannot pisse in a Noblemans shoe, but it must be sprinkled into the Chronicles, so that I never could remember my Treasure more full, and never emptier of Honourable, and true Heroicall actions.[86]

Thus careful reading was figured as a kind of profitable destruction: an act of discrimination that, recalling the Latin *legere*, plucked out the few worthy titles while leaving the rest (the chap books, the pamphlets, the bad plays) to the 'consuming looks' of fire (as Jonson put it). We might expect censorious reading to be figured as the erasing of the unwanted, to leave the virtuous behind. This is how John Brinsley, in *Ludus Literarius: or, The Grammar Schoole* (1612), describes the teaching of troubling pagan

---

[83] Robert Burton, *The Anatomy of Melancholy* (1621), pp. 8–9; John Cotgrave, *The English Treasury of Wit and Language* (1655), 'To the Courteous READER'.
[84] Thomas Tomkis, *Lingua: or, The combate of the tongue, and the fiue sences for superioritie. A pleasant comoedie* (1657), sig. C5. My thanks to Carla Mazzio for pointing me in the direction of this text.
[85] Tomkis, *Lingua*, sig. D7v.   [86] Tomkis, *Lingua*, sig. C6.

authors: 'filthy places in the Poets would be wisely passed ouer, or warily expounded. It were well if there were an *Index Expurgatorius*, to purge out all the filth out of these, by leauing it out, or changing it.'[87] But all reading in the period exercised a similar concern with excision, with uncoupling the sententious from the unwanted whole, with separating the good from the less good: reading was always a kind of burning away of the rest. When Lucius Cary celebrated Jonson's 'exact' literary 'judgement', he suggested that had we his reading notes, it wouldn't matter if everything else was lost.

> His Learning such, no Author old nor new,
> Escapt his reading that deserv'd his view,
> And such his Iudgement, so exact his Test,
> Of what was best in Bookes, as what bookes best,
> That had he joyn'd those notes his Labours tooke,
> From each most prais'd and praise-deserving Booke,
> And could the world of that choise Treasure boast,
> It need not care though all the rest were lost.[88]

In Johann Comenius' *Orbis sensualium pictus* (1685), the space and function of 'The Study' is illustrated by a picture of a reader, bent over his desk, reading one text while others line the shelves. The accompanying prose unpacks this little scene. Reading is solitary ('a Student, a part from men, sitteth alone'), and is accompanied by – indeed is coterminous with – the transcription of text-parts: the reader 'picketh all the best things out of them into his own Manual'. Indeed, the text being read is positioned top left on the desk in such a way so as to make the copying the central physical activity of reading. But such is the reader's absorption – he is 'addicted to his studies' – that while he works, outside his window, and just visible to us, but not to the reader in the scene, smoke and flames tumble from a neighbours' house. Is this an image of good reading, or of reading gone wrong? Is the occupant of the neighbouring house a similarly absorbed reader (we note our reader's array of fire hazards: candle, lantern, torch)? Should we, as readers absorbed in this text, check that nothing is burning in our world?

If it is hard to identify the register of this scene, and thus a stable sense of what exactly it stands for, then it clearly does present reading as the process of extracting part from whole, of leaving behind, untranscribed, the unwanted, the superfluous – and this textual pruning is framed by pluming flames.

---

[87] John Brinsley, in *Ludus Literarius: or, The Grammar Schoole* (1612), sig. G3.
[88] Lucius Cary, Lord Falkland, 'An Eclogue on the Death of Ben Jonson, between Melybaus and Hylas', in *Jonsonus Virbius, or, The Memorie of Ben: Johnson* (1638), pp. 1–9, p. 4.

CHAPTER 3

Errors and Corrections: 'My Galley Charged with Forgetfulness'

'I would add that the ore, such as it is, lies near the surface and is plentiful.'[1]

Where does a book begin?

The first two poems in *Hesperides* (1648) are not in 'Hesperides'. Before Robert Herrick begins his lyric collection with '*The Argument of his Book*' – 'I sing of *Brooks*, of *Blossomes, Birds*, and *Bowers*: / Of *April, May*, or *June*, and *July*-Flowers' – he opens his book with two prefatory verses: a pre-beginning beginning; a clearing of the throat. First, a ten-line dedication to Charles, Prince of Wales, which attributes the 'Glories' in the book to Charles who is 'The *Flame* of it, and the *Expansion*'. And then, and with a sense of bathos signalled by the shrunken type, four lines of verse by Herrick that introduce a list of printing errors:

> For these Transgressions which thou here dost see,
> Condemne the Printer, Reader, and not me;
> Who gave him forth good Grain, though he mistook
> The seed; so sow'd these Tares throughout my Book.

The errata list, compiled by Herrick or perhaps a print-shop worker, begins 'Page 33. Line 10. Read *Rods*' (where the book has 'Gods'), and itemises 16 corrections.[2]

Taken together, these two poems – the dedication, and the errata verse – complicate the question of who, exactly, is responsible for *Hesperides*:

---

[1] R. W. Chapman, *Cancels* (London and New York: Constable, 1930), p. 10.
[2] *The Complete Poetry of Robert Herrick*, ed. Tom Cain and Ruth Connolly (Oxford: Oxford University Press, 2013), 2 vols, vol. 1, p. 422, assert with conviction that Herrick drew up the errata list, while noting that the errata list of 16 errors missed a further 69 mistakes in the book. Stephen Dobranksi, *Readers and Authorship in Early Modern England* (Cambridge, UK: Cambridge University Press, 2005), p. 154 suggests that the errata list 'could have been made by a member of the printing house instead of Herrick', and notes that 'other books published and/or sold by Francis Eglesfield and John Williams frequently included errata'. Dobranski is here pursuing a larger argument about Herrick's relative lack of control over the printing of *Hesperides* and his reliance on other agents, including readers.

dedicatee Prince Charles is the '*Creator*' ('So all my *Morne*, and *Evening Stars* from You / Have their *Existence*'), but what Charles creates, Herrick notes with careful proprietorship, is '*my* Works'.[3] At the same time, the errata verse invites the reader to condemn the printer as a corrupting but nonetheless shaping agent in the making, or sowing, of Herrick's book. These two prefatory verses thus insist on textual precision even as they blur the idea of the author-as-source.

Herrick's errata verse figures Herrick supplying the grain from which the volume grew, only for the printer to ignorantly sow tares. Tares are corrupting weeds that, when young, resemble corn: errors, the comparison suggests, are damaging because they initially look like the intended words, but grow to become distortions. Herrick's reference invokes Matthew chapter 13 and the parable of the tares: 'while men slept, his enemy came and sowed tares among the wheat, and went his way', a narrative that Jesus explains in eschatological terms: 'He that soweth the good seed is the Son of Man ... but the tares are the children of the wicked *one*; The enemy that sowed them is the devil; the harvest is the end of the world; and the reapers are the angels.'[4]

One effect of this intertextuality – of Herrick establishing a bridge between his four-line verse and Matthew's New Testament – is to moralise *Hesperides*' typographical errors: not just slips of the compositor's fingers, they become now sins that mark out the fallen. Another effect is to make Herrick's errata poem literary: the poem does one of the things that poems often do, which is to make partially buried allusion to a canonical text, and so creates a verse that is more than merely documentary. The relationship with the parable of the tares means the reading process becomes more complicated, requiring the reader to track between Herrick's errata verse and Jesus' parable in the Gospel of Matthew. The bookish facts that the errata page relays come at the reader through literature's twisting mediations.

Modern editors of Herrick haven't quite known what to do with this errata verse and list of corrections. Tom Cain and Ruth Connolly's 2013 edition enacts the 16 changes – that is, they correct the errors the 1648 text tells them to correct – and so the errata list, while printed in their edition, no longer applies. Moreover, by paginating their edition differently from the 1648 text, while maintaining the original page and line numbers in the errata list ('P. 41 l. 19. R. *Gotiere*'), the list becomes impossible to use, like a broken online link.[5]

---

[3] My italics.   [4] King James Bible, Matthew 13.25, 37–39.
[5] *Complete Poetry of Herrick*, ed. Cain and Connolly, vol. 1, p. xxx. F. W. Moorman's 1915 edition follows a similar policy but adds the editorial note 'The Errata have been corrected in the reprint. The page-numbers and line-numbers quoted above are those of the original text.' (F. W. Moorman (ed.),

We'd call 'Gods' for 'Rods' an error, but Renaissance England had a richer field of terms: faults (or 'fautes'), faults escaped, errata, castigations, castigata, escapes, oversights, blemishes, imperfections, corrigenda. Over time, from the mid-sixteenth to the early seventeenth centuries, there was a shift from 'Faults escaped' to 'Errata' as the most common term. What can we do with these things? What we normally do is correct them: perhaps with a handwritten note in the margin (if we are a reader), or an emendation in an edition (if we are an editor). Criticism finds it hard to endure mistakes, finds it hard to let them live on, just as it finds it hard to endure the meaningless, the random, the inexplicable, the untidy, the contingent. The discourse of textual studies is full of moralised terms for variants and errors – terms like 'corruptions' and 'imperfections' – a conflation that goes back to the sixteenth century, and before: one hostile history of Thomas Wolsey concludes with an errata list and the note that 'there is no reason that a Booke should be without faultes, when the person of whom the booke intreateth had so many in his life.'[6] But to correct an error is to refuse to reread an error – we don't want to see it again – and in this chapter I'd like to resist this urge to correct, and instead consider the usefulness of printed errors for bibliographers and literary critics.[7]

'Concerning *Mistakes* in the *Press;* They are not much vers'd in *Books*, that look for none'.[8] Early modern books were conspicuously fallen: authors, printers, publishers, and readers expected printed books to carry mistakes. There were technical reasons why errors were so common – printing was difficult, particularly when dispersed across agents, presses and print shops, with the pressures of deadlines and economics – although some authors framed errors as expressive less of technological challenges

---

The Poetical Works of Robert Herrick (Oxford: Clarendon Press, 1915), p. 4.) The 1921 version of this edition – 'prepared, not for the scholar, but for the lover of poetry' – includes the four-line errata verse but omits the errata list, noting 'In the original text this address is followed by Errata, which have been duly corrected in this reprint' (F. W. Moorman (ed.), *The Poetical Works of Robert Herrick* (London: Oxford University Press, 1921), with preface by Percy Simpson, p. vi). L. C. Martin's 1965 edition omits the four-line errata poem and the errata list, while including the other prefatory poem to Prince Charles; but, bafflingly, it includes reference to the errata poem in its index of first lines.

[6] Thomas Storer, *The life and death of Thomas Wolsey Cardinall Diuided into three parts: his aspiring, triumph, and death* (1599), sig. k3v.

[7] By 'printed error' I mean text (whether letter, word, phrase, or number) that appears in a form that was unintended by any of the agents of a book's production: authors, compositors, printers, publishers. I don't mean views that other readers might condemn as wrong but which were printed correctly (that is, as intended) – although, as I will explore, there is a productive overlap between my narrower definition of printed error and other conceptions of mistake, most obviously in the discourse of Reformation polemic.

[8] Robert Croft, *The plea, case, and humble proposals of the truly-loyal and suffering officers* (1663), p. 12.

than of the fallen state of the world. In his *The Fall of Man* (1618), Godfrey Goodman discussed his book's typographical blunders as not only the products of an error-fraught book trade (although they were that too), but also more fundamentally as a register of what Goodman calls 'a general corruption' of the cosmos – thus proving the thesis of this text:

> the subject of my booke, was onely to proue a generall corruption; which corruption I should in effect seeme to disproue and denie, vnlesse it might eueryhwere appeare... in the author, then in the pen, then in the presse... How happie was I to make choice of such a subiect, which seems to excuse all the errors of my Pamphlet?[9]

What interpretative potential might errors have for students of the book? This chapter's discussion is organised around four mechanisms of bibliographical correction: the errata list, the handwritten annotation, the pasted insert-slip and the cancel page. Rather than bundle these four modes into a single category of 'correction', I hope to discuss each with some specificity in order to analyse the particular way of working of each, and to draw out their interpretative potentials. It is, after all, a very different thing to strike through a word with a stroke of the pen than to paste over the top of the word a new piece of text, even if both actions serve to correct a text. At the same time, running across these local discussions are two broad commitments. First, I want to think about errors and corrections as moments when a book breaks down and admits, with rare candour, its own materiality. This means reading errors as potential sources for the process of book production. In an error, and in a meditation on error, like Herrick's errata verse, some of the labour and physical processes of printing a book, normally effaced, might briefly be on display. This, then, is to read the error as a bibliographical document: as a momentary source for the history of the book – a glimpse inside the print shop.[10]

Second, I would like to consider the error and the correction as literary forms. While the relationship between error and the printed book varied according to form and genre – mathematical treatises, for example, were more preoccupied with mistakes than, say, almanacs – it is true to say that error was not a rare anomaly but a defining trait of print. Errors and

---

[9] Godfrey Goodman, *The Fall of Man* (1618), sig. [Ff7]v. See William Poole, 'The Evolution of George Hakewill's *Apologie or Declaration of the Power and Providence of God*, 1627–1637: Academic Contexts, and Some New Angles from Manuscripts', in *The Electronic British Library Journal* (2010), article 10.

[10] This strand is a particular emphasis in my discussion of errata lists, but it pervades the whole chapter.

corrections might contribute to the literary, aesthetic or thematic effects of a book. Indeed, in various ways authors reflected on the presence of errors in their texts; what they wrote, and how they wrote, was in part shaped by an expectation that the printed book would be error-stuffed, and that various post-publication forms of correction were already circling round their text like hawks. This second strand means considering the connections between a bibliographical and a literary critical analysis of a book.

Looking at printed errors today, it is hard not to turn to the dominant twentieth-century paradigm for thinking about mistakes, which is Freud. In *The Psychopathology of Everyday Life* (1901), Freud is mostly interested in speech and in handwriting – slips of the tongue and slips of the pen. His notion that buried, repressed thoughts break out through verbal or written slips – that something true, that we may not even realise, is conveyed when our guard drops and we trip on a word or misspell a name – probably seems to most of us familiar to the point of being naturalised. Freud's influence is so profound, even as it is often denied, that his model just seems to be the way things are. His brief discussion of printing errors maintains the same central idea: that errors are meaningful as moments when 'the real thinking ... broke through'.[11] He also suggests that revelatory errors are particularly likely in print, because the slower, mechanical production of texts means it is harder to inhibit those buried meanings. Amid the sustained physical strain of printing, meaningful errors are more likely to spring forth – to 'escape', in the language of early modern errata lists.

The Psychopathology of Everyday Life is one of my favourite books, but there are two immediate questions that any early modernist will have. The first is history, and the degree to which Freud's thinking can accommodate an historicist's interest in cultural distance. Do selves, does language, work then as it does now? The second, more particular question relates to the condition that printing, in the Renaissance, is always a collaborative process, spread across agencies – author, scribe, compositor, pressman and others, sometimes involving multiple presses and even print shops. If books are collaborative things, there is the question of exactly whose thinking is breaking through, or where it comes from, or what repressive forces it ruptures.

---

[11] Sigmund Freud, *The Psychopathology of Everyday Life* (London: Penguin, 2002), p. 116. For a critique of Freud's conception of error in terms of textual studies, see Sebastiano Timpanaro, *The Freudian Slip: Psychoanalysis and Textual Criticism* (London: Verso, 1985).

80   Material Texts in Early Modern England

But there is a more fundamental difference between Freud's conception of error and the kind of early modern mistakes this chapter will discuss. To put it starkly: Freud works with a model of depth; errors are moments when buried meanings burst through. A Renaissance conception of bibliographical error works with a model of surface: errors in books show how easily one word can turn into another. A Freudian conception of error imagines a text and buried meanings beneath it; and indeed I deploy a version of this model when reading printing errors as moments when the normally hidden work of the print shop can be reconstructed: the error here is a path, suddenly open, to the repressed labour of book making. But a Renaissance writer might imagine a text with all the other texts it nearly is, hovering around it.[12]

To cite an example that will appear later: in the poetry miscellany and conduct book *The Mysteries of Love and Eloquence* (1658), a list of errors includes the accidentally Petrarchan 'for killed, read kissed'.[13] The word 'kiss' is close to the word 'kill', and that is interesting, and could be the source of comedy or tragedy, but for Renaissance readers not because a buried sense of violence is breaking through the kiss, or a buried sense of eroticism is lurking in the violence. A model of Renaissance error is less vertical, and more horizontal: the word 'kiss' is only precariously itself – it can easily become kill, or kith, or kick, or kids, or kine – just as any printed text might, at any point, with the alteration of one letter, slide across and become a different thing.

I   Errata Lists

Errata lists, or pages of 'castigata', were one mechanism of correction in printed books, alongside overprinting, stamped text, handwritten alterations, cancels and pasted-in slips. One important difference between manuscript and print production was, as David McKitterick has noted, 'the removal of correction [in print] from *after* marking the page, to *before* it'.[14] Errata lists, however, are evidence of this culture of correcting-before-printing breaking down; they were one of the last parts of a book to be printed, 'at the end of a sequence that included the author's drafts and

---

[12] For the Freudian model of depth as a key (and often naturalised) influence on literary criticism more generally, see Rita Felski, *The Limits of Critique* (Chicago: University of Chicago Press, 2015), chapter 2, 'Digging Down and Standing Back'.
[13] *The Mysteries of Love and Eloquence*, sig. A4v.
[14] David McKitterick, *Print, Manuscript and the Search for Order 1450–1830* (Cambridge, UK: Cambridge University Press, 2003), p. 99. My italics. See also p. 115.

Errors and Corrections: 'My Galley Charged with Forgetfulness' 81

redrafts, transcription (sometimes) by an amanuensis, editing, composition, proofing and printing'.[15] If most of the stages of correction and proofing are concealed in the final printed book, errata lists give us some sense of the process.

Errata lists were one of print's innovations and flourished from the early sixteenth century until they started to decline towards the end of the seventeenth.[16] Sometimes they took the form of a note of a necessary global change ('Towards the midst, till the end of this Booke, for Getulia, alwaies reade Natolia')[17], but more common was the litany of substitutions, pegged to page and sometimes line number – or, in one particularly careful instance, to 'quayre … page … [and] syde'.[18] These lists might be short, or they might be (as in the case of Robert Chambers' *Palestina* (1600)), very long: for 'seede, reade feede'; for 'rake, reade take'; for 'annoynted, reade accounted'; for 'stayres, reade stories'; for 'miage, reade image'; for 'his armes, reade her armes.'[19] Certain kinds of books produced particularly extensive lists of errata: mathematical works, in particular – both popular guides to reckoning and also more scholarly works – had a thematic concern with accuracy which combined with the difficulty of setting vertical calculations to prompt meticulous, lengthy litanies of errors and corrections ('D. ii. a. in the example, set 9, for 6, in the seconde rowe').[20]

The list of faults escaped was often accompanied by a brief, typically one-paragraph prose, or occasionally verse, introduction or gloss: a usually anonymous passage of text written by author, publisher or occasionally

---

[15] McKitterick, *History*, vol. I, p. 240.
[16] The most important scholarship on error and errata lists is McKitterick, *Print, Manuscript*, pp. 97–165 (see p. 138 for notes on the errata list's chronology of rise and decline); McKitterick, *History*, vol. I, pp. 235–253; Ann Blair, 'Errata Lists and the Reader as Corrector', in *Agent of Change: Print Culture Studies after Elizabeth L. Eisenstein*, ed. by Sabrina Alcorn Baron, Eric N. Lindquist and Eleanor F. Shevlin, pp. 21–40 (particularly for errata lists in humanist reference books); Seth Lerer, *Error and the Academic Self: the Scholarly Imagination, Medieval to Modern* (New York: Columbia University Press, 2002), pp. 15–54. For pre-print manuscript cultures of correction, see Daniel Wakelin, *Scribal Correction and Literary Craft: English Manuscripts 1375–1510* (Cambridge, UK: Cambridge University Press, 2014). Wakelin argues that scribes and sometimes readers exercised great intelligence, skill and care in correcting errors (correcting 'is ubiquitous in manuscripts in English from the late fourteenth century to the very early sixteenth' (p. 5)), and in doing so, they contributed to that tradition of attentive critical reading of the vernacular that we now call philology or literary criticism.
[17] Emanuel Ford, *Parismus, Part 2* (1599), sig. A4v.
[18] Robert Record, *The ground of artes teaching the worke and practise of arithmetike* (1552), 'fautes escaped', sigs a1v-a3v.
[19] Robert Chambers, *Palestina* (1600), 'Faults escaped'.
[20] Robert Record, *The ground of artes teaching the worke and practise of arithmetike* (1552), where an eight-line verse from 'The Printer to the Reader' on the accuracy of books (p. 13) is followed by a detailed five-page list of errors, sigs av–aiiiv. For errors in elite books, see Euclid, *The Elements of geometry* (1570), final page 'Faultes escaped'. For other extensive lists of errata, see, for example, Philippe de Mornay, *Fowre Bookes* (1600), where the 'Faultes escaped' fill the final six pages.

printer that presents a particular compound of humility, irritation, prescription, wit and regret.[21] This errata preface typically sought the reader's patience and forgiveness for the presence of the errors following; requested some variation of the formula 'Reader, Correct these Errors with thy Pen, before thou read the Book';[22] and noted that other errors not cited are to be ignored or corrected by the reader as they see fit. This errata preface is also often a space in which one agent involved in the production of the book (usually author or publisher, but sometimes printer) shifts responsibility for errors on to another agent (usually printer, but sometimes corrector, author (often blamed for supplying illegible copy) or translator). All of these functions combine in Johann Oberndorf's brief but generically orthodox final-page message in his *The anatomyes of the true physition, and counterfeit mounte-banke* (1602):

> Diuers faults haue escaped the Printer; which as they are easily discerned, so I entreat thee (friendly Reader) to amend with thy Pen, as thou goest along: and to pardon me, who by occasion of some Businesse, haue not looked so narrowly to them, as I should, and (otherwise) would haue done.[23]

At times the separation between bibliographical list and moralised narrative blurs. The 'faults' listed in Anthony Munday's *A discouerie of Edmund Campion* (1582) are conveyed in a semi-narrativised list which attributes cause and blame and creates the sense of a voice speaking the errata ('In the first Page of B. among the names, thou shalt finde *Iames Bosgraue* by misaduenture left out: I desire thee to beare with the Printers fault, and to allowe the name there').[24] Authors might also bend the purpose of errata lists to include not corrections but versions of authorial regret (retrospective glosses, expansions, clarifications): when the main text of *A new method of Rosie Crucian physic* (1658) refers to one '*E.A.*', author John Heydon includes within the list of errata the knife-twisting note: 'p. 44. l. 33. r. do not think by E.A. I mean not Elias Ashmole'. George Hakewill's *Apologie of the Power and Prouidence of God in the Gouernment of the World* (Oxford, 1627) converts the errata list into a four-page retrospective set of textual adjustments which he titles 'A Revise', in which

---

[21] Ann Blair, 'Errata Lists', p. 28, citing Richard Westfall's *Never at Rest*, notes that occasionally the compilation of an errata list was 'delegated to a third party: Isaac Newton ... drew up the list of errata for his teacher Isaac Barrow's edition of Archimedes.' Blair provides an overview of the form, pp. 31–36.
[22] George Mackenzie, *Aretina, or, The Serious Romance* (1660), sig. A8v.
[23] Johann Oberndorf, *The anatomyes of the true physition, and counterfeit mounte-banke* (1602), p. 43.
[24] Anthony Munday, *A discouerie of Edmund Campion, and his confederates, their most horrible and traiterous practises, against her Maiesties most royall person* (1582), sig. A8.

Hakewill offers a sustained reflection on errors of commission and omission within his book: details of passages to be inserted ('*Pag.* 47. In the Section of the revolution and circulation of all things in their times and turns may properly be inserted these excellent verses of *Manilius* . . . '); mistranslations ('Pag. 163. *Vndevicesimo* is translated *twenty one*, whereas it should bee *nineteen*, which makes more for my purpose, it being spoken of the wife of *Quintilian*, who by his owne testimony was not full *nineteen* when shee did, yet had shee borne him two sonnes'); and various kinds of post-publication authorial doubts ('Pag. 170. I doubt mine information touching *prescriptions* is not sufficient, but my meaning is . . . ').[25]

Conventional errata lists of substitutions are straightforward – instead of *this*, read *that* – but they are also not straightforward: they are inherently literary, in that they are acts of metaphor (one thing read as another). Perhaps it is for this reason that several contemporary poets are drawn to the interpretative richness of the form. Ian Hamilton Finlay's 'Errata of Ovid', cut into stones in Stockwood Park, Luton, casts classical myth as a series of printing errors, turning Ovidian metamorphoses into faults escaped in the press.

>for 'Daphne'
>read 'Laurel'
>
>for 'Philomela'
>read 'Nightingale'
>
>for 'Cyane'
>read 'Fountain'
>
>for 'Echo'
>read 'Echo'
>
>for 'Atys'
>read 'Pine'
>
>for 'Narcissus'
>read 'Narcissus'
>
>for 'Adonis'
>read 'Anemone'.[26]

Similarly, Geoffrey Hill's *Triumph of Love* (1999) finds poetic resonance in the cadence of errata:

---

[25] George Hakewill, *Apologie of the Power and Prouidence of God in the Gouernment of the World* (Oxford, 1627), sigs Ooo -Ooo2v. Percy Simpson, *Proof-Reading in the Sixteenth, Seventeenth and Eighteenth Centuries* (Oxford: Oxford University Press, 1935; second edition 1970), p. 116.
[26] Ian Hamilton Finlay, *Selections* (Berkeley: University of California Press, 2012), p. 190. My thanks to Charles Boyle for drawing my attention to this poem.

> Take out supposition. Insert suppository.
> For definitely the right era read: deaf in the right ear.²⁷

Reading errata creates a particular combination of clarity and confusion. One word, or phrase, is neatly substituted for another (for 'battering, reade bettering'),²⁸ and that seems unambiguous; but we are left to observe, imagine, laugh at, or worry about, the relationships between the two, which means speculating on a causal link between mistake and correction. This blend of exactness and abundance is one device for hearing (in Colin Burrow's description of Geoffrey Hill's verse) 'truths pitched just beyond our capacity'.²⁹ Notes of errata sometimes do what poets like to do: they yoke together unlike things; they switch suddenly between registers and worlds, between the quotidian and the transcendent: 'for *laughing*, reade, *languishing*'.³⁰

The errata list often came near the start of the book, as the last item of prefatory material, or at the very end: the list hovered at the fringes, a supplement to, and not quite a constituent of, the central text, although, as we shall see, its rhetoric often leaked into the body of the work. Errata lists were 'more often included in books in which blank pages were left', and so didn't incur any extra paper costs, their level of detail often reflecting the available blank space rather than the actual extent of errors in the text.³¹ Certainly, they are often squeezed into small spaces, or pasted in some (but not all) copies of a book, sometimes at different places in the text,³² which creates the effect of an afterthought, a late arrival, a passage of text whose status is not clear.

These little confessional spaces look at first like emblems of a new culture of accuracy, and this is how earlier historians of the book have understood them: Elizabeth Eisenstein noted that 'the very act of publishing errata demonstrated a new capacity to locate textual errors with precision and to transmit this information simultaneously to scattered readers.'³³ But the errata list's relationship to error was paradoxical and sits uneasily amid these kinds of Whiggish

---

²⁷ Geoffrey Hill, *Broken Hierarchies: Poems 1952–2012* (Oxford: Oxford University Press, 2015), p. 269.
²⁸ Chambers, *Palestina*, 'Faults escaped'.
²⁹ Colin Burrow, 'Rancorous Old Sod', review of Geoffrey Hill's *Broken Hierarchies*, in *London Review of Books* 36.4 (20 February 2014), 11–13, 12.
³⁰ Richard Bellings, *A Sixth Booke to the Countesse of Pembrokes Arcadia* (Dublin, 1624), sig. A4v. The British Library copy reproduced on *EEBO* shows a reader's handwritten enactment of this change on p. 8.
³¹ Blair, 'Errata Lists', p. 26.
³² With Thomas Browne, *Hydriotaphia, Urne-Buriall* (1658), the pasted-in errata list is in BL C.71.e.24, sig. O6v, but not in Eve.a.166 (John Evelyn's copy). In BL C.116.bb.22 the errata list is pasted in on the next page (sig. O7v).
³³ Elizabeth L. Eisenstein, *The Printing Revolution in Early Modern Europe* (Cambridge, UK: Cambridge University Press, 1983), p. 51.

histories of print. If a declaration of errors created the effect of book production diligence, books seeking to create the effect of accuracy did so by parading their mistakes. Was a short errata list more or less of a signal of an accurate text? Did a long errata list suggest print shop neglect or care? Errata lists are quite often subsequently augmented by further printed paste-in slips of corrections: a second wave of error-spotting that both shores up and weakens the book's claims to accuracy.[34] A four-line errata slip is pasted over a three-line in one copy of John Dryden's *The Hind and Panther* (1687).[35] In Figure 12, a slip detailing three additional errata has been pasted into a copy of William Penn's *The Great Case of Liberty of Conscience Once More Briefly Debated & Defended* (1670).[36]

Sometimes errata lists themselves contained further errors – as was the case with Milton's *Paradise Regain'd* – often prompting further slips to be pasted on.[37] Samuel Mather's *The figures or types of the Old Testament* (1685) is significant in part because the errata list constructs a hierarchy of mistakes, ignoring errors 'which the Reader … will not be stumbled by' – mispointing; slips in font, the recording of which 'would be needless exactness'[38] – and so supporting David McKitterick's observation that arguments between authors and printers were less about absolute standardisation than about 'what degree … [of] variation was acceptable.'[39] But the list is also significant because a reader has made handwritten corrections to a series of numerical errors contained within the printed list of corrections: page numbers and also dates of sermons.[40]

---

[34] William Perkins, *A Discourse of Conscience: Wherein Is Set Downe the Nature, Properties, and Differences Thereof: As Also the Way to Get and Keepe Good Conscience* (Cambridge, 1596), sig. L7v. Robert Glover, *Nobilitas Politica Vel Ciuilis* (1608), sig. R6v.
[35] Bod. Ashmole 1023 (1).
[36] Some copies of William Perkins, *A Discourse of Conscience: Wherein Is Set Downe the Nature, Properties, and Differences Thereof: As Also the Way to Get and Keepe Good Conscience* (Cambridge, 1596), have nine lines of errata pasted over the original seven (sig. L7v); variant copies of Robert Glover's *Nobilitas Politica Vel Ciuilis* (1608) have a 30-line errata slip pasted over the original 14-line errata (sig. R6v); and some copies of William Prynne's *Anti-Arminianisme. Or the Church of Englands Old Antithesis to New Arminianisme* (1630) have a slip of additional marginal errata pasted to the last page.
[37] John Milton, *Paradise Regain'd* (1671), sig. P4r, noted by Dobranski, '*Samson* and the Omissa', 154–155. See also *The second Punick War* (1661), HN 22208.
[38] Compare John Donne, *A Sermon Vpon the XV. Verse of the XX. Chapter of the Booke of Judges* (1622), A4v, which lists five errata with the note, 'Those Errors which are committed in mis-pointing, or in changing the forme of the Character, will soone be discerned, and Corrected by the Eye of any deliberate Reader'.
[39] McKitterick, *Print, Manuscript*, p. 111.
[40] Samuel Mather, *The figures or types of the Old Testament* (1685), HN 440070, sig. A4v.

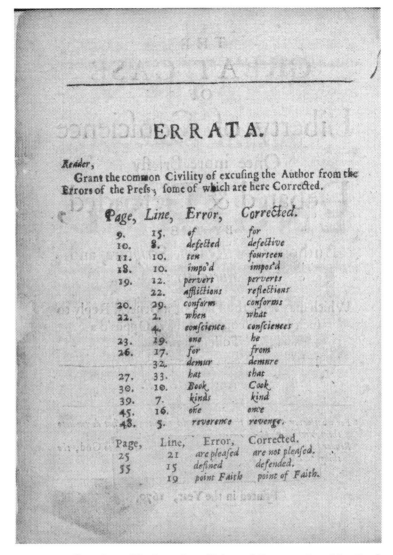

Figure 12 William Penn, *The Great Case of Liberty of Conscience Once More Briefly Debated & Defended* (1670), 'Errata'. By permission of The Huntington Library (8870)

Like other mechanisms of print correction, errata lists serve less to correct than to mark out error. They cast error as one of print's signature traits. And just as one overlooked consequence of print was the creation of huge numbers of books that were never read,[41] so the printing press was also a radical force for the dissemination of blunders. In Thomas Heywood's *An Apologie for Actors* (1612), the errata page has been narratavised into a general fuming at what Heywood calls the 'disworkemanship' of William Jaggard, who had (Heywood claims) printed his earlier book with mistakes: 'The infinite faults escaped in my booke of *Britaines Troy*, by the negligence of the Printer, as the misquotations, mistaking of sillables, misplacing halfe lines, coining of strange and neuer heard of words.'[42]

As Bill Brown has reminded us, we understand an object better when it breaks down and is therefore denaturalised: the parts of the TV remote control become stranger, and more visible, when they refuse to work. Errors are moments when a book admits its own clumsy materiality, confesses its contingency, and hints at the labour that brought it into the world.[43] This is the basis of Claire Bolton's recent analysis of the late-fifteenth-century printing practices of Johann Zainer. Compared to his contemporaries, 'Zainer's work seems to stand out as being consistently poorer than many, perhaps most', and Bolton considers moments of bibliographical breakdown to analyse Zainer's printing techniques.[44] These mistakes include bad register (the misalignment of pages printed back to back); slurred impression; off-set (ink transferred from page to tympan and back to another page); set-off (ink transferred from one wet page to another page resting on top); poor inking; marks from inked, raised spaces; fallen type (loose type resting on top of type, leaving an impression in printing); and traces from bearing type (type intended to support paper which, due to accidental inking or too vigorous pulling of the press, leaves an inked or blind (uninked but embossed) impression). In the context of the present study, I will seek to read lists of errata and the prefaces that

---

[41] Blair, 'Errata', p. 41, citing Hugh Amory.
[42] In fact, Heywood claims Jaggard refused to publish a conventional list of errata, despite these mistakes, out of a reluctance to 'publish his owne disworkemanship', preferring instead to 'let his owne fault lye upon the necke of the Author.' Thomas Heywood, *An Apologie for Actors* (1612), sig. G4r. Noted in Maguire, 'Craft of Printing', p. 446. The context for this dispute was as follows: Jaggard issued an expanded edition of *The Passionate Pilgrim* in 1612 with additional poems about Helen of Troy (the title page records 'Whereunto is newly added two Love Epistles, the first from Paris to Hellen, and Hellen's answere back again to Paris') taken from Thomas Heywood's *Troia Britannica* (William Jaggard, 1609). Here, in *Apology for Actors*, Heywood complains against the piracy, noting also that Shakespeare was 'much offended'.
[43] Bill Brown, 'Thing Theory', in *Critical Inquiry*, vol. 28, no. 1 (Autumn, 2001), 1–22.
[44] Claire M. Bolton, *The Fifteenth-Century Printing Practices of Johann Zainer, Ulm, 1473–1478* (Oxford: Oxford Bibliographical Society, 2016), p. 34.

accompany them in a comparable manner, that is as potential documents of the process of book production, to put alongside canonical, albeit idealising, sources such as Joseph Moxon's *Mechanick exercises on the whole art of printing* (1683–4).[45] The implications for the early modern reader were similarly revelatory: the effect of reading books which regularly foregrounded their own errors was to make the book hyper-embodied, not a transcendent thing but the product of a particular time and place – a tangle of tatters (to quote Samuel Beckett).

What, then, do errata lists suggest about printing books? Errata lists suggest printing was fast: or at least that a discourse of haste and cut corners often ushered books into the world.[46] Some books had lists of errata covering only the final pages, suggesting that proofs had been printed, errors spotted and corrections implemented for the bulk of the book, but that the print shop didn't have time to finish all the alterations.[47]

Errata lists show that some copies of a book might have faults, but others, in the same edition, might not: Thomas Sorocold's *Supplications of Saints: A booke of prayers* (1612) introduces its list of five errors with 'The faults escaped *in some copies* amend thus'; John Chester's *An Orthographie* (1569) lists 'Faultes escaped in part *of the Copies of this first impression*'.[48] The fact that some but not all copies contain errors suggests that the correcting process – reading proofs, marking them up, scurrying across to the presses to unlock the formes and unpick that upside down 't' – went on during a print run, and so books printed later on in the same run wouldn't have the errors that earlier books possessed. Thus Sir Thomas Urquhart, *Ekskybalauron: or, The discovery of a most exquisite jewel* (1652) lists 'these ensuing *errata's;* which though not all to be found in any one of the copies, yet each of them being in the whole impression, I chused rather to insert more, then that an industrious spirit should be debarred the

---

[45] Errata prefaces are one of the textual forms used in James Binns, 'STC Latin Books: Evidence for Printing-House Practice', in *The Library* 5th series, 32.1 (1977), 1–27, and 'STC Latin Books: Further Evidence for Printing-House Practice', in *The Library* 6th series, 1.4 (1979), 347–354.

[46] For speed of production – as opposed to textual stability – as a feature of early print, see McKitterick, *Print, Manuscript*, pp. 100–101. Of course, not all books were printed quickly: production might indeed be spread over many months or even years. My concern here is with the rhetoric of haste.

[47] *The familiar epistles of Sir Anthony of Gueuara, preacher, chronicler, and counceller to the Emperour Charles the fifth. Translated out of the Spanish* (1575), 'The favvtes that be escaped in printinge', final page (n.p.).

[48] Thomas Sorocold, *Supplications of Saints: A booke of prayers* (1612), n.p. (my italics); John Chester, *An Orthographie, conteyning the due order and reason, howe to write or paint thimage of mannes voice* (1569), sig. Av.

conveniency of amending any.'[49] One book was not identical with another book, even if they both came from the same edition.[50]

'Print', as David McKitterick notes, 'is an exercise in communal responsibility',[51] and fallen books vividly convey book making as a collaborative process: lists of errata describe the various individuals involved in the work of print, and their relationships – relationships often characterised by a kind of reluctant, irritated dependency. Often the compositor is described in unfavourable terms. Asking that the reader 'correct with thy penne these faults', one 1580 text describes the compositor's lack of skills and print-shop hardware:

> for although I haue had great care and bene very diligent in the correcting thereof, yet because my Compositor was a straunger and ignorant in our Englishe tongue and Orthographie, some faultes are passed vnamended of me. The other, that thou wilte not like the worse of this learned worke, because it hath not the varietie of letters which is requisite in such a booke, and as the Printers in England do customably vse, my abilitie was not otherwise to do it, and hauing these Characters out of England, I could not ioyne them together with any others, and so was forst to vse one Character both for the words of Fulke, and for all Allegations.[52]

Complaints about compositors lacking language skills, and print shops lacking the correct type, particularly for foreign language publications, are common. (Alexander Gil added extensive corrections to the first edition of his own *Logonomia Anglica* (1619) because the printers lacked the specialised type he wanted.)[53]

George Turbeville's *The Booke of Faulconrie or Hauking* (1575) includes an address from 'the printer to the reader'. Since 'printer' might at this point mean 'publisher' – 'printed by' could mean 'caused to be printed by' or 'printing paid for by'[54] – there is a slipperiness of terminology which reflects the fact that these professional identities are not yet quite distinct: so this may be publisher Christopher Barker, or it could be his printer,

---

[49] Thomas Urquhart, *Ekskybalauron: or, The discovery of a most exquisite jewel* (1652), sig. A8v.
[50] David McKitterick, *A History of Cambridge University Press* (Cambridge, UK: Cambridge University Press, 1992), vol. 1, p. 239: 'within an edition sheets can be found varying one from another, each forme in different stages of amendment and different volumes made up of different permutations of the sheets.'
[51] McKitterick, *Print, Manuscript*, p. 117.
[52] John Lyon, 'The Printer to the Reader', in Richard Bristow, *A reply to Fulke, In defense of M. D. Allens scroll of articles, and booke of purgatorie* (1580), p. 416.
[53] Alexander Gil, *Logonomia Anglica* (1619), Bod. 4° G 30 Art.
[54] Peter Blayney, *The Stationers' Company and the Printers of London, 1501–1557* (Cambridge, UK: Cambridge University Press, 2013), 2 vols, vol. 1, p. 30.

Henry Bynneman, describing the little network of relationships revealed as a result of things going wrong.[55]

> Gentle Reader, if *Argus* with all his eyes shoulde peruse an impression, yet some thing mighte of him bee unseen: so I must of force confesse sundry faultes to haue escaped in printing this booke of Falconrie, by whiche some places are made obscure, and sundrie termes quite abused, contrarye to the Authors meaning and myne: whiche is not my small griefe, neyther yet coulde I muche helpe the same, the copie being obscurely penned and not legible in sundrie places, for that it was the translaters originall. And therfore when haply they do occurre, or that thou lyght on them, blame not the booke or me, but runne ouer to the *Errata*, where thou shalte be satisfied in euery pointe, as hereafter ensueth.[56]

This address provides a description not only of a book full of errors, but also of a set of relationships, and a process: a handwritten 'copy' comes from the translator; it is difficult to read ('obscurely penned'; 'not legible in sundrie places'); the compositor struggles to make it out, and has to guess, but gets bits wrong; the errors are missed in proof, but spotted after printing; a list of errata is needed; the publisher appeals to the reader for help. Complaints of bad handwriting in manuscript copy are common as a source of printed mistakes, and remind us, among other things, that one way of complicating a binary between print and manuscript is to remember that manuscript copy preceded and enabled print: printed books were a product of a process of textual transmission that began with the handwritten word, and the relationship between the two might be figured less as a binary than as a continuum. If a compositor was setting a new edition of a book already in print, he would probably work from the old printed book, marked up with revisions; but a new book meant working from handwritten copy – sometimes prepared by a professional scribe, but more likely a mess 'because subject to be irregularly Writ',[57] and full of little ambiguities and cruxes that the compositor would have to improvise around in the moment of setting: 'for this he likes not,' writes Moxon, 'and is by *Compositers* call'd . . . *Bad, Heavy, Hard Work*.'[58] There are many descriptions of such texts: 'the Copie was somewhat obscurely written, as b[e]ing the first original', or was written 'in a difficult and unacquainted hand', or was '*Interlin'd,* and with *a Differing Hand,* and *Ink,* from that which wrote

---

[55] For the trickiness of book-agent terminology, and the relative merits of the terms publisher, stationer, and editor, see John Jowett, 'Henry Chettle: "Your old Compositor"', in *Text* 15 (2003), 141–161, 144.
[56] George Turbeville, *The Booke of Faulconrie or Hauking* (1575), 'The printer to the reader'.
[57] Moxon, *Mechanick Exercises*, p. 250.   [58] Moxon, *Mechanick Exercises*, p. 211.

the Body of them.'[59] Henry Chettle claims he transcribed Robert Greene's 'il written' *Groatsworth of Wit* (1592) to provide a clearer fair copy for the licensers – although he probably also wrote at least parts of the text, too.[60] Thomas Taylor admitted that errors in his *The Beawties of Beth-el* (1609) were due 'partly by the vnacquaintance of the workeman with my hand',[61] while one corrector, peering incredulously at an authorial text, asked 'do hens have hands?'[62]

But perhaps the figure who is conjured most frequently in errata lists is the author: the absent author, the sick author tucked up in his bed, the author travelling abroad, the author for one of any number of reasons negligently away from the print shop as the proof sheets are pulled, still wet, from the press and scanned for mistakes. In a blend of authorial centrality and absence, errata addresses frequently stress the importance of the author by invoking his nonattendance as the cause of mistakes.[63]

In his 1618 *Fall of Man*, Godfrey Goodman laments that 'the copie was not of mine owne writing, whereby many things were defac't and omitted: and liuing not in towne, I could not be alwaies present at the presse, so that I confesse many faults haue escaped, especially in the first sheetes, being begun in my absence, points displaced, words mistaken, peeces of sentences ommitted'.[64] The publisher or printer of Sir John Smythe's *Instructions, obseruations, and orders mylitarie Requisite* (1595) listed 'Faults happened in the printing of this Booke, by reason *that sir* Iohn Smyth *was absent from London at the time of the imprinting thereof.*' The book becomes, briefly, a polyphonic text: Smythe's lengthy opening 'Epistle Dedicatorie' is followed by an errata address written by someone else, describing the author's absence. It's difficult to know the degree to which this particular address is admonitory, but there are certainly many errata addresses that do convey irritation with absent authors. Reginald

---

[59] Ludwig Lavater, *Of ghostes and spirites walking by nyght and of strange noyses, crackes, and sundry forewarnynges* (1572), 'An aduertisement to the Reader'; Thomas Heywood, *The exemplary lives and memorable acts of nine the most worthy women in the vvorld three Iewes. Three gentiles. Three Christians* (1640), 'Errata'; Croft, *The plea, case*, p. 12. For other complaints about 'obscure copy', see *The arte and science of preseruing bodie and soule* (1579), and Joseph Hall, *Contemplations vpon the principall passages of the holy storie* (1612), in which the list of errata is explained 'Through fault of the copie'.
[60] Jowett, 'Chettle', 147; John Jowett, 'Johannes Factotum: Henry Chettle and *Greene's Groatsworth of Wit'*, in *The Papers of the Bibliographical Society of America* 87 (1993), 453–486.
[61] Thomas Taylor, *The Beawties of Beth-el* (1609), 'Errata'.
[62] Anthony Grafton, *Bring Out Your Dead: The Past as Revelation* (Cambridge, MA: Harvard University Press, 2002), p. 145.
[63] For authorial absence and errata lists in books printed in Cambridge, see McKitterick, *History*, vol. I, pp. 238–239.
[64] Goodman, *Fall of Man*, sig. [Ff7]v.

Scot's *A perfite platforme of a hoppe garden* was printed by Henry Denham in 1574 as a guide '*for all men ... which in any wise haue to doe with hops*', and features illustrations to direct 'him that cannot reade at all.' But the author's absence from the print shop meant that the printer struggled to work out where to deploy the illustrations: Scot sent the figures, and some notes explaining placement, but Denham got in a tangle 'conferring the wordes with the figures.' In an address from 'The Printer to the Reader', distinguished typographically from Scot's preceding 'To the Reader', Denham explains that

> [f]or as much, as M. Scot could not be present at the printing of this his Booke, whereby I might have used his advise in the correction of the same, and especiallye of the Figures and Portratures contayned therein, whereof he deliuered unto me such notes as I being unskilfull in the matter, could not so th[o]roughly conceyue, nor so perfectly expresse ... I shall desire you to let his absence serue for mine excuse in this behalf[.][65]

Such errata narratives suggest a hope, or an expectation, that authors might be physically present as a book was printed. To many students of the early modern book, this may seem surprising, in part because early modern literary criticism has often operated with an unhelpfully Shakespearean paradigm of authorship: the author who – despite the recent efforts of Lukas Erne to reverse the large lorry that is Shakespeare criticism – separates himself from the inky world of print.[66] This ethereal conception of writing has obscured a different early modern sense of the author-in-the-print-shop, and if much literary criticism has moved away from authorship as the dominant category of literary definition it was for much of the twentieth century, then errata discourse makes texts more authorial than we expect – although the version of the author they promote is not the lone genius of post-Romantic criticism, but the author always in collaboration with others, the author as one agent among several. Partly there are practical print-shop reasons for this desire for the author to be present: due to cost and limited resources,[67] printers would not want to keep lots of formes locked up pending corrections, so errata lists thus want the author to be there, checking proofs, telling the printer where to insert the illustrations of hop poles. Ben Jonson is the most obvious example of the author present in the print shop – obsessively, overbearingly present, we might

---

[65] Reginald Scot, *A perfite platforme of a hoppe garden* (1574), sig. B3.
[66] Lukas Erne, *Shakespeare as Literary Dramatist* (Cambridge, UK: Cambridge University Press, 2003), and *Shakespeare and the Book Trade* (Cambridge, UK: Cambridge University Press, 2013).
[67] Blair, 'Errata Lists', p. 26.

imagine – for the production of his 1616 folio: the most recent editorial discussion of stop-press corrections suggests Jonson was heavily involved in changes found in the first four or five plays, although his engagement subsequently declines.[68] But lists of mistakes that lament a missing author imply a present author was not a Jonsonian anomaly, but something like an expectation. Literary genre might be a variable here: certain kinds of publication may well have been more powerfully connected with a print-shop author, and it is tempting to suggest that literary works, like Jonson's, called out more loudly for a present author to check and correct as the pages came off the press. But this may be to conflate our sense of literary eminence with an early modern conception of canon, and many of my examples come from less illustrious, more practical kinds of publication. There may also be other factors influencing authorial print-shop presence, alongside genre, that are harder for us to perceive, including perhaps the nature of the relationship between author and publisher-printer: Jonson presumably chose William Stansby due to Stansby's high standing in publishing, and a relationship of (wary) mutual respect perhaps encouraged Jonson's presence.

Moreover, one consequence of this mapping of a set of relations is that the category of the author can emerge in (sometimes fine) distinction from other agents of book making: in the accounting for error, roles are described, and 'the Authours naughty pen', as John Florio puts it, emerges through a process of contrast with 'the Compositors wauering hande, the Correctors daseling eye, and the Printers presse.'[69] Thus William Penn separates the author from printing, asking his readers to 'Grant the common Civility of excusing the Author from the Errors of the Press.'[70] Thus Thomas Blount puffs and fumes to distinguish author from printer, or, metonymically, the study door from the printer's case:

> Besides the many failings both of the Author and Continuator, the Printer has, with supine negligence, added a grosse number of Errata's, without any advertisement of them, but leaving all upon the Authors account, yet the understanding Reader wil, for the most part, discern, which ought to be laid at the Authors Study dore, and which at the Printers Case.[71]

---

[68] David Gants, 'The 1616 Folio (F1): Textual Essay', in *Cambridge Edition of the Works of Ben Jonson Online*, http://universitypublishingonline.org/cambridge/benjonson/k/essays/F1_textual_essay.
[69] John Florio, *Florio his firste fruites which yeelde familiar speech, merie prouerbes, wittie sentences, and golden sayings* (1578), p. 13.
[70] Penn, *The great case*, 'Errata'.
[71] Thomas Blount, *Animadversions upon Sr. Richard Baker's Chronicle* (1672), sig. A3v.

94		Material Texts in Early Modern England

Thomas Coryate tracks through the 'many errors' in his *Crudities Hastily gobbled up in five Moneths trauells* (1611) – 'false pointing'; 'false figuring of the leaues'; 'some grosse faults [that] haue passed, as *authologine* for *anthologium*, *morarchie* for *monarchie*, *ratria* for *patria*, *imptolijs* for *impolitic*' – in an attempt to mark out his authorial work from the slack corrector's: 'Most of which ascribe I pray thee (candid Reader) to the negligence of the Corrector, and not to my vnskilfulnesse.'[72] (Technical works were particularly prone to manglings of learned or specialist words: the rhetorical terms in Henry Peacham's *Garden of Eloquence* (1577), for example, were incorrectly set by compositors, as a list of 'Faultes escaped' records: 'for Tantologia, reade Tautologia'; 'for Cacosmtheton, read Cacosintheton'; 'for Polysmdeton, reade Polysindeton.'[73]) Sometimes this process of calibrating various agents – separating out who, exactly, was responsible for what – can become complicated. The 1582 edition of *The grounde of artes teaching the perfect vvorke and practise of arithmetike* breaks down writing into temporally separated stages of production: the book, which seeks to teach 'arithmetike, both in whole nu[m]bers and fractions', was '*Made* by M. Robert Recorde, D. in Physick', was 'afterwards *augmented* by M. Iohn Dee', was then 'lately diligently *corrected*, [and] *beautified* with some new rules and necessarie additions' before being 'further *endowed* with a thirde part, of rules of practize . . . By Iohn Mellis of Southwark, Scholemaster.'[74] The text is normally attributed to Robert Recorde, but what we would call writing is dispersed across a series of related but non-identical processes, in which error-spotting plays a central part: making, augmenting, correcting, beautifying, endowing. That this book is a guide to arithmetic contributes to its sense of book writing as an accumulating series of additions, like the calculations it seeks to explain 'after a more easie and exact sort'.[75] The governing, or final voice, is John Mellis', to whom the book is attributed on the title page: Mellis gathers and coordinates the other agencies that precede his. He also writes the list of errata, which requests that the reader continue this process of production by 'amend[ing] in the Margente of the booke, these faultes that haue escaped in the Printing'.[76]

---

[72] *Crudities Hastily gobbled up in five Moneths trauells* (1611), noted in Simpson, *Proof-Reading*, pp. 113–114.
[73] Henry Peacham, *The Garden of Eloquence* (1577), sig. A4. Discussed by William Poole, 'The Vices of Style', in *Renaissance Figures of Speech*, ed. Sylvia Adamson, Gavin Alexander and Katrin Ettenhuber (Cambridge, UK: Cambridge University Press, 2007), pp. 236–251, p. 239.
[74] Robert Record, *The grounde of artes teaching the perfect vvorke and practise of arithmetike*, title page, my italics.
[75] Record, *The grounde of* artes, title page.   [76] Record, *The grounde of artes*, final page.

Errors and Corrections: 'My Galley Charged with Forgetfulness'

While error-discourse invokes authors alongside other print shop agents of production, it also looks forward to readers. Books of mistakes appealed to readers for patience and goodwill, but most commonly they appealed to readers to intervene in the book: to make changes to the material text; to do the work of correcting themselves. 'Correct these Errors with they Pen', reads one 1660 romance, 'before thou read the Book.'[77] Errata pages recruited readers into the process of book making, the task of altering errors devolving down on to them: 'take they pen', instructs John Ludham's *The Practis of Preaching* (1577), 'and (before all thinges) correct'.[78]

An anonymous but first-person errata list in a 1611 collection of Lancelot Andrewes sermons requests that readers mark the book by hand, converting the printed text into a print-manuscript hybrid: 'for thine owne good, amend these following faults (committed in printing) with thy pen, before thou enter vpon the body of the booke'.[79] This is an example of that dynamic Peter Stallybrass has described as printing-for-manuscript: of print, as a medium, not seeking to replace manuscript, as it is sometimes figured in Darwinian narratives of the triumph of print, but rather actively catalysing handwritten additions.[80] But what role, exactly, is the reader being asked to assume here? Is she still a reader? A co-author? The author of the errata list – perhaps Francis Burton, who initialled the opening 'Epistle Dedicatory' – seems to have a quite exact idea: his expectation that the book buyer would work through the alterations, one by one, before entering the book as a reader, figures her as a kind of supplementary print house worker: a second corrector. Readers usually bought books unbound, and organised the binding themselves, so the process of binding a book can be thought of as an early act of reception, rather than a final act of production. Something similar is going on here, with these error lists: at least in the ideal prescribed by Burton, readers bought and then corrected their book, extending the process of book production both temporally – it carries on, after the moment of purchase – and geographically, dispersing bookmaking beyond the print shop.[81]

But did readers do what they were told? Did they care about mistakes? There is certainly archival evidence to suggest readers often did take

---

[77] George Mackenzie, *Aretina, or, The Serious Romance* (1660), sig. A8v.
[78] John Ludham, *The Practis of Preaching* (1577), pp. 6–7.
[79] Lancelot Andrewes, *Scala coeli: Nineteen sermons concerning prayer* (1611), sig. A8. See also Ben Jonson, *Execration against Vulcan. With divers epigrams by the same author* (1640), final page.
[80] Peter Stallybrass, 'Printing-for-Manuscript', unpublished 2006 A. S. W. Rosenbach lecture.
[81] Blair, 'Errata Lists', p. 41.

96   Material Texts in Early Modern England

mistakes seriously.[82] The list of 'Faultes escaped' in one copy of John Chester's *An Orthographie, conteyning the due order and reason, howe to write or paint thimage of mannes voice* (1569), has been cancelled out by hand, with the note, 'But in this book now corrected.'[83] A reader of Izaak Walton's *The life of Mr. Rich. Hooker* not only struck through the errata list after enforcing the prescribed changes, but also went further, correcting unlisted errors.[84] Other readers cut out and discarded the errata list once the changes had been made by hand, indicated by stubs suggesting a once-present, now removed list. Readers might also cut out errata lists and glue them to the back-boards of books.[85] Not only did errata lists hover at the edges of books – at the start, before the main text begins; at the very end – but they were materially mobile, too, not quite integrated into the form of the book. Brian Gerrard uses the term *papiliones*, Latin for butterflies, to describe such pieces of paper that flutter across a book, carrying text including errata lists; unlike pasted-in correction slips, the *papilio* does not need to be located at any particular point in the book.[86] If errata lists occupied discrete leaves, they might be snipped out, shunted around, reshuffled, used then discarded.[87] (Errata lists which shared a page or leaf with other printed text were not likely to be mobile in this way, and their application was often signalled by readers adding a single diagonal stroke through the errata.) Readers might even add their own lists of errors: Figure 13 shows a copy of Francis Wolferston's English version of Ovid's *Art of Love*, now in the Huntington, which has a print-style list of errata carefully added at the end of the volume.[88]

---

[82] McKitterick, *Print, Manuscript*, p. 142, suggests that the archival evidence for readers enacting errata corrections is surprisingly thin.
[83] John Chester, *An Orthographie, conteyning the due order and reason, howe to write or paint thimage of mannes voice* (1569), sig. Av. BL G.7481.
[84] Izaak Walton, *The life of Mr. Rich. Hooker* (1665), HN 106572, sig. A8. For unlisted corrections, see, for example, p. 106.
[85] *The Diall of Princes* (1557), HN 47821. Errata lists might be bound in the wrong place. *A mirrour or looking-glass both for saints, and sinners* (1671), HN 120052, contents and errata relating to vol. 2 misbound after sig. 1A; William Prynne, *The antipathie of the English lordly prelacie* (1641), HN 147406, has an errata leaf bound preceding B1 of pt. 1 instead of at the end of pt. 2. Thomas Chafie, *The seventh-day Sabbath* (1652), HN 227443: the final page errata list has been implemented and then cut out in this copy.
[86] Brian Gerrard, 'A new taxonomy of post-impression corrections', in *An index of civilisation: Studies of printing and publishing in honour of Keith Maslen*, ed. R. Harvey, W. Kirsop and B. J. McMullin (Melbourne: Monash University, 1993), pp. 45–54, 47.
[87] An errata list is pasted in at end of Edward Pelling, *A Practical Discourse Concerning God's Love to Mankind* (1694), pasted on p. 135. BL 227.e.4.
[88] Francis Wolferston, *The three books of Publius Ovidius Naso, De Arte Amandi* (1661), HN 17112.

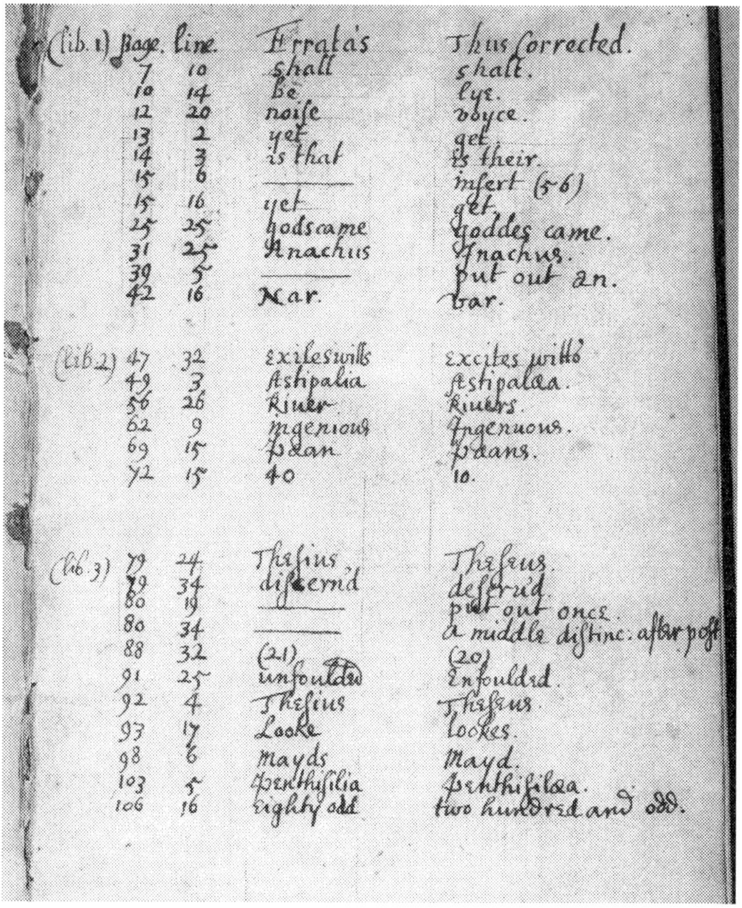

	Page.	line.	Errata's	Thus Corrected.
(lib. 1)	7	10	shall	shalt.
	10	14	be	lye.
	12	20	noise	voyce.
	13	2	yet	get.
	14	3	is that	is their.
	15	6	———	insert (5-6)
	15	16	yet	get.
	25	25	godscame	goddes came.
	31	25	Anachus	Inachus.
	39	5	———	put out an.
	42	16	Nar.	bar.
(lib. 2)	47	32	exileswills	excites wills
	49	3	Astipalia	Astipalaa.
	56	26	River	Rivers.
	62	9	ingenious	ingenuous.
	69	15	pean	peans.
	72	15	40	10.
(lib. 3)	79	24	Thesius	Theseus.
	79	34	discernd	deserud.
	80	19	———	put out once.
	80	34	———	a middle distinc: after post
	88	32	(21)	(20)
	91	25	unfoulded	Enfoulded.
	92	4	Thesius	Theseus.
	97	17	Looke	lookes.
	98	6	mayds	mayd.
	103	5	penthisilia	penthisilaa.
	106	16	eighty odd	two hundred and odd.

Figure 13 Francis Wolferston, *The three books of Publius Ovidius Naso, De Arte Amandi* (1661). By permission of The Huntington Library (17112)

But the flip-side to signs of diligent readers is a body of evidence suggesting not quite that readers didn't care about errors, but certainly that printers, publishers and readers had a more playful, even literary relationship to error: that an error was neither something to be corrected, nor ignored, but a piece of text with potential. This introduces a second way of approaching slips and errata lists: not as overlooked documents of book production, but rather as genres of writing that had their own, established conventions that authors, printers and publishers might recognise, play with and develop. If we think about the errata list as a literary genre – which means asking, How does this errata page do something similar, or something different, from other errata lists? – then we are inclined to read it less in terms of the practical work of the print shop, and more as a passage of text in dialogue with other passages of text.

Printed books certainly nudge us in this direction. *The Mysteries of Love & Eloquence* (1658) is a miscellany of verse and prose excerpts for the socially ambitious: 'a Magazin richly furnist . . . [with] such nimble applications [which], if rightly directed, are most absolutely useful.'[89] Alongside its opening list of errors – including the aforementioned 'for killed, read kissed' – there is a note to the 'Courteous Reader':

> there are some more Errata's besides these committed, but since it is a custom to print Errata's and few or none takes notice of them, I intreat thee favourably to pass them by, and as thou readest, correct them by thy own judgement.[90]

Variations on this half-hearted sense of error-spotting are legion, and most frequently take the form of errata lists which convey insufficient specificity. Noting only, for example, a word and a page number ('eurse, curse 28, but will, but who will 50')[91] means it is practically difficult to implement the corrections: the reader has to scan an entire page for the single mistaken word. This suggests the errata list is drifting away from a utilitarian function – it is less about actually correcting – and is becoming a rhetorical set piece, something printed books did to introduce themselves as printed books, rather as title pages boast that a new edition is 'enlarged', or 'augmented', or 'corrected', or 'revised', even if the truth may be otherwise. (The Latin '*postrema*' ('*postrema editio*': the latest edition) is used shamelessly.) There is also space for something like sarcasm, or irony, or a clowning around that raises the prospect of Sterne, Borges or Calvino to come: 'The Auther being a farre off, some faults may haue passed mee: I pray you impute them to mere ignoraunce.'[92]

This printer's *laissez-faire* attitude to error was perhaps in part a product of the available space: these words are squeezed into the remaining few lines of the final page. But there is, particularly in the seventeenth century, a consistent use of error as a source of creativity and wit: an overlapping of

---

[89] *The Mysteries of Love and Eloquence* (1658), sig. A5.
[90] *The Mysteries of Love and Eloquence*, sig. A4v.
[91] Robert Allott's *Englands Parnassus* (1600), sig. A8v.
[92] Henoch Clapham, *An abstract of fayth grounded on Moses, and applyed to the common Creede; plainely and briefly* (1606), p. 43.

what might be regarded as the bibliographical and the literary, as authors write within a conception of the book as error-prone, as decked out with errata lists and other mechanisms of correction. Ann Blair has considered errors in humanist reference works, while Seth Lerer has analysed the ways in which questions of textual accuracy were recruited into confessional debates during the early Reformation: Thomas More constructs Protestant texts as books of error and elides typographical and moral mistakes as he presents himself as his own corrector, while William Tyndale educates the vernacular reader in using the errata sheet to become a diligent reader.[93] My analysis will therefore focus on more literary works that respond to the potential of the errata list.

The potential for errata list wit is plentiful: a list of errors is already close to satire, and it only takes a gentle nudge to tip the errata list into something critical. John Taylor, writer and Thames waterman – and hence 'The Water Poet' – used the form as one strand in his adventures in ludic bibliography. *Sir Gregory Nonsence His Newes from no place* (1622) – a text 'plentifully stored with want of *wit, learning, Iudgement, Rime and Reason*' – has a mock title page, a prefatory address 'To Nobody', and a list of authors including 'Ready money' and 'Yard of Ale'. It also itemises 'Faults escaped in the Printing' and offers a series of satirical jokes:

> IN the 25. page. 44. line, for a *Friers mouth* read a *Pudding*.
> If the 170. page 53. line, for a *foole* read a *Bable*.
> In the 90. page, 27. line, for *friend* read *rare*.
> In the 30. page 6. line 78. for a *Whore* read a *Bridewell*.
> In the 100. pace [sic], line 40. for a *Bawd* reade a *Cart*.
> In the 12. page 11. line, for *noone* read *dinner*.
> In the 16. first, and all the Pages following for *Tobacco* read a *Witch*.
> In the 40. page, and 80. line, for a *Calues head* read *Bacon*.
> In the 37. page, and 1. line, for *vice* read *plenty*.
> In the 000. page, and 3. line for *money* read *scarce*.
> In the last Page, for *conscience,* read *none*.
> In euery page for *sence* read *nonsence*.[94]

The errors are not actually present – there aren't even enough pages in the book – but Taylor dances across the conventions of the form: this is sufficiently late in the history of the errata list for its norms to be widely known, and thus for playful reworkings to be possible. Eight years later, Taylor turned to the other part of the errata list – the little narrative that

---

[93] Blair, 'Errata Lists', passim; Lerer, *Error and the Academic Self*, pp. 23–29.
[94] John Taylor, *Sir Gregory Nonsence His Newes from no place* (1622), sig. A5v.

introduced and glossed the list of errors – and converted it into a rambling, idiosyncratic verse preface, titled 'Errata, or Faults to the Reader':

> *Faults,* but not *faults escap'd,* I would they were,
> If they were faults escap'd, they were not here:
> But heere they are, in many a page and line,
> Men may perceiue the Printers faults, or mine.
> And since my faults are heere in prison fast,
> And on record (in print) are like to last,
> Since the Correcters let them passe the Presse,
> And my occasions mix'd with sicknesses,
> And that foure Printers dwelling farre asunder,
> Did print this booke, pray make the faults no wonder.
> I will confesse my faults are scap'd indeed,
> If they escape mens Censure when they read.
> No Garden is so cleare, but weedes are in't,
> All is not Gold that's coined in the Mint;
> The Rose hath prickles, and the spots of sinne,
> Oft takes the fairest features for their Inne.
> Below the Moone no full perfection is,
> And alwaies some of vs are all amisse.
> Then in your reading mend each mis-plac'd letter,
> And by your iudgement make bad words sound better.
> Where you may hurt, heale; where you can affect,
> There helpe and cure, or else be not too strict.
> Looke through your fingers, wink, conniue at mee,
> And (as you meet with faults) see, and not see.
> Thus must my faults escape, (or escape neuer,)
> For which, good Readers, I am yours for euer.[95]

This verse, appearing at the start of Taylor's *Workes* (1630), certainly performs many of the roles performed by a conventional prose or verse errata preface. Taylor makes an appeal to readers for patience, and asks them to correct errors 'by your iudgement'. Blame is distributed ('Men may perceiue the Printers faults, or mine') and, in the process, a map of the agents of book production is briefly sketched: 'Correcters' who 'let them [i.e., errors] passe the Presse'; an author hindered 'with sicknesses'; and 'foure Printers dwelling farre asunder', who shared the printing. Dividing printing between presses was a common source of error,[96] and may, in this instance, have been compounded by the involvement of the notorious

---

[95] John Taylor, *All the Workes* (1630), sig. A4v.
[96] See, for example, Brathwaite's translation of Mariano Silesio, *The Arcadian Princesse* (1635): the book 'was divided upon severall Presses; no marvaile if he suffer in the one or other.' Noted in Simpson, *Proof-Reading*, p. 114.

John Beale,[97] who, despite being a senior member of the Stationer's Company and a Master Printer since 1613, had a dubious reputation: 'My printer and I shall afford subject enough for a tragicomedy', wrote Ben Jonson of Beale's printing of the 1631 second folio of his *Workes*, 'for with his delays and vexation I am almost become blind[.]'[98]

But Taylor's conventional errata pleas are enlivened by a literary inventiveness and wit: Taylor, like Geoffrey Hill 350 years later, uses the cadences of the errata list to request his reader's patience ('Where you may hurt, heale'), and the poem plays on the phrase 'faults escaped', suggesting that print gives a kind of permanence to error: print fixes, in the sense of locking in, rather than making right, mistakes that can no longer flee.

We see a similar entangling of the conventions of the errata page with literary invention in Thomas Watson's sonnet collection *The hekatompathia or Passionate centurie of loue* (1582). In his prefatory address 'To the frendly Reader', Watson asks the reader to forgive 'faultes herein escaped', which he describes as the 'ouersightes of a blinde Louer'; as 'idle toyes proceeding from a youngling frenzie'; and as the (poetic) limpings of a 'maiemed man'. Watson tries to separate what we might call these thematic errors, which sit with consistency alongside his Petrarchan discourse of 'my paines in suffering', from those 'escaped eyther by dotage, or ignorance [which] ... I ... lay ... vpon the Printers necke.'[99] But even as Watson effects this separation, he draws attention to the potential of the press to participate in what Watson calls 'my trauaile in penning these louepassions'.

One of the reasons for this frequent overlap between what might be considered print shop discourse and literary writing was the striking number of authors who worked and even lived in print shops. In addition to being the wittiest writer of his age, Thomas Nashe (a close friend of Thomas Watson) lodged with John Danter, a printer with a reputation for piracy and the man behind the first printed Shakespeare play, *Titus Andronicus* (1594). Nashe seems to have worked as a corrector or 'overseer' – a role close to our modern sense of the editor – and probably, given his literary standing, a more general literary adviser.[100] Nashe's print shop

---

[97] Simpson, *Proof-Reading*, p. 114. Initials on the second title page indicate Beale's involvement.
[98] Jonson's letter is *CWBJ*, 6.343. Jonson was writing to his patron William Cavendish, then the Duke of Newcastle. John Creaser, 'The 1631 Folio (F2(2)): Textual Essay', in *Cambridge Edition of the Works of Ben Jonson Online*, http://universitypublishingonline.org/cambridge/benjonson/k/essays/F2-2_textual_essay/2/.
[99] Thomas Watson, *The hekatompathia or Passionate centurie of loue* (1582), 'To the frendly Reader', n.p.
[100] Charles Nicholl, *A Cup of News: The Life of Thomas Nashe* (London: Routledge, 1984), p. 225: 'For a man of his [Nashe's] accomplishments, this would mean general reader, editor and adviser on MSS, as well as more menial proof-reader.'

career is alluded to in the academic play *Second part of the return from Parnassus*, acted at St John's College, Cambridge in 1601–2, where Ingenioso – usually taken as a representation of Nashe – is shown engaged in the unseemly task of press correction, and a version of Danter is on stage acquiring the manuscript of *A catalogue of Cambridge cuckolds* from Ingenioso.[101] Gabriel Harvey assumed a similar role when he lived and worked with printer John Wolfe in 1593 (running up a huge bill for his 'diet' which he never paid),[102] while Harvey's work was printing, and as plague spread outside: Nashe mocked Harvey 'lying in the ragingest furie of the last Plague . . . inck-squittring and printing against me at *Wolfes* in *Poules Church-yard*'.[103] Prolific playwright, pamphleteer, epistle-writer and master stationer Henry Chettle was the author of *Kind-Harts Dreame* (1592), dozens of lost plays, and was perennially short of cash. He signed himself in print as 'your old compositor', and worked as a printer, corrector and literary patcher on texts including the controversial first edition of *Romeo and Juliet* (1597), and as a middle-man between authors and printers such as Danter and William Hoskins, as John Jowett has described.[104] Playwright and London writer Anthony Munday worked as an apprentice to printer John Allde, who with Danter printed *Romeo and Juliet*.[105] And William Baldwin worked for printer Edward Whitchurch in the 1540s, shortly before, or even while he wrote his *Marvelous History Entitled Beware the Cat* (written ca. 1552; printed 1570), and edited the influential *A Mirror for Magistrates* (ca. 1554).

These and other writers constitute what we might call print-shop authors: authors with printer's ink on their hands, whose literary imaginations were shaped, to a degree, by the messy, collaborative, noisy world of the print shop. To what degree was writing, for them, not about the pen hovering over the page, but about plucking pieces of type and correcting text? Here are two brief suggestions.[106]

Martin Marprelate's final text, *The Protestatyon of Martin Marprelat* (1589), is a text all about error, not least (as noted in the introduction: see

---

[101] *The Three Parnassus Plays (1598–1601)*, ed. J. B. Leishman (London: Nicholson and Watson, 1949), p. 228. Discussed in Jowett, 'Henry Chettle', 142–143; McKitterick, *A History*, vol. I, pp. 237–238.
[102] Nicholl, *Cup*, p. 225. [103] Simpson, *Proof-Reading*, p. 31.
[104] Chettle's compositor reference comes in his letter to Nashe printed in Nashe's *Have with you to Saffron Walden* (1596). Jowett, 'Henry Chettle', 155–156; Harold Jenkins, *The life and work of Henry Chettle* (London: Sidgwick & Jackson, 1934), 1–29.
[105] Jowett, 'Chettle', 148. [106] These print-shop authors will be the subject of my next book.

Figure 2) because the first gathering was set by an amateur printer, as the sliding left margin and the irregular spaces between words make clear.[107]

The pamphlet deploys the errata list as a literary form to work with: starting conventionally ('Page 6, line 23, read single for siuule'); becoming loquacious ('Page 31. There is something twice set down, mend that thy self if thout wilt, for I promise thee I cannot'); and then morphing into a ranging, buttonholing address ('Yet here me a word afore thou goest, an thou be a goodfellow, commend me to George Bullen Dean of Lichfield'). Readers then get a series of (to us today) semi-comprehensible comments on Bullen's sermons, his faults, and his obsession with his dog. This all takes place on a page that is misnumbered 23, instead of 32. Moments like this, when a paratext's utilitarian function is left behind, or is folded into the literary project of the text, peak at times of satirical stress: the late 1580s and 1590s and the 1650s.[108]

Authors also regularly situate themselves in the print shop. In *Lenten Stuffe*, Nashe signs off his address 'To his Readers' with *'I am cald away to correct the faults of the presse, that escaped in my absence from the Printing-house'*.[109] His note is informed by the genre of the errata plea: mistakes are linked to authorial absence, as was common. But Nashe animates it, takes it to a different place, and the prospect of him dashing back to the print shop creates a weird temporal doubling: we're reading the printed text, but Nashe has just told us he has to run to check the proofs; perhaps if we stop reading we can give Nashe time to race back to perfect the text we have in our hands. Even authors who didn't formally work in the print shop (that is, those who don't belong to my group of print shop authors) might spend considerable time there checking the production of the book, and as a result might regularly describe, or have their work described, using the language of composing and correcting. In his *Seconde Tragedie of Seneca entituled Thyestes* (1560), Jasper Heywood ruefully remembered spending time checking the proofs of his *Troas* (1559) as they were printed at Richard Tottel's print shop at the 'sygne of Hande and Starre', in Fleet Street:

> To Printers hands I gaue the worke:
> by whome I had suche wrong,
> That though my selfe perused their prooues

---

[107] Joseph Black (ed.), *The Martin Marprelate Tracts: A Modernized and Annotated Edition* (Cambridge, UK: Cambridge University Press, 2008), pp. 193–194.
[108] Nicholas McDowell alerted me to Quaker Samuel Fisher's use of the errata list in *Rusticus ad Academicos* (1660) to mock the idea that the Bible could be an error-free source of faith.
[109] Thomas Nashe, *Lenten Stuffe* (1599), sig. A4v. Thanks to Philip Schwyzer for reminding me of this moment.

> the first tyme, yet ere long
> When I was gone, they wolde agayne
> the print therof renewe,
> Corrupted all: in such a sorte,
> that scant a sentence trewe
> Now flye abroade as I it wrote.[110]

Presumably as a result of this struggle with printing and proofing, Heywood's translation of Seneca's *Hercules Furens* makes print shop correction central to the work's title page definition and to the book's sense of what it is an author does when he writes: *The first Tragedie of Lucius Anneus Seneca, intituled Hercules furens, newly perused and of all faultes whereof it did before abound diligently corrected ... By Jasper Heywood student in Oxford* (1561).

One answer to the daunting question, 'What is writing?', might be, for authors like Nashe and Heywood, the error-prone process of seizing lead-alloy from a case; of checking proofs; of altering a forme.

II Handwritten Corrections by Authors

It was relatively common for authors to correct books after their printed publication through the addition of handwritten annotations: many authors wrote with an expectation that making hand-corrections on published books was part of what an author did.[111] In part this was a consequence on the pressures of book production that meant that authors, often absent from the print shop, were unable to see proof sheets.[112] Authors continued writing – to use that term expansively to mean working on a text – long after they had 'finished' their work, in the sense that manuscript copy was handed over to publisher or printer, and a printed book appeared in the world. Izaak Walton added corrections to so many copies of his *Lives* that, in the words of one bibliographer, 'uncorrected copies may almost be considered as bibliographical rarities',[113] and most extant copies of William Davenant's incomplete epic *Gondibert* (1651) contain corrections in the author's hand, including presentation copies to John Selden and the parliamentarian Major John Wildman.[114] Presentation copies were

---

[110] Jasper Heywood, *The Seconde Tragedie of Seneca entituled Thyestes* (1560), 'The Preface', sigs *8v-[trefoil]1.
[111] My subject here is not authors correcting print-shop proofs, although there is evidence of this happening. For proofs, see McKitterick, *History*, vol. I, pp. 244–248.
[112] McKitterick, *History*, vol. I, pp. 236–237.
[113] G. and A. Tillotson, 'Pen-and-ink corrections in mid-seventeenth-century books', in *The Library* 4th series, 14.1 (1933–4), 59–72, 59.
[114] D. H. Woodward, 'The Manuscript Corrections and Printed Variants in the First Edition of *Gondibert* (1651)', *The Library*, 5th series, 20.4 (1965), 298–309; Niall Allsopp, '"Lett none our

particularly likely to be revised in this way, post-print. At the request of librarian John Rouse, John Milton presented to the Bodleian eleven of his prose writings (the five anti-prelatical and the four divorce pamphlets, *Areopagitica* and *Of Education*)[115] in late 1646, and re-presented his 1645 *Poems*[116] with his manuscript ode to Rouse[117] in January 1647 upon the loss in transit of the *Poems*. Many of these texts bear Milton's (or at least his authorised) corrections.[118]

Recent work on annotations in books has been dominated by the figure of the reader and has made the act of writing in books virtually synonymous with reading: always scrambling for reliable evidence, the history of reading has relied, paradoxically, on the act of writing. This attention to written traces has meant that the history of reading has been overwhelmingly organised as case Studies of marginal annotations – which, in turn, has led to accounts of reading which stress appropriation and use by the reader, and the reader's lack of reverence for, or of interest in, author or origin. This kind of narrative finds one founding moment in Lisa Jardine and Anthony Grafton's study of Gabriel Harvey's Livy, where Jardine and Grafton set in motion a sense of early modern reading as active, 'purposeful' in terms of political action, keyed to particular occasions, and 'intended *to give rise to something else.*'[119] This model of reading, informed by Michel de Certeau's work on consumers as improvisers,[120] proposes that readers appropriate texts away from their authors, towards some future use, and it has underpinned much recent work.

Annotations of a book by its author present a different category of book-use evidence. Unlike reader's marks, these annotations are authorial: they put the author back into the book, even if this is the author at a later point in time, and even if this is the author who is also now a reader of his or her own work. If we are concerned with authorship as a variable of literary and critical definition, we need to think carefully about such marks, with an emphasis that is different from reader-centric studies of annotations.

Lombard author rudely blame for's righteous paine": An Annotated Copy of Sir William Davenant's *Gondibert* (1651)', in *The Library* 16.1 (2015), 24–50, esp. 25–28.

[115] Bod. Arch. G e.44.   [116] Bod. Arch. G f.17.   [117] Bod. Arch. F d.38.

[118] Simpson, *Proof-Reading*, pp. 27, 29; Helen Darbishire, 'Pen-and-Ink Corrections in Books of the Seventeenth Century', in *The Review of English Studies* 7.25 (January 1931), 72–73. My thanks to Will Poole for helping to clarify the narrative of Milton's donated books.

[119] Lisa Jardine and Anthony Grafton, '"Studied for Action": How Gabriel Harvey Read His Livy', in *Past and Present* 129 (1990), pp. 30–78, 32, 30.

[120] Michel de Certeau, *The Practice of Everyday Life*, translated by Steven Rendall (Berkeley: University of California Press, 1984), esp. p. 174 for the 'ruses' and 'turns' enacted by readers to resist imposed readings.

Perhaps the best known instance of an author-annotated book is the 'Bordeaux Copy' of the *Essais* of Montaigne: a copy of the fifth edition (1588) heavily annotated by Montaigne and his secretaries in the years before his death in 1592 (although some of those annotations have been lost through the trimmings of a later bookbinder).[121] Montaigne supplies additions, corrections, deletions and also extensive revisions and augmentations, often starting in the margins but creeping out into the body of the text; he also marked the text as the '6th edition', and the annotations, sent to Montaigne's literary executor Marie de Gournay, functioned as the basis for her 1595 edition. Montaigne's revisions have received extensive critical and editorial commentary; I would like to think a little about two texts by Milton, both of which feature post-publication pen-and-ink corrections: 'Lycidas', a printed copy of which carries Milton's handwritten alterations; and *Areopagitica*, which has an important handwritten reworking that has been long thought, but not universally accepted to be, by Milton. I want to consider how critics have responded to these interventions, and what the interpretative possibilities of each might be.

'Lycidas' is the final and longest poem in *Obsequies to the memorie of Mr. Edward King*, the second part of *Justa Edouardo King* (1638).[122] Edward King drowned on 10 August 1637; the autograph draft of Milton's pastoral elegy in his poetical notebook, in the library of Trinity College, Cambridge, is dated November 1637;[123] and the quarto *Obsequies*, including 'Lycidas', was printed by Cambridge University Printers Thomas Buck and Roger Daniel in 1638. Later printings of 'Lycidas' followed in the *Poems* of 1645 and 1673.[124] The 1638 book, which sought to remember King and lament his early death, is expressive of the variability of print at this point in the seventeenth century. The book circulated in different forms:

---

[121] The Bordeaux Copy is preserved at the Bibliothèque municaple in Bordeaux. For details and facsimiles of the text, see The Montaigne Project, hosted online by the University of Chicago, at www.lib.uchicago.edu/efts/ARTFL/projects/montaigne.

[122] *Obsequies to the memorie of Mr. Edward King* (1638), pp. 20–25.

[123] Trinity College, Cambridge, MS R.3.4.

[124] Also extant is a fragment of the proof conveying lines 23 to 58, complete with handwritten corrections marked before the final printing in the hand not of Milton but a worker at the print shop. The handwritten changes to the proof insert a hyphen in 'eye lids' (line 26) and 'a field' (line 27), and a full stop after 'wheel' (line 31), and invert a turned 'u' in 'Snch' (line 49) – all changes incorporated into the final 1638 printing – in addition to noting broken fonts and loose setting and what printers referred to as 'botches'. The proof sheet is CUL Adv.d.38.6; McKitterick, *History*, p. 247, prints a facsimile; on p. 246 McKitterick suggests that the 'proofs show, in their attention to details of presentation as well as to textual error, typographical standards that by the next decade were becoming unusual in London.' For a near-contemporary comparison, see D. F. Foxon, 'The varieties of early proof: Cartwright's *Royal slave*, 1639, 1640', in *The Library* 5th series, 25.2 (1970), 151–154.

Errors and Corrections: 'My Galley Charged with Forgetfulness' 107

the two parts of the volume commemorating King, containing respectively classical and English verses, were usually bound together with the English following the classical, with the effect that 'Lycidas' was the last poem in the whole volume, obtaining a prominence that literary history has endorsed; but there is at least one extant copy in which the sections' order is reversed (that is, the 13 English poems precede the classical, with 'Lycidas' appearing mid-book, a last vernacular gasp before the 20 Latin and 3 Greek poems take up the task of elegiac lament), and another in which the English section appears alone.[125] Moreover, the first page of 'Lycidas' is printed in two states, with an indentation at line 15 ('Begin the, Sisters of the sacred well') and an exclamation mark at line 14 ('Without the need of some melodious tear') in some, but not all, copies.[126]

There are also pen-and-ink corrections in what editors agree to be Milton's hand in a Cambridge University Library copy.[127] The Cambridge University Library copy's handwritten corrections are as follows (alterations in bold):

1. line 10
'*Who would not sing for Lycidas? he knew*':
changed to
'*Who would not sing for Lycidas? he* ∧ *knew* ∧ **well**'

2. line 51
'*Clos'd ore the head of your lord Lycidas?*'
changed to
'*Clos'd ore the head of your* ~~lord~~ *Lycidas?* ~~**Lov'd**~~ **Lov'd**'

3. line 53
'*Where the old Bards the famous Druids lie*'
changed to
'*Where* **the** *old Bards the famous Druids lie* **your**'

4. line 67
'*Were it not better done as others do,*'
changed to
'*Were it not better done as others* ~~**do**~~**, use**'

---

[125] BL C.21.c.42 has only the English section; BL Ashley 1167 has the parts reversed. Noted in *Shorter Poems*, ed. Lewalski and Haan, p. clix.
[126] *Shorter Poems*, ed. Lewalski and Haan, p. clix.
[127] CUL Adv.d.38.5. Another copy (BL C.21.c.42) also has sustained alterations in a hand that has been claimed as Milton's, but now appears not to be. These annotations seem to be copies of the Cambridge corrections. Some but not all of the annotations in both these books are detailed in Hugh C. H. Candy, 'Milton Autographs Established', in the *Library*, 4th series, 13.2 (1932), 192–200. Candy argues that in both copies the annotations are in Milton's hand, a view contemporary scholarship rejects.

5. line 157
'*Where thou perhaps under the humming tide*'
changed to
'*Where thou perhaps under the* ~~humming~~ *tide* **whelming**'

6. line 175
'*With Nectar pure his oazie locks he laves,*'
changed to
'*With Nectar pure his o*~~a~~ ˚*zie locks he laves* **oosie**'

7. after line 176
'*And heares the unexpressive nuptial song;*'
line added in margin
'in the blest kingdoms / meeke of Joy and Love'

8. final initials 'J.M.'
changed to
'J. M. **ilton**'

Milton's corrections return the 1638 text to the Trinity Manuscript readings in four of six occasions: the exceptions are his alteration of 'oazie to 'oosie' at line 175 (where the Trinity Manuscript has 'oozie' and the 1645 *Poems* has 'oazie'), and, more significantly, his change of 'humming tide' to 'whelming tide'. Since the Trinity Manuscript has 'humming tide', and the 1645 *Poems* 'whelming tide', Milton's handwritten annotation perhaps represents his post-Trinity Manuscript preference, taken up by later editions.

Despite these alterations, Milton does not emerge as an entirely meticulous corrector of his own text: he neglected to note errors deriving from either the transcriber or from the compositor(s) at the print shop at lines 39 ('shepherds' for 'shepherd'), 56 ('Ah' for 'ay'), 64 ('uncessant' for 'incessant'), 66 ('stridly' for 'strictly'), 73 ('where' for 'when'), 112 ('mitred' for (according to the Trinity MS) 'mitre'd'), 131 ('smites' for 'site'), 149 ('beauty' for 'beauties'), and 151 ('Lycid' for 'Lycid").[128] If this suggests a less than thorough process of correcting, then Milton here resembles other authors whose corrections to their own printed texts were often irregular and disorderly. This is true of Davenant's corrections and of Edward Benlowes's to copies of his *Theophila* (1652).[129] Thomas Browne marked at least 12 copies of his *Hydriotaphia, urne burial* (1658) with varying numbers of corrections – some copies have over 40; one has 77; others

---

[128] John T. Shawcross, 'Establishment of a text of Milton's poems through a study of *Lycidas*', in *Papers of the Bibliographical Society of America* 56 (1962), 317–331. Shawcross argues that 'editors have been all too prone to hold the early editions as sacrosanct' (318).
[129] G. and A. Tillotson, 'Pen-and-ink corrections'.

have fewer than 20. What McKitterick calls Browne's 'unsystematic labour' probably reflects changing material circumstances: at times Browne may have been relying on memory; at other times he may have been working from the printed errata list that is pasted in some but not all copies of the book.[130]

Most diligent editions of 'Lycidas' note Milton's annotations, but simultaneously bury them away in textual notes that offer no reflections on their significance.[131] Scholars who have considered them have been preoccupied with two very reasonable questions: first, whether these alterations are the work of Milton himself;[132] and second, what use these alterations may serve in terms of establishing a reliable text.[133] Thus these annotations have been understood as Milton's corrections of errors made by the print shop compositor or by the transcriber of Milton's manuscript. Hugh C. H. Candy notes that '[i]n the original draft Milton used an abbreviated *your* which transcriber, or compositor, has mistaken for y^e and has accordingly interpreted *the*; in the same draft Milton wrote *oozie*; the *oazie* of our text looks like a printer's error. In 1645 the printed version has *your* and *oozy*.'[134]

But is there anything more to be said? We might think about the interpretative consequences of this print-and-manuscript hybrid, a mode of reading we could call copy-specific literary criticism: a reading that considers the interpretative possibilities (and not just the bibliographical or textual significance) of unique features of a book. We might consider, for example, the annotations as a new voice in the poem: 'Lycidas' is a monody (a funeral song by a single singer), but the coda adds a brilliant jolt when it reframes through the narrator's perspective what we have just read with a growing sense of immediacy ('Thus sang the uncouth swain . . . ').[135]

---

[130] McKitterick, *Print, Manuscript*, p. 129. For a counter example of care, see Richard Hooker's 5th book of *Lawes of Eccleiasticall Politie* (Bod MS Add.C.165), corrected by Hooker himself, and the text from which John Windet printed the 1597 folio. Simpson, *Proof-Reading*, p. 78, calls this 'a wonderful tribute to both author and printer'.

[131] See, for example, John Milton, *Complete Shorter Poems*, ed. Stella P. Revard (Oxford: John Wiley & Sons, 2009), p. 560; and *Complete Shorter Poems*, ed. John Carey (London: Longman, 1968; Pearson Education, 2007), p. 238.

[132] Candy, 'Milton Autographs', argues that '[t]he evidence as a whole makes it very difficult to doubt that Milton made *all* these marginal corrections [that is, in both CUL Adv.d.38.5 and BL C.21.c.42], that he wrote them between 1638 and 1645, and that "C.21.c.42" now deserves more honourable and explicit mention in the General Catalogue of the British Museum than it has hitherto received' (200).

[133] Shawcross, 'Establishment', 323.

[134] Candy, 'Milton Autographs', 193. Candy notes that since line 67 ('do' for 'use') 'is not easily explained as a careless transcript, it may be a liberty of the Obsequies' editor' (198).

[135] The descriptive heading in the Trinity MS ('In this Monodie the author bewails a lerned freind unfortunately drown'd in his passage from Chester on the Irish seas 1637') is not in the 1638 memorial volume, since that collection's title page had already described the occasion, but was

The handwritten annotations add one more sense of a frame, another vantage point from outside, in. Or we might consider the annotations as elements which disrupt the calm of the poem – the calm of both *mise-en-page* and verse form – rather as the short lines and irregular rhyme scheme disrupt the iambic pentameter, and as the waves of the Irish Sea knocked off-course Edward King's boat. The scribbled annotations accentuate a sense of the irregular, the tense, the difficult, the unresolved, like the extra-syllable 'well' added to line 10 ('*Who would not sing for Lycidas? he ⋏ knew ⋏**well***'), also in the Trinity Manuscript but generally refused in later printed editions from 1645 to this day.[136] The annotations convey that same sense of untimely interruption with which 'Lycidas' begins, a beginning that figures the writing of elegy, like the act of correcting, as arduous, violent manual work that has to destroy in order to create:

> Yet once more, o ye laurels, and once more,
> Ye myrtles brown, with ivy never-sere,
> I come to pluck your berries harsh and crude,
> And with forc'd fingers rude
> Shatter your leaves before the mellowing yeare.

We might also consider the annotations and their relation to a sense of tradition. 'Lycidas' is a powerful poem in part because it stages the twin pull of adherence to, and departure from, literary convention. Writing in the immediate aftermath of Edward King's death, Milton's poem asks whether the inherited patterns and depths of pastoral elegy can speak to the tragic circumstances of the present, and we feel the strain of diachronic convention being bent to the synchronic moment. 'Lycidas' is thus a poem that is preoccupied with literary genealogy and with its own place in literary genealogy: 'it is, paradoxically', writes Barbara Lewalski, 'at once the most derivative and most original of elegies', each line echoing earlier pastoral elegies by classical, neo-Latin and vernacular poets including Theocritus, Virgil and Spenser, while the poem moves beyond all precedents in terms of profundity and range.'[137]

Milton's handwritten corrections strengthen this restless concern with genealogy. One consequence of the handwritten corrections is that the 1638 text becomes two texts: as we read CUL Adv.d.38.5 copy-specifically, we

added for the 1645 *Poems*, with a second sentence: 'And by occasion foretels the ruine of our corrupted Clergy then in their height'.
[136] The extra-syllabic 'well' is included in *The Poetical Works of John Milton* (Oxford: Clarendon Press, 1955), vol. 2, ed. Helen Darbishire, p. 165.
[137] Barbara K. Lewalski, *The Life of John Milton: A Critical Biography* (Oxford: Blackwell, 2000), p. 82. Lewalski judges that 'no previous, or I think subsequent, funeral poem has the scope, dimension, poignancy and power of *Lycidas*' (p. 82).

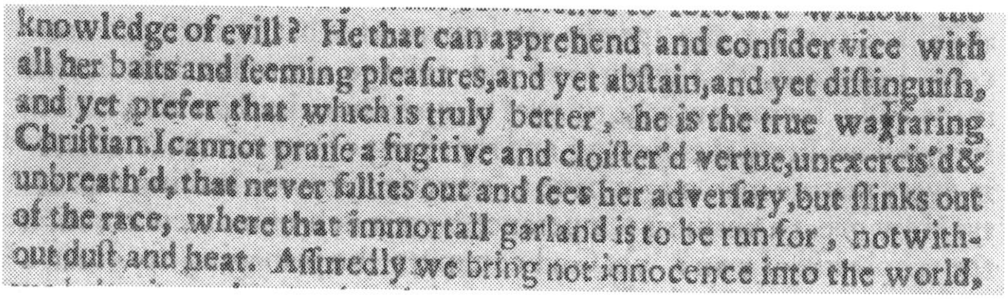

> knowledge of evill? He that can apprehend and confider vice with all her baits and feeming pleafures, and yet abftain, and yet diftinguifh, and yet prefer that which is truly better, he is the true wayfaring Chriftian. I cannot praife a fugitive and cloifter'd vertue, unexercis'd & unbreath'd, that never fallies out and fees her adverfary, but flinks out of the race, where that immortall garland is to be run for, notwithout duft and heat. Affuredly we bring not innocence into the world,

Figure 14 John Milton, *Areopagitica* (1644), p. 12. Beinecke Rare Book and Manuscript Library, Yale University (2111653)

encounter both an earlier, unannotated printed text, and a later, hand-revised text, and we are probably inclined to consider the relationship between the two. Both of these texts are authorial (with the caveat that the printed text comes to us via the mediations of the print shop): the usual opposition between authorial and reader-annotated variant won't do. The annotations thus create two texts, and suggest, or invite us to think about, a retrospective genealogy that connects Milton's marked poem with the earlier unmarked poem we read at the same time. The annotated copy invents a tradition that it immediately departs from, strengthening 'Lycidas'' struggle with literary history.

If the Cambridge copy of 'Lycidas' shows Milton working to correct, then in *Areopagitica* (1644) (Figure 14) Milton makes the case for the ethical importance of getting things wrong. Writing to the sound of Civil War, and with Spenser's *Faerie Queene* in mind, he described 'the true warfaring Christian' as one whose virtue could only emerge through entanglements with vice, and 'all her baits and seeming pleasures'. A virtue that 'slinks out of the race' to remain 'fugitive and cloister'd' is no virtue at all ('a blank vertue, not a pure'); a 'survey of vice is ... necessary to the constituting of human vertue', and 'the scanning of error to the confirmation of truth.'[138] We need mistakes, Milton argues: the Latin root of error is *errare*, meaning to wander, and, like knights in a romance, Milton's readers should meander into forests of bad texts to establish and test their virtue. Indeed, at this point Milton infamously makes a (non-typographical) error, writing how 'our sage and serious Poet *Spencer* ... describing true temperance under the person of *Guion*, brings him in with his palmer through the cave of Mammon.'[139]

---

[138] John Milton, *Areopagitica. A Speech of Mr. John Milton For the Liberty of Unlicenc'd Printing, To the Parlament of England* (1644), pp. 12–13.
[139] Milton, *Areopagitica*, p. 13.

But the Palmer does not accompany Guyon in Book 2 of *The Faerie Queene*.[140]

In this emphasis on the relationship between 'scanning ... error' and virtue, Milton echoes some of the rhetorical register of errata lists which often present errors as valuable moral tests of attentive reading: they become a means to instil a culture of diligent study. A 1622 printed sermon by John Donne lists five errors before noting a second class of mistakes, unlisted, to which the reader need attend: 'Those Errors which are committed in mis-pointing [punctuation], or in changing the forme of the Character, will soone be discerned, and Corrected by the Eye of any deliberate Reader'.[141] Such mistakes constitute a little examination of readerly deliberation: an exercise in becoming assiduous.[142] Thomas Taylor's book offers blunder-spotting as a way for readers to prove themselves civilised: listing errors that 'alter the sence', the writer leaves 'the other to thine owne humanity, and curtesie to correct.'[143] One function of error is to catch out fools – the kind of bad reader who, as described in Robert Greene's *The defence of conny catching* (1592), ponders the 'small scape' while letting 'grosse faultes passe without any reprehension.'[144]

But there is a bibliographical footnote to this. While Milton's 1644 text – the only free-standing edition from the seventeenth century, printed unlicensed, unregistered and with no note of publisher or printer – prints 'wayfaring', rather than 'warfaring', in many of these copies the 'y' of 'wayfaring' has been struck through with an 'r' added above.[145]

This alteration is added with sufficient regularity in at least eight copies (of which at least four are presentation copies) to suggest, if not, as some have

---

[140] Harold Bloom argues that Milton's error is an unconscious but anxious attempt to distance himself from his predecessor, 'to make his own belatednesss into an earlines, and his tradition's priority over him into a lateness' (*A Map of Misreading* (Oxford: Oxford University Press, 2003), p. 131). George F. Butler suggests Milton's Palmer 'is not as egregious an error as critics have generally suggested ... [but is] more deliberate than accidental and is part of his rhetorical strategy rather than a mistake' ('Milton's "sage and serious Poet Spencer": Error and Imitation in *The Faerie Queene* and *Areopagitica*', in *Texas Studies in Literature and Language*, 49.2 (Summer 2007), 101–124, 102).

[141] John Donne, *A Sermon Vpon the XV. Verse of the XX. Chapter of the Booke of Judges* (1622), sig. A4v.

[142] Lerer, *Error*, p. 28, discusses errata sheets at the end of Tyndale's English translation of the New Testament, arguing that Tyndale educates the reader in error-spotting and, more broadly, inculcates a kind of Protestant readerly diligence.

[143] Taylor, *Beawties*, 'Errata'.

[144] Robert Greene, *The defence of conny catching* (1592), final page of 'To the Readers'.

[145] Milton, *Areopagitica*, p. 12. The revision is contained in BL C.55.c.22(9), Bod Wood B.29(5) (a copy with 'Edw: Rigby', 'Alice Rigby', 'Lucy Hesketh' and 'pd – 4^s – 6^d' on the opening flyleaf), and the copy held at the University Library at Lausanne. BL G. 608 and BL C.120.b.12(1) do not have the revision.

argued, Milton's own hand, then at least an authorised revision.[146] The change perhaps indicates a mistake by the compositor or the scribe who prepared the print-shop copy; but it might also represent a post-print, authorial second-thought. Certainly, the new reading is thematically consistent with a passage that describes the inevitable entwining of error and truth – that sense of 'the knowledge of good and evil as two twins cleaving together leapt forth into the World' – and the need for readers to fight their way through both: thus the Yale edition of Milton's prose, and most modern editors, print 'warfaring'.[147]

The handwritten annotation over the printed page performs the argument of the passage. The switch from wayfaring ('travelling or journeying by road')[148] to warfaring is a movement from an arduous journey to a battle: of reading, and of life, as an exterior, and not only an interior, conflict. It chimes with Biblical precedents such as Ephesians 6.1 ('Put on the whole armour of God') and also with Spenser's *Faerie Queene*, which opens with Redcrosse 'Ycladd in mightie armes and silver shielde, / Wherein old dints of deepe wounds did remaine.'[149] And certainly Milton's conception of the 'sage and serious Poet *Spencer*' is threaded through this section. But the point lost in textual debates about best or correct readings is that both readings are present, visible, viable and real: the significance of the correction is precisely that it does not replace the earlier version. In *Of Grammatology*, Derrida deployed the idea of writing '*sous rature*', or 'under erasure', to convey, in the spirit of a heuristic, the use of words and concepts that are flawed but necessary: a way of bringing a word to the surface while also holding it at bay. Thus a word is written, crossed out, both word and deletion are printed, and the layering that is

---

[146] G. A. Bonnard, 'Two Remarks on the Text of Milton's *Areopagitica*', in *Review of English Studies* 4.16 (1928), 434–438, 437–438, makes the case for Milton's hand, based on the repeated appearance of the change in presentation copies. Darbishire, 'Pen-and-Ink Corrections', responding to Bonnard, is certain that the revision is not Milton's hand ('I have no shadow of doubt that this *r* is not his' (72)), but is rather the hand of the printer or bookseller. Ernest Sirluck (ed.), *Complete Prose Works of John Milton* (New Haven: Yale University Press, 1959), vol. II, states that while the identity 'cannot be proved . . . [i]t can scarcely be doubted, however, that the change has Milton's authority, and was made, if not by himself, by the printer or bookseller' (p. 515, n. 102). Sirluck notes that the colour of the ink suggests '[t]he changes were probably not made out of the same inkwell'. More recently, Nigel Smith, *Is Milton Better Than Shakespeare?* (Cambridge, MA: Harvard University Press, 2008), says the emendation is 'in Milton's own hand' (pp. 27–28), but doesn't indicate why he thinks this is the case.

[147] Balachandra Rajan, *Milton and the Climates of Reading: Essays*, ed. by Elizabeth Sauer (Toronto: University of Toronto Press, 2006), p. 139.

[148] *OED*, '*wayfaring*, adj.', a.

[149] Noted in John Milton, *The Major Works*, ed. Stephen Orgel and Jonathan Goldberg (Oxford: Oxford University Press, 2003), p. 826.

created is a response to '[t]he predicament of having to use resources of the heritage that one questions'.[150]

Derrida's method – 'at first very exciting,', according to A. D. Nuttall, 'but in time merely tiresome'[151] – might be usefully deployed to analyse a range of palimpsestic early modern textual forms, including deleted references to the Pope and Thomas Becket in prayer books, prescribed by legislation in 1535 and enacted by readers who crossed out, coloured in, glued over, and scratched out these words.[152] As Juliet Fleming has shown, the workings of these and other acts of erasure were more complicated than unproblematic deletion (if unproblematic deletion can ever be imagined): 'to systematically blot the name of the Pope from the pages of a book', for example, 'is to produce a blot *as* that name.'[153] While way/warfaring shares with Derrida's *sous rature* and many of those prayer books the idea of legibility in deletion (we can still read the printed word), the *Areopagitica* example is in fact more complex: what we read is not just a deletion, but a deletion ('y') and a new version (way'faring'). The post-print handwritten 'r' in *Areopagitica* deposits a new reading over an old, and it is impossible to read one without the other: we note the handwritten correction, then the crossed-out but legible printed text that seems both spatially and temporally prior (it is beneath, and before), and then we toggle between the two, beginning to think about the differences between wayfaring and warfaring, about Milton's intention, about whether other copies contain this change, about the compositor, about the moment of printing, about the moment of annotation, about which reading to use, about the annotator, about all the other lexical paths not taken by this passage of prose. What is created is an oscillation between 'way' and 'war' that doesn't resolve; a sense of mistake and correction as continually growing out of and into each other; and a conception of error as morally and hermeneutically productive.

III Paste-in Slip-Insertions

Books and glue enjoyed an intimate relationship in early modern England. Most of the recipes in William Bullein's *Bulwarke of Defense* (1579) – a text

---

[150] Jacques Derrida, *Of Grammatology,* translated by Gayatri Chakravorty Spivak (Baltimore: Johns Hopkins University Press, 1974, 2013), pp. xiv, p. 318, n. 13.
[151] A. D. Nuttall, *A New Mimesis: Shakespeare and the Representation of Reality* (New Haven: Yale University Press, 2007), p. 35.
[152] Dunstan Roberts, 'The Expurgation of Traditional Prayer Books (c. 1535–1600)', in *Reformation* 15 (2010), 23–49.
[153] Juliet Fleming, *Graffiti and the Writing Arts of Early Modern England* (London: Reaktion, 2001), pp. 73–78, 76.

designed to assuage the 'sicknesse, soarenesse, and wouudes that doe dayly assaulte mankinde' – concern glues used in medical treatments, either 'made of the skyns of … the strongest beastes, as Bulles, Oxen, red Deare', or 'made of Fyshes, as of the Bellyes of Whales or other great Fyshes' for treating, among other things, 'skalding & burning of the body' and 'red spots from the face'. But Bullein also describes 'another Glew made of Corne, as Wheat. &c. good for Paste for Stacyoners, which *Galen* doth remember *libro. vij. simplic. Medic.*'[154] In his *Naturalis Historia*, Pliny the Elder describes a 'common paper paste' composed from 'the finest flour of wheat mixed with boiling water and some small drops of vinegar sprinkled in it', like the 'paste' Joseph Moxon describes in the print shop, 'made of fine Wheaten Flower, well boiled in fair Water to the consistency of Hasty-pudding [i.e., porridge]', applied with a brush to cover the frames of the tympans with skin.[155] Animal-based glue might be used on books, too: a recipe in the commonplace book of a late sixteenth-century Yorkshire yeoman 'To make glewe for bookes' uses the bladders of stockfish – soaked in clear water; cleaned with a knife; beaten in a mortar; strained through a cloth until 'yt waxethe thyke', and tempered with ale and flour – to produce an adhesive the compiler, a scrivener, probably used to join together sheets of parchment into a codex.[156]

Glue, along with stitching, held together the architecture of a book through its boards and binding. Glue also pasted up title-pages 'on Posts, or Walls, / Or in Cleft-sticks, advanced to make Calls', or broadsides like *The Humble Petition of the Post-Masters of the Several Roads of England* (1653) 'pasted upon ye posts 2d of Aprill', as pamphlet collector George Thomason noted.[157] And glue also enabled narrow slips of new text to be layered over the old.

The addition of paper slips glued over a section of an existing page was a regular mechanism of book alteration, although it has proven harder for bibliographers to fix on a single term to describe them. In 1993 Brian

---

[154] William Bullein, *Bulleins bulwarke of defence against all sicknesse, soarenesse, and vvoundes that doe dayly assaulte mankind* (1579), ff. 60v, 61. Thanks to Andy Gordon for advice on glue.

[155] James Ward, *Adventures in Stationery: A Journey through Your Pencil Case* (Profile Books: London, 2014); Joseph Moxon, *Mechanick Exercises on the Whole Art of Printing*, ed. Hebert Davis and Harry Carter (London: Oxford University Press, 1958), p. 277.

[156] Steven W. May, Arthur F. Marotti, *Ink, Stink Bait, Revenge, and Queen Elizabeth: A Yorkshire Yeoman's Household Book* (Ithaca: Cornell University Press, 2014), p. 221. The manuscript is BL Add. MS 82370.

[157] Ben Jonson, 'To my Bookseller', *Epigrams* II. *To the Right Honorable, the Councel of State: and to the Honorable Committee, by them appointed in the case of the Post-Masters. The humble petition of the Post-Masters of the several roads of England* (1653), BL 669.f.16 (91).

Gerrard, irritated at the way bibliographers had 'botched' the language of post-impression correction (that is, correction after printing), suggested the glued-in slip be called a *tegens* (plural *tegentia*), since a 'tegens is hiding, or concealing, whatever lies beneath ... [deriving] from the Latin *tegere*, to hide.'[158] The problem with Gerrard's term is that these slips, as we will see, often fail to hide or conceal. Deborah Leslie, English rare materials cataloguer at the Folger Library, has recently given them the less emotive label 'author/publisher slip-insertions'.[159] Such paste-ins might convey a single letter, word, phrase, or a more sustained passage of text, or simply blank space. Paste-ins are often copy-specific in their placement: that is, different copies of the same edition carry different arrangements of paste-in revisions – as seen, for example, in extant copies of Samuel Morland's *The Urim of Conscience* (1695).[160] Sometimes the slips seem to have been added by the author (as in the case of Margaret Cavendish, below), but the slips were 'generally but not invariably executed in the printing house' by a print shop worker, perhaps following the advice of the corrector if such a figure was present.[161] (Multiple print-shop roles were often performed by a single individual: as one 1610 text put it in discussing printing 'negligence', the 'Printer, Compositor, or Corrector ... I repute as one man.'[162]) They are generally but not exclusively a means to correct errors, or to revise a text in the light of changing contexts – some copies of *The Booke of Common Praier* (1612) have a slip substituting Prince Charles for Prince Henry, who

---

[158] Gerrard, 'A new taxonomy', p. 47.
[159] William H. Sherman and Heather Wolfe, 'The Department of Hybrid Books: Thomas Milles between Manuscript and Print', in *The Renaissance Collage: Towards a New History of Reading*, special edition of *Journal of Medieval and Early Modern Studies*, ed. Juliet Fleming, William H. Sherman and Adam Smyth, 45.3 (September 2015), 457–486, 465. I will use Leslie's term (or 'paste-ins', or 'pasted-in slips') to refer to strips of paper smaller than page-size cancels, added to previously printed pages. The word 'slip' is useful in that it draws attention both to materiality (slip *qua* 'A piece of paper or parchment, esp. one which is narrow in proportion to its length', *OED* 2) and to the passage of text requiring alteration that the material slip marks out (slip *qua* 'A mistake or fault, esp. one of a slight or trivial character, inadvertently made in writing, speaking', *OED* 3).
[160] Compare, for example, pp. 12, 14 and 21 of Bodleian (OC) 141 m.863 with copies held at the British Library, Folger Shakespeare Library, Emmanuel College Cambridge, Trinity College Cambridge and Dr Williams's Library.
[161] McKitterick, *Print, Manuscript*, p. 127; see p. 115 for the presence or absence of correctors. Elsewhere, McKitterickk notes that 'there was no talk of such a figure [a corrector] until the late 1620s' (*A History*, vol. 1, p. 239). For correctors more generally, particularly from a European perspective, see Anthony Grafton, *The Culture of Correction in Renaissance Europe* (London: British Library, 2011)
[162] Thomas Bell, *The Catholique triumph conteyning, a reply to the pretensed answere of B.C. (a masked Iesuite,)* (1610), p. 335.

Errors and Corrections: 'My Galley Charged with Forgetfulness' 117

died in November 1612, in the State Prayers[163] – but they might also supplement the page with additional material: augmenting, rather than rewriting, the text. Slips appear at the very start of books, on title pages, and imprint details of publication are often changed.[164] Slips appear within the main body of the text: they might, for example, correct pairs of lines that had been set in the wrong order by the compositor, particularly in poetry and verse drama where the error is clear from the rhyme words. This occurs in copies of *A most pleasant comedie of Mucedorus* (1598) and Samuel Daniel's poem 'Musophilus' (1601).[165] Slips might also come at the very end: the final list of individuals who contributed to William Somner's *Dictionarium Saxonico-Latino-Anglicum* (1659) is expanded with pasted-in slips and manuscript additions, creating the effect of a series of deferred conclusions and of a book that doesn't want to close.[166]

Very often this form of revision was enacted alongside other modes: thus John Dee used pasted-in slips together with handwritten annotations to make corrections to 60 copies of his *General and Rare Memorials* (1577).[167] And thus, in perhaps the most spectacular performance of error and correction in early modern book history, Augustine Vincent's *A Discovery of Errors in the first edition of the Catalogue of Nobility published by Raphe Brooke, York Herald* (1622). Vincent's book was an attack and meditation on the many errors in Ralph Brooke's *A Catalogue and Succession of the Kings, Princes, Dukes, Marquesses, Earles, and Viscounts of this Realme of England* (1619), but it itself contained countless mistakes and a torrent of leaf cancels, paste-in slips, overprintings, inserted revisions and an errata list of the 61 slips 'of most Consequence', together with a shoulder-shrugging acceptance that 'the rest … I must leave to thine own Obseruation and courteous correction'.[168]

---

[163] *The Booke of Common Praier* (1612), General Theological Seminary, New York.
[164] Gerhard Mercator, *A geographicke description of the regions, countries and kingdomes of the world* (1633), St John's College, Oxford, HB 4 Folios 531, has letterpress English title and imprint slips pasted over the original engraved French title and imprint. Similar layering of English title and imprint details over Dutch occur in Samuel Marolois, *The Art of Fortification, or Architecture Militaire As Well As Defensiue* (1638); Wleem Janszoon Blaeu, *The Light of Nauigation* (1622); and Jacob Aertsz Colomm, *The New Fierie Sea-Colomne* (1649).
[165] *A most pleasant comedie of Mucedorus* (1598), BL C.34.b.34, sig. B1; *The works of Samuel Daniel newly augmented* (1601), Bod Buxton 27, sig. A5v. My thanks for Holger Syme for sharing the Daniel details.
[166] Balliol College, Oxford, 515e1, sig. Ttt2v.
[167] R. J. Roberts, 'John Dee's Corrections to His "Art of Navigation"', in *The Book Collector* 24 (1975), 70–75. Noted in Sherman and Wolfe, 'Hybrid Books'.
[168] For leaf cancels, sigs M1, 2Z4, 3Z1; paste-in cancels, 2D2, 4C1, 4S3v; overprinting, pp. 125–126; inserts, after p. 166; errata, sig. 4X4. See also E. R. Wood, 'Cancels and corrections in *A discovery of errors*, 1622', in *The Library*, 5th series, 13.2 (1958), 124–127.

Sometimes the pasted alterations were subsequently appropriated in later printings; the slips thus create a text that hovers between a first and second edition.[169] The paste-ins to Thomas Cooper's anti-Martinist *An admonition to the people of England: wherein are answered ... the slaunderous untruethes, reprochfully vttered by Martin the libeller* (1589) – the word 'can' over the word 'dare'; the phrase 'That is not yet proued' over 'I will not deny it' – are printed in the second edition, as the paste-ins in effect dissolve into the page.[170]

While some paste-ins were used to alter relatively minor details – paste-ins in copies of *Tables of interest: Whereby questions of interest or use of money, and valuations of purchases, leases, annuities, or pensions* (1630) allow for new handwritten and stamped page signatures[171] – glued-in slips were in general applied only to significant places in a text: like a hermeneutical heat map, paste-ins draw attention to points of pressure, discord or conflict. They mark out what matters: places where an error counts, or where a text is meaningfully insufficient. Stephen Gosson's anti-theatrical *Playes confuted in fiue actions: prouing that they are not to be suffred in a Christian common weale* (1582) was in part written to counter 'the cauils of Thomas Lodge' in the form of Lodge's *Defence of Poetry, Music, and Stage Plays*, itself an answer to Gosson's earlier *Schoole of Abuse* (1579).[172] When Gosson's text prints 'And William Lodge in that patchte pamphlet of his wherein he taketh upon him the defence of playes', the error is corrected with a slip printed 'Thomas', the paste-in reminding readers of the intimate, *ad hominem* nature of these debates about dramatic representation.[173] We might call this a manuscript-style sense of the coterie, but the frequency with which printed texts generate the impression of dialogic directness (in the Martin Marprelate texts, for example, or in Civil War pamphlets) unsettles any exclusive link between this kind of intimacy-effect and manuscript culture.

Reformation fault-lines might also be instantiated in the form of pasted slip-insertions. When John Knox attacked, with characteristic thunder,

---

[169] Lists of corrections might serve a similar role. One of the reasons Erasmus attached to the second, revised edition of his *Apologia ad monachos Hispanos* (Basel, 1529) 26 octavo pages of corrections of several of his books was perhaps that he didn't expect these books to appear in new editions. Simpson, *Proof-Reading*, p. 116.

[170] BL RB.23.A.17194, pp. 40, 135; the revised text appears in second editions on pp. 40, 140.

[171] St Edmund Hall, Oxford, Quarto.G.18 (7).

[172] Lodge's *Defence* was untitled and the given title is a nineteenth-century scholarly suggestion. J. Dover Wilson, 'The Missing Title of Thomas Lodge's Reply to Gosson's "School of Abuse"', in *The Modern Language Review* 3.2 (1908), 166–168.

[173] Brasenose College, Oxford UB/S III 6(6), sig. B4v, line 6. The cancel slip is now missing in this copy, but its presence is remembered in glue marks. Other copies retain the slip.

Errors and Corrections: 'My Galley Charged with Forgetfulness' 119

what he saw as lingering Popish elements in the 1552 *Book of Common Prayer*, the 'Order for the Administration of the Lord's Supper' was duly revised with a protestant gloss (the 'Black Rubric') on kneeling during Communion as gratitude, not adoration: printers Richard Grafton and Edward Whitchurch scrambled to print correction slips to be added to as many unsold copies as possible, and distributed to those who had already bought the book.[174] The *Book of Common Prayer* thus went on being made after its publication date, the process of book production spilling out of the print shop. Extant copies reflect this fast-shifting theological terrain: earlier copies often omit the revision; some carry the text on a separate page ('it is not ment therby, that any adoration is doen ... for that wer idolatry'); and later copies incorporate the change among the Communion instructions.[175]

The slip-insertion complicates the book's relationship with time by extending its moment of production, and works concerned with predicting the future were particularly prone to material revision or supplement as their anticipated telos arrived early, late, or not at all. The paste-in slip-insertion was a useful technology for conveying prophesy, a slippery form best suited to oral culture, in print. In Digby Bull's fiercely anti-Catholic *A letter of a Protestant clergy-man to the reverend clergy of the Church of England, and to all other good Protestants* (1695), the printed title page warns 'of the Evil which he apprehends to be coming upon THE PROTESTANT CHURCH, &c.' In some copies, the publication date has been scratched out, '1710' has been added by hand, and the prophetic tone has been over-pasted with a slip evidently cut from a larger sheet proclaiming 'that POPERY and the second Dreadful WO are certainly now at hand; And also when the third Dreadful WO is like to be executed; And when the Dreadful FIRE at the End of the World is like to come.'[176] Other slip-insertion modifications – as many as seven in some copies – further rework passages that are concerned with the future.[177] The original reads:

> I know not the Day and Hour when this second Woe will fall, nor the Day and Hour when the End of the World will be. Thro' the good Hand of God, so much Light I have as to be able to give warning of these two Woes, and to advertise men to take care that they do not perish therein, and to let them know

---

[174] Peter W. M. Blayney, *The Stationers' Company and the Printers of London, 1501–1557* (Cambridge, UK: Cambridge University Press, 2013), p. 744.
[175] For the incorporated revisions, see *The Boke of common prayer* (1652), Bod C.P. 1552 d.4.
[176] BL T.1839 (7).
[177] BL T.1839 (7) has paste-in slips on the title page, and sigs D1v, D2, E4v, G, H3, H3v. There are also handwritten alterations to dates (for example, sig. E3).

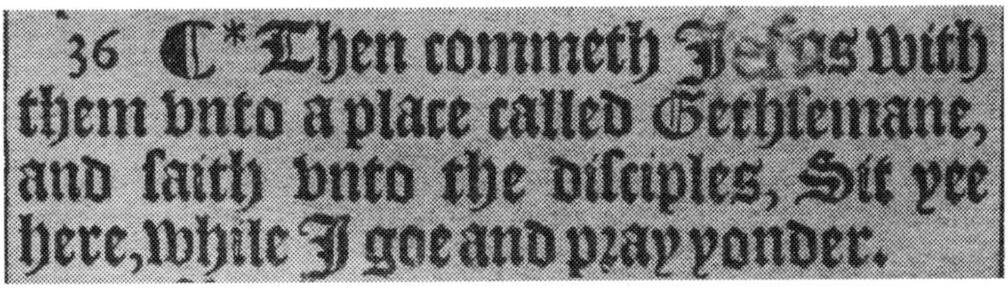
36 ¶*Then commeth Iesus with them vnto a place called Gethſemane, and ſaith vnto the diſciples, Sit yee here, while I goe and pray yonder.

Figure 15 Robert Barker's King James Bible (1611), Matthew 26.36 (R.1.1). Reproduced by kind permission of the President and Fellows of Queens' College, Cambridge

> when they are approaching; but not to tell them the Day and Hour when they will come, nor the Day and Hour when the End of the World will be.

In some copies a slip of printed text produces a set of predictions altered in the light of experience:

> I know that this second Wo is certainly now at hand; And I have some ground to expect it in the year 1721. And I believe that the third Wo will be executed about the year 1826, or soon after that year; And that the End of the World will be about the year 3000; but I know not the day thereof.[178]

In at least one copy, the pasting is imperfect – it starts a line too late – and the opening grammatical sense is scrambled.[179]

Sometimes these pasted slip-insertions are inconspicuous, particularly with a quick scan of the page, but any reader consuming the text with some degree of care is likely to notice the slightly embossed, often imperfectly aligned pasted-in slip: passages of text which, in Jeffery Masten's phrase, 'rise up from the texture of the page.'[180] In the 1611 Authorized Version of the Bible, printed by Robert Barker, Matthew 26.36 had it that it was not Jesus coming to 'a place called Gethsemane' but Judas: the error meant that Jesus had to be pasted over Judas (Figure 15 shows a copy with 'Judas' scratched out and rewritten). Reading closely, as Protestants should, the disruption is clear in many copies: an off-kilter son of God, the 'J' of Judas peaking out beneath.[181]

This is, then, a mode of modification that calls attention to itself. It is also common to see the signs of lost slip-insertions: a former presence

178 BL 108.f.19. 179 BL T.1839 (7).

180 Jeffrey Masten, 'Material Cavendish: Paper, Performance, "Social Virginity"', in *Modern Language Quarterly* 65.1 (2004), 49–68, 52.

181 For other examples of Bibles containing printing errors (including the 'Printers' Bible' (1702) and 'Vinegar Bible' (1717)), see S. H. Steinberg, *Five Hundred Years of Printing* (London: Faber and Faber, 1959), p. 204.

betrayed by marks of dried glue or, if the slip fell away late in the book's life, the lighter band of text it once concealed – the latter reminding us through contrast just how ink-marked and dirty a 'blank' space actually is.[182] There was much that could go wrong when applying paste-in corrections. John Ferne's *The Blazon of Gentrie: Deuided into Two Parts. The First Named The Glorie of Generositie. The Second, Lacyes Nobilitie* (1586) is a book of heraldry celebrating the Lacy family. Half of the genealogical tree on sig. 2D1v was printed upside down – inverting succession, precisely the opposite of what was meant to be depicted and celebrated. Attempts were made at correction with a new tree, but the new text was often just bound in, so what readers find now is the upside-down page and the corrections together (for examples, BL 9917.ccc.3). In BL G.1058 the new pages were once glued down to cover the old, but they have come away, leaving the pages separate, although we can see the dried brush marks where the glue was applied. In BL 138.a.3, the old pages have been struck through with a single pencil line, but the second corrected page has been bound in upside down.

We encounter a combination of paste-in slips present and absent in *Englands Helicon* (1600), an anthology of pastoral poetry masterminded by London grocer John Bodenham – who also published a series of vernacular commonplace collections of verse – and published by John Flasket. The volume is inspired by Philip Sidney's writing and features some 150 verses by Sidney, Thomas Lodge, George Peele, Robert Greene, Edmund Spenser and others: 'dainty little masterpieces', according to A. H. Bullen, along with what Hyder Rollins more wearily described as 'some second-rate . . . harping on shepherds and flocks and Arcadian dales.'[183] In copies of *Englands Helicon*, including one owned by Staffordshire bibliophile and collector of English literature Frances Wolfreston (1607–77), there are paste-in slips as well as marks of dried glue indicating former slips now lost. These slip-insertions all relate to authorship: the slips change the attributions at the end of many poems, switching one name for another; supplying a name where there previously was none; or changing a named author to 'Ignoto'. Thus in Wolfreston's copy, a slip with 'N. Breton' is pasted over 'S. Phil Sidney', and 'Ignoto' is pasted over 'S. W. R.' and 'M. F. G.'[184] (In the 1614 second

---

[182] For a vividly missing cancel slip, see, for example, *Where of late tyme there hath ben a certayne staye and intermission of the auncient free entercourse for marchaundise* (1564), Queen's College, Oxford, Sel.b.230 (62).

[183] Hyder E. Rollins (ed.), *England's Helicon 1600* (Cambridge, MA: Harvard University Press, 1935), p. 3.

[184] BL C.39.e.48, sigs H, L3, O4. Wolfreston is discussed in Paul Morgan, 'Frances Wolfreston and "Hor Bouks": A Seventeenth-Century Woman Book-Collector', in *The Library*, 6th series, 12.1 (1989), 197–219; Masten, 'Margaret Cavendish', 53.

> **ENGLANDS HELICON.**
>
> Since then that *Phillis* onely is,
> > the onely Sheepheards onely Queene:
> And *Coridon* the onely Swaine,
> > that onely hath her Sheepheard beene.
> Though *Phillis* keepe her bower of state,
> > shall *Coridon* consume away:
> No Sheepheard no, worke out the weeke,
> > and Sunday shall be holy-day.
>
> *FINIS.*   *N. Breton.*

Figure 16 A present and absent slip-insertion, in *Englands Helicon* (1600), sig. H. By permission of the Bodleian Library (Crynes 920)

edition of *Englands Helicon*, the first two changes had been incorporated into the text, while the third poem is newly attributed to 'I. F.')[185] Other copies of *Englands Helicon* contain very similar but not quite identical alterations, although all concern authorial attribution.[186]

The attribution slips have the effect of making the author both central – something worth fighting about, and getting right – and supplementary: a belated layering, a *post hoc* variable that is settled only after the poem is written and published. Figures 16 and 17 show the end of the poem beginning 'Faire in a morne', and titled in this volume 'Astrophell *his Song* of Phillida *and* Coridon'. To read the poem in Figures 16 is to experience Breton's authorship as a careful correction, but one that peels away to show the contestation beneath. (A slip-insertion at the end of a Walter Raleigh poem in another copy of *Englands Helicon* has been aggressively scratched away to create an even more vivid sense of dispute.)[187] The legibly missing cancel slip in Figure 17

---

[185] *Englands Helicon* (1614), sig. E5, G5v, I5.
[186] For varied attribution paste-ins, see Bod J-J Sidney 98. For a *nuancing* of authorship in a different text, see Richard Watson, *The Royall Votarie Laying Downe Sword and Shield* (1660), HN 56126, the only known copy, where the words 'In part metrically paraphrased by Ri. Watson' are printed on a slip pasted over the words 'By Ri. Watson'.
[187] Bod Crynes 920, sig. N4: the damaged slip carries the attribution 'S.W.' and was pasted at the end of the previously anonymous verse beginning 'Praysed be Dianaes faire and harmlesse light'. The volume carries the title page annotation 'Edward Pierson his Booke'.

Errors and Corrections: 'My Galley Charged with Forgetfulness'   123

> ENGLANDS HELICON.
> Since then that *Phillis* onely is,
>   the onely Sheepheards onely Queene:
> And *Coridon* the onely Swaine,
>   that onely hath her Sheepheard beene.
> Though *Phillis* keepe her bower of state,
>   shall *Coridon* consume away:
> No Sheepheard no, worke out the weeke,
>   and Sunday shall be holy-day.
>
> FINIS.   *S. Phil. Sidney.*

Figure 17   A present and absent slip-insertion, in *Englands Helicon* (1600), sig. H. By permission of the Bodleian Library (J-J Sidney 98)

produces a poem whose attribution to Sir Philip Sidney is cast simultaneously as a mistake (the true author's name is missing), as nostalgic (this is how the book once defined this poem) and as a triumphant reassertion (Sidney bursts through, flinging the usurper aside). (Modern scholarship concurs with the Breton attribution, but the real animating agent of the poem was Thomas Morley, who included it in his *First Booke of Ayres* (1600), where he attributed the poem to himself.)[188] If Sidney's name is like a ghost – it has been banished; it occupies (with its clean page) a different time; it is still flickering – then Breton's authorship seems to have only the strength of the glue and a strip of paper to keep it from literary oblivion.

The fragile technology of the paste-in slip might also engage with the thematic content of literary texts. Henry Constable's *Diana: The praises of his mistres, in certaine sweete sonnets* (1592) is a Petrarchan sonnet sequence of 23 poems, each verse numbered in Italian. At the foot of 'Ultimo Sonnetto', the catchword 'Blame' has been retained in error from the skeleton forme used to print an earlier page (Figure 18).[189]

The word 'Blame' – now the volume's final word – was covered with a blank slip-insertion which has subsequently, in the copies I have seen, fallen away. On one level such a slip and correction recalls the process and order of printing, and suggests – along with a hand correction and an upside-down woodcut border illustration[190] – hasty print-shop

---

[188] Thomas Morley, *First Booke of Ayres* (1600), sig. D3v.
[189] CCC Library Δ.22.9 (5), sigs D3v, B1v.   [190] Sigs A3 and Dv.

> ## Vltima Sonnetto.
>
> Faire Sunne, if you would haue me praise your light:
>   when night approacheth, wherefore doo you flie?
>   Time is so short, Beauties so manie bee,
>   as I haue need to see them day and night:
> That by continuall view, my verses might
>   tell all the beames of your diuinitie;
>   which praise to you, and ioy should be to mee,
>   you liuing by my verse, I by your sight.
> I by your sight, and not you by my vearse:
>   neede mortall skill immortall praise rehearse?
>   No, no, though eies were blinde, and verse were dumb,
>   your beautie should be seene, and your fame knowne,
>   For by the winde which from my sighes doo come,
>   your praises round about the world is blowne.
>
> Blame

Figure 18 Henry Constable, *Diana* (1592), sig. D3v. By permission of the President and Fellows of Corpus Christi College, Oxford (CCC Library Δ.22.9 (5))

production. But as a Petrarchan sequence, the simultaneous presence and absence of 'Blame' becomes meaningful. The prefatory sonnet, 'To his absent Diana', describes with the imprecision required of the genre the 'fault' and subsequent banishment of the narrator, 'forc'd ... from thy sight', and also the hoped-for reading of these 'pictures of thy praise' by Diana. The final sonnet that has 'Blame' flickering at the foot of the page (printed, but blanked, but revealed) is concerned, as all Petrarchan poems are, with a sight that is glimpsed but also denied ('your beautie should be seene, and your fame knowne'). In this sense, the little drama of the paste-in slip (its concern with transgression and blame, with seeing and non-seeing) enacts an oscillation between presence and absence (the slip is missing; is applied; falls away) that is also the concern of Constable's sequence. Which is not to say that this paste-in was introduced with such aesthetic aspirations in mind; but it does suggest that the inclusive model of reading advocated by D. F. McKenzie – where 'the fine detail of typography and layout, the material signs which constitute a text, do signify'[191] – brings newly enriched literary, and not only bibliographical, possibilities.[192] Problematically, such readings require the suspension of intention (of author, printer or any of the agents behind this book), since I am reading the 'Blame' and the fallen-away slip in ways that were not imagined. I return to the potentials and limits of such an interpretative mode in Chapter 4, on reading printed waste.

But perhaps the most compelling use of the slip-insertion occurs across the printed corpus of Margaret Cavendish.[193] To most if not all copies of her 1668 *Plays Never Before Printed*, Cavendish made approximately 22 post-publication alterations in a careful italic hand, often mimicking the appearance of print,[194] and also (Figure 19) pasted in up to six thin slips of paper next to particular scenes or songs, bearing the note 'Written by my

---

[191] D. F. McKenzie, 'The Book as an Expressive Form,' in *Bibliography and the Sociology of Texts* (Cambridge, UK: Cambridge University Press, 1999), pp. 9–30, 25.

[192] For a more sceptical assessment of reading the literary potential of bibliographical features of a text, see Chapter 4, on printed waste.

[193] Jeffrey Masten, 'Material Cavendish: Paper, Performance, "Social Virginity"', in *Modern Language Quarterly* 65.1 (2004), 49–68; Heather Wolfe and Georgina Ziegler, 'A newly uncovered presentation copy by Margaret Cavendish', in *The Collation* (26 January 2012), http://collation.folger.edu/2012/01/a-newly-uncovered-presentation-copy-by-margaret-cavendish; James Fitzmaurice, 'Margaret Cavendish on Her Own Writing: Evidence from Revision and Handmade Correction', in *Papers of the Bibliographical Society of America*, vol. 85 (September 1991), 297–307.

[194] Cavendish's post-print hand revisions are evident in many copies of her *Orations* (1662), *Philosophical and Physical Opinions* (1663), *Grounds of Natural Philosophy* (1668) and *The Description of a New World Called the Blazing-World* (1668), although it is *CCXI Sociable Letters* (1664), *The life of . . . William Cavendish* (1667) and *Plays Never Before Printed* (1668) that are most thoroughly marked. Fitzmaurice, 'Margaret Cavendish', p. 307, suggests that the consistency of Cavendish's corrections to these three titles indicate that these works were of particular importance to her (p. 307). For a discussion of Cavendish 'as thoughtful reviser of her own works', effecting 'a thoroughgoing reconception of her style', see Elizabeth Scott-Baumann, *Forms of Engagement: Women, Poetry, and Culture 1640–1680* (CUP, 2013), pp. 60–80 (p. 62).

> ### SCENE IV.
>
> *Enter Sir* William Sage, *with all the Gentlemen, his Bridal-Guests, passing over the Stage, and going away again; after them comes Sir* John Amorous, *as going to bed in his Night-Gown,* Madam Mediator *and the Ladies usher him, and when he passes, this* Epithalamium *is sung.*
>
> VVritten by my Lord Duke.
> Epithalamium.
>
> NOw *at the Door*
> *You'l stand no more,*
> *But enter the Bridal-bed:*
> *Where you will prove*
> *The Sweets of Love*
> *With God* Hymen'*s banquet fed.*

Figure 19 Margaret Cavendish, *Plays Never Before Printed* (1668). By permission of the Folger Shakespeare Library (N867)

Lord Duke'.[195] Cavendish probably had sheets of this note of attribution printed at different times (the 'W' of 'Written' is sometimes but not always a 'VV'), and then cut and glued each slip: there are precedents for something similar in the Folger Shakespeare library's second copy of Thomas Milles' *The Misterie of Iniquity* (1611), which contains 'pre-printed but as yet undistributed slip-insertions' of the sort that both Milles and Cavendish deployed in their respective augmented books.[196] As William

---

[195] In *Plays Never Before Printed* (1668) BL 79 l.15, there are paste-ins with 'VVritten by my Lord Duke' glued in at *Scenes*, p. 146 (before Scene XXIX) and p. 152 (before Scene XXVII); *The Bridals*, p. 13 (before 'Epithalamium'); and *The Convent of Pleasure*, pp. 38 (before 'You've won the prize'), 39 (before 'The Jolly Wassel now do bring'), and 47 (before 'O Gentlemen, that I never had been born', the line opening scene 5.2, so perhaps indicating William's authorship of the whole scene). The paste-ins in other copies of this book are close but not identical and the exact number of handwritten revisions also varies: BL 79.l.15 and BL G.19053 (2) have 22; BL C. 102.K.18 has 21; and Bod Vet.A3.c.113 has 16. The latter Bodleian copy does not include pasted-in slips.

[196] Sherman and Wolfe, 'The Department of Hybrid Books'.

Sherman and Heather Wolfe have demonstrated, Milles (1550?–1627?) is a crucial but hitherto largely overlooked figure in the history of the slip-insertion. A prolific author of at least 12 printed books on antiquarianism, religious controversy and economic policy, Milles regularly augmented his printed publications with bespoke printed paste-ins: he seems to have published books with a semi-coterie readership in mind, and adapted his books to appeal to these individuals, sometimes addressing particular named readers through the pasted inserts.[197]

Cavendish probably, then, followed a similar method to Milles, slicing up printed sheets of repeated attribution notes, but she just might have used a book stamp of the kind described by Hugh Plat to mark blank slips,[198] or – more eccentrically still – could have possessed a small collection of printer's sorts to hand-stamp text which she then pasted in. When the Oxford epigrammatist John Reinolds died in 1614, the inventory of his rather meagre goods recorded, among the 'books in his studdy' and 'wearing apparell', 'certayne letters to print with'. Valued at only 2s 6d, this probably indicates not a full printer's fount, but a small collection of letters, perhaps to hand-stamp his name in books.[199] Cavendish may have used a similar technique.

Whatever the exact technology, Cavendish's paste-in slips do not correct existing attributions, and in this sense they are a departure from the slip-insertions discussed thus far, which were always layered over printed text. What Cavendish's insertions do is provide new information where there was none: her slips are supplements, corrections to insufficiencies. One consequence of these slips is that what had been a finished, single-author printed text becomes a hand-revised, collaborative work, produced by husband and wife.[200]

In part this reflects Cavendish's awareness of the wobbly nature of print, a consequence of her own chaotic compositional methods ('I did many times not peruse the Copies that were transcribed, lest they should disturb my following Conceptions; by which neglect, as I said, many Errors are slipt into my Works'), the inadequacies of her scribes (who 'neither

---

[197] Thomas Milles, *The misterie of iniquitie* (1611), New College Oxford, BT3.83.13(1), for example, has numerous pasted-in marginal annotations and glosses in addition to half-page inserts.
[198] Hugh Plat, 'The Art of Moulding and Casting', in *A Jewell-House of Art and Nature* (1594), p. 67; Plat provides further details, and demonstrates his invention by printing his name, in BL Sloane MS 2197 f. 16r. Noted in Knight, *Bound to Read*, p. 221, n. 45.
[199] William Poole, 'John Reinolds, Dead Poet (1614), or, What Did Fellows Own When They Died In College?', in *New College Notes* 5 (2014), www.new.ox.ac.uk/new-college-notes. My thanks to Will Poole for alerting me to Reinolds.
[200] Masten, 'Material Cavendish', 54.

understood Orthography, nor had any Learning'),²⁰¹ and the mistakes of the print house: some of Cavendish's instructions to her printers John Martin and James Allestrye, such as 'This is to be placed next my Tale of the Philosopher, which my Lord writ', were mistakenly included in the final text of *Natures Pictures* (1656), for example.²⁰² But Cavendish's pasted-in and handwritten alterations also reflect the way in which Cavendish responded with a kind of bibliographical scrupulousness to those who dismissed her authorship: her careful attribution of small parts to William was a way of both exactly caveating, and therefore shoring up, her claims to authorship: of showing how precise her claims were. In a prefatory letter to her *Playes* (1662) – which does not include printed slips, but does print 'the Lord Marquess writ' and '*Here ends the Lord Marquess of Newcastle*' next to particular passages²⁰³ – Cavendish noted that

> My Lord was pleased to illustrate my Playes with some Scenes of his own Wit, to which I have set his name, that my Readers may know which are his, as not to couzen them, in thinking they are mine; also Songs, to which my Lords name is set, for being no Lyrick Poet, my Lord supplied that defect of my Brain with the superfluity of his own Brain.²⁰⁴

Cavendish was not only aware of the inevitable flowering of error in the temporally and spatially dispersed process of producing a book; she also had a conception of the author as an agent who continues to work on the book, post-print, performing activities not always associated with writing, such as pasting in printed slips or making handwritten alterations or, indeed, distributing her own titles to the world. Cavendish sent dozens of her own books to eminent cultural institutions and individuals: letters thanking Cavendish for books were sent from many Oxford and Cambridge College libraries, from Leyden University, and from individuals including Kenlem Digby, Thomas Hobbes and Jasper Mayne.²⁰⁵ It is hard to know quite how sincere these expressions of thanks in fact were: as with modern donors, polite letters of thanks may have masked a weariness at yet more books to accommodate. But what is certain is that for Cavendish, the author-function included the roles of book distributor, corrector and reviser, and the paste-in slip was one mechanism for enacting the latter.

---

²⁰¹ *Plays* (1668), 'To His Grace the Duke of Newcastle'.
²⁰² *Natures Pictures* (1656), pp. 395, 396: noted in Scott-Baumann, *Forms of Engagement*, p. 62.
²⁰³ Masten, 'Material Cavendish', 55.   ²⁰⁴ Margaret Cavendish, *Playes* (1662), prefatory letter.
²⁰⁵ *Letters and Poems in Honour of the Incomparable Princess, Margaret, Duchess of Newcastle* (1676), passim. See Fitzmaurice, 'Margaret Cavendish', 300.

IV Cancel Pages

The death of Elizabeth Hastings (*née* Stanley), Countess of Huntingdon, on 20 January 1633 at Whitefriars, London, ended a life of learning, piety, artistic patronage (Donne addressed two verse epistles to her), devotional and epistolary composition, political lobbying (Hastings strengthened links between Huntingdon and Whitehall) and even dramatic performance: Hastings danced in *The Masque of Queens* (1609), and was, according to Lucius Cary, 'Born learneder than Hippatia / And might be called the philosophos truer than she.'[206]

At Hastings' funeral at Ashby-de-la-Zouch on 9 February, 'J. F.' – perhaps the minor poet Joseph Fletcher – preached a sermon which circled around John 11.25, 'He that Beleiveth in mee though he were Dead yet shall he liue'. On death, urged Fletcher, '[o]ur life is not lost, but hid'; but maintaining this belief requires a kind of 'wonder: which is nothing els but Contemplation broken off, or loosing it selfe'. Keeping faith is hard because man is inclined towards doubt and inconstancy: 'a propension, and flexiblenesse in our selves to waver with every contrarie Ayre'.[207] Amid this discussion of resurrection, Hastings is weirdly absent, although she is the purported subject. Entirely unmentioned until three-quarters of the way in, Hastings is then only addressed as an unnamed, hardly defined figure of spiritual virtue – as 'this renowned Ladie', with 'a mind of a most excellent composure', who worked carefully on devotional writing 'with her owne hand ... till within very few dayes before her death': 'she did with exceeding diligence search, and with great Iudgement choose, whatsoever the Scripture could afford her for the ... building up of her assurance in the Lord Iesus.'[208] The Biblical subject matter and what appears to modern eyes the unremitting imprecision – the sense of an outline, not a particular life – is characteristic of devotional writing, and devotional life-writing, from this period, built as it so often was around the alignment (and not the distance) between writer and existing patterns and narratives. We see this in many of Hastings' devotional texts that survive.[209] In

---

[206] James Knowles, 'Hastings, Elizabeth, countess of Huntingdon (*bap.* 1587, *d.* 1633)', *Oxford Dictionary of National Biography* (Oxford: Oxford University Press, 2004; online edn, May 2006) [accessed 26 August 2015].
[207] *A Sermon preached at Ashby De-la-zouch in the countie of Leicester* (1635)
[208] *A Sermon*, pp. 32, 33, 41.
[209] Hastings is the author of five Huntington Library manuscripts: four of devotional meditations, prayers, and Biblical extracts (HM 15369; EL 6871; Hastings Literature, Box 1, Folder 6; Hastings Religious, Box 2, Folder 8), and one of sermon notes (Hastings Religious, Box 1, Folder 13). Forty-six of her letters survive as HA 4809–4854.

this sense, the sermon's slight engagement with Hastings as an individual is a fitting response to Hastings as an individual.

The sermon was printed two years later, in 1635, by William Jones.[210] A printed funeral sermon seems like the final word, but Hastings' posthumous life in print was surprisingly animated. The sermon appeared two other times: in 1635, in a new state, identical except for a new imprint ('Printed by W[illiam] I[ones] and T. P[aine] and are to be sold by Matthew Simmons'), and in 1636, with a reset title page and an imprint noting 'Printed by T. P[aine] and are to be sold by Iohn Greenesmith'.[211] Although the 1636 issue announces itself as coming a year later, the text is the same as the first two appearances, with the exception of a replacement (or cancel) title page. Some copies include a portrait of Hastings, serene and about to be crowned by two angels, engraved by John Payne; some include an epitaph attributed to 'him who saies what he saw / Falkland' – that is, Lucius Cary, Second Viscount Falkland; some include neither.[212]

There is a further internal difference, a kind of vitality, within what appears at first to be the same text. Within some but not all copies of the sermon, two leaves have been removed and replaced by new leaves carrying revised text.[213] Such a process of cutting, removing and replacing was not uncommon in early modern books: it was a form of correction which, unlike pasted in slips, hand-corrections or errata lists, left little or sometimes no trace of its process. Since R. W. Chapman's 1930 *Cancels*, bibliographers have tended to call the leaf to be excised a cancellandum (plural cancellanda) and the new leaf to replace it a cancellans (plural cancellantia), although a defining trait of much of the scholarship on cancelled pages is precisely a frustration with terminology. Brian Gerrard calls on bibliographers to abandon the noun 'cancel' – except when referring to R. W. Chapman's book *Cancels* – since past discussion has definitively 'botched the usage'. He gives examples of unspecified catalogue entries that include, among other oddities, 'The cancel at A4 is not present in this copy', or, even better, 'The cancel found at A4 in this copy appears not to be present.'[214] R. W. Chapman similarly prefaces his book-length study with a

---

[210] *A Sermon Preached at Ashby De-La-Zouch in the countie of Leicester: At the Funerall of the Truly Noble and Vertuous Lady Elizabeth Stanley one of the Daughters and Coheirs of the Right Honourable Ferdinand Late Earle of Derby, and Late Wife to Henrie Earle of Huntingdo [sic] the Fifth Earle of that Familie. The 9. of February. Anno Dom. 1633. By I.F.* (1635).

[211] Respectively, STC 10644, 10645, 10646.

[212] BL 1419.b.19 has neither image nor epitaph; BL 1415.k.12 has no image, but has the epitaph; BL C.53.k.16 has image and epitaph.

[213] BL C.53.k.16, BL 1419.b.19 and BL 113.f.13 feature the original, uncancelled leaves; BL 1415.k.12 and the Cambridge University Library EEBO copy have the cancellantia.

[214] Gerrard, 'A new taxonomy', p. 45

note of the 'ambiguity' of terminology: 'When a bookseller', he asks, 'catalogues a copy of a book as "having the cancelled leaves," does he mean that it has the leaves which were (normally) cancelled, or that it has the leaves which replaced them?'[215]

This frustration is, like most frustrations, instructive, and what it illuminates is the paradox of dealing with missing text. How can we tell a cancellandum is not there? How can we spot a replacement leaf? What do we call an absent page?

The most common form of cancel was the single-leaf cancellans: the text of the leaf to be removed was reset and printed on a new leaf, along with any other cancels required, usually on a vacant section of a sheet later on in the book – and this was pasted onto the stub left behind after the cancellandum was cut out with scissors or knife. Less common but sometimes used for plates was the 'turn-over', where a cancellans with a wide margin was folded around the adjacent leaves; or, if the cancellanda were a pair of conjugate leaves (that is, joined leaves from a single sheet of paper, such as, in octavo, A1 and A8, or A2 and A7), the old pair of leaves could be removed and the new pair inserted in its place.[216] Whole sheets might be excised, reset, reprinted, and restored, although this is difficult to detect except by comparing cancelled and uncancelled versions of the sheet.[217] For a pasted single-leaf cancellans – the most common variety – there is often a stub that has been left behind after the cancellandum is excised; and for all varieties of cancellantia, the new pages might not align quite with the old, or their chain lines and watermarks might not match, or they might be printed in a visibly different ink,[218] or they might carry an altered running title, or a different signature – cancellantia sometimes have signature marks which would not normally appear on regular pages (such as A8), but which are there to guide their placement.

Cancellantia might add in text that was omitted, usually through compositorial error: a missing line in the 1612 quarto of Jonson's *Alchemist*, for example; or, in the *Faerie Queene* (1590), seven additional dedicatory sonnets to augment the original ten.[219] Cancelled preliminaries could also give a book a new moment and form. Shakespeare's 1609 quarto *Troilus and Cressida*, printed by George Eld for Richard Bonian and Henry Walley, exists in two states (Qa and Qb): in the second, the title page has been cancelled and

---

[215] Chapman, *Cancels*, 'Preface', p. 6.   [216] Chapman, *Cancels, passim*.
[217] Philip Gaskell, *A New Introduction to Bibliography* (Oxford: Clarendon Press, 1972), p. 134.
[218] In the EEBO copy of *A Sermon Preached at Ashby De-La-Zouch* (STC 10645), sig. B2r-v is clearly in a different, more thickly applied ink, almost to the point of illegibility, compared to the surrounding pages.
[219] Herbert Davis, 'Note on a Cancel in *The Alchemist* 1612', in *The Library*, 5th series, 13.4 (1958), 278–280; Andrew Zurcher, 'Getting It Back to Front in 1590: Spenser's Dedications, Nashe's Insinuations, and Ralegh's Equivocations', in *Studies in the Literary Imagination* 38:2 (2005), 173–198, 174.

replaced by a half sheet with a revised title, eliminating previous mention of performance at the Globe and adding, on the second page of this cancellans, an address to the 'euer reader' in which the play is said to be 'a new play, neuer stal'd with the Stage, neuer clapper-clawd with the palmes of the vulgar.'[220] Zachary Lesser argues that such a reframing (including the new preface's emphasis on wit and commodities) in effect resituates the play in the kind of city comedy context that was more available in 1609 than it was in 1603 when the play was first performed.[221] Richard Dutton has suggested the shift from Qa to Qb is a shift from a theatrical to a literary text, a transition reflecting Shakespeare's investment in both forms.[222] Certainly, the work of cancels significantly repositions the play.

Cancels might reflect errors noticed by the corrector or another print shop worker or they might be introduced at the wish of the author. Most extant copies of Robert Herrick's *Hesperides* (1648), with which this chapter began, contain three cancels replacing cut-out leaves (sigs C7, M8, O8). These cancels, pasted onto the stubs remaining after the faulty leaves had been excised, include significant corrections: in 'Kissing Usurie' an inverted stanza; a series of mistakes including 'lively food' for 'lively-hood' in 'To his peculiar friend Sir Edward Fish'; and an omitted stanza in 'The Wassaile'. Indeed, R. W. Chapman suggests that the three cancels were important as an early example of 'purely literary' cancel alterations, and Cain and Connolly similarly argue that they are enactments of Herrick's command.[223] At the same time, the cancels convey a sense of rushed work: they introduce new mistakes (including the unfortunate 'warty' for 'watry' in 'To Dean-bourn'), and in one copy the O8 cancel is inserted the wrong way round.[224]

Some copies of Elizabeth Hastings' funeral sermon have cancellantia at sigs B2r-v and D4r-v. The differences between the cancellandum (the excised former leaf) and the cancellans (the revised leaf) are set out in the table below.

---

[220] Philip Williams, Jr., 'The "Second Issue" of Shakespeare's *Troilus and Cressida*, 1609', in *Studies in Bibliography* 2 (1949–50), 25–33, 25–26.

[221] Zachary Lesser, *Renaissance Drama and the Politics of Publication: Readings in the English Book Trade* (Cambridge, UK: Cambridge University Press, 2004), pp. 1–3. For other significant literary cancellantia, see Fredson Bowers, 'Dryden as Laureate: the Cancel Leaf in "King Arthur"', in *Times Literary Supplement* 2671 (10 April 1953), 244.

[222] Richard Dutton, 'The Birth of the Author', in *Elizabethan Theater: Essays in Honor of S. Schoenbaum*, ed. R. B. Parker and S. P. Zitner (Newark and London: University of Delaware, 1996), pp. 71–92, 84.

[223] Chapman, *Cancels*, p. 47. *Complete Poetry of Herrick*, ed. Cain and Connolly, pp. 422–423. For a counter view, see Dobranski, Readers and Authorship, pp. 158–9.

[224] *Complete Poetry of Herrick*, ed. Cain and Connolly, pp. 422–423; The inverted cancel is BL E.1090.

Errors and Corrections: 'My Galley Charged with Forgetfulness'   133

sig. B2r cancellandum	sig. B2r cancellans
l. 5 *lyars,*	l. 5 *lyars.*
l. 5 notes,	l. 5 notes
l. 6 aduentured	l. 6 adventured
l. 6 alte-	l. 6 alte
l. 7 f eates	l. 7 feates
l. 15 faith [t fading]	l. 15 faith
l. 22 cleaue	l. 22 cleave
	spacing of final 5 lines

sig. B2v cancellandum	sig. B2v cancellans
l. 5 Resurrection	l. 5 resurrection
l. 9 wils	l. 9 wills
ll. 11–12 ding rich and precious mercies, pro-[/]mises	ll. 11–12 exceeding rich and precious promi[/]ses
l. 14 crosse	l. 14 Crosse
l. 16 The	l. 16 the

sig. D4r cancellandum	sig. D4r cancellans
l. 1 ve-	l. 1 ve
l. 4 Ignorance,	l. 4 ignorance
l. 4 and	l. 4 &
l. 4 insiblenesse	l. 4 insiblenes
l. 6 &	l. 5 and
l. 8 did,	l. 8 did:
l. 10 people;	l. 10 people,
l. 11 Now	l. 10 now
l. 12 are	l. 11 are,
l. 14 virtue	l. 14 vertue
l. 16 Gospell	l. 16 Gospel
l. 17 Gospell	l. 17 Gospel
ll. 18–9 sum-moned [long s]	l. 18 sūmoned
l. 21 this	l. 21 this,
l. 22 mouthes	l. 22 mouths
l. 22 Covenant	l. 22 covenant
l. 23 Angells of the Churches	ll. 22–3 angels of the churches
ll. 24–5 And here both that voice which sounded from mount *Sion* have their	l. 23–5 & here both that voice which sounded *from mount Sinai, and that which sounded*

sig. D4v cancellandum	sig. D4v cancellans
l. 1 part in the action.	ll. 1–2 *from mount Sion,* have their part in the [/] action.
l. 2 and	l. 3 &
l. 6 person	l. 7 persó
ll. 9–10 gospell quicken	l. 10 gospel quickĕ
l. 10 and life,	l. 11 & life
l. 11 see,	l. 11 se
l. 11 runne	l. 12 run
l. 12 Arms	l. 12 arms
l. 12 Restorer.	l. 12 Restorer

(cont.)

l. 12 Law	l. 13 law
ll. 16–17 Christ in the Go-[/]spell	ll. 16–17 *Christ* [/] in the Gospel
l. 17 summoneth	l. 17 sŭmoneth
l. 17 and	l. 18 &
l. 19 and	l. 19 &
l. 20 and	l. 20 &
l. 21 for us. And now, catchword has misaligned t	l. 21 us & now catchword corrected

Does this table tell us anything worth knowing, or is it an instance of profitless bibliographical industry? We note that the changes to D are more numerous than to B, by a ratio of 35 to 12. B's changes concern small shifts in punctuation (a full stop for a comma), spelling ('wills' for 'wils'), capitalisation, broken type, an error in spacing and the removal of an apparently superfluous mercy: 'rich and precious mercies, pro-[/]mises' becomes 'rich and precious promi[/]ses'. It was probably the case that the latter error prompted the cancelling of the leaf, and that the other changes were then introduced while the page was being altered. The relative slightness of these changes suggests considerable care in printing: a sense that the print shop and perhaps the author felt it was important to get things right, or, at least that, once correcting had begun, it was worth catching other errors at the same time. This is not to imply that the printers imagined they were reaching for some kind of textual perfection – there are, unsurprisingly, other uncorrected errors scattered throughout the text,[225] and in fact cancellans Dv introduces a new error, omitting a full stop at line 12. But if early modern printing was, among other things, a constant calculation about how much error is acceptable in a book for it to remain a legitimate publication (that is, for a book to be recognizably the object it claimed to be), then these cancellantia indicate that a line had been crossed in terms of the standards of the print shop of William Jones and his partner Thomas Paine.

The changes on D are more numerous. Most once more concern small shifts in capitalisation, compression or expansion ('&' for 'and') and punctuation. The most substantial difference comes at the turn from recto to verso: what had been 'And here both that voice which sounded from mount *Sion* have their [/] part in the action' is amplified into '& here both that voice which sounded *from mount Sinai, and that which sounded* [/] *from mount Sion*, have

---

[225] On sig. B4r, for example, 'went went' at lines 7–8; or on sig. D2, a tilted 'd' at the end of 'parted' at line 21.

their part in the action.' I suspect this lapse was sufficiently striking to induce cancellation of the leaf, and once undertaken, and as with B, the other corrections were made – corrections which in themselves might not have catalysed cancellation. The compositor, presumably suffering from eye-skip with the similar Sion / Sinai, originally missed Sinai: we know this because the 'both' in the original signals two examples to come. The cancellans restores the omitted Sinai. The voice that sounded at Mount Sinai is described in Exodus 19 as God's address to Moses ('if ye will obey my voice indeed, and keep my covenant, then ye shall be a peculiar treasure unto me above all people'); the 'the sound of a trumpet, and the voice of words' at Mount Sion or Zion is in Hebrews 12.[226] One effect of this significant addition of text is that space on Dv became pressured: the subsequent changes in cancel D$4v$ are largely attempts at compression, a race to condense the text under the pressure of the new additions, so that it can fall in line with the final word 'evident' in order to align with the next page. Thus '& life' for 'and life', and 'run' for 'runne', and the various other shortenings.

A comparison of cancellandum and cancellans can thus tell us something about the post-print remaking of a book, and about a print shop's conception of the degree of variance that was deemed tolerable before a book needed to be remade. There are also ways in which the lively post-publication life of Hasting's funeral address feeds into the subject of Joseph Fletcher's address. The theme of *A Sermon Preached at Ashby De-La-Zouch* is resurrection, of Hastings living on, despite death, and of the need for Christians to maintain faith in this afterlife. In a small but significant way, the bibliographical animation of this sermon after printing – the varying appearances of epitaph and of portrait; the reissuing of the sermon under different imprints; and the substitution of two altered leaves for their predecessors – contributes a material enactment of this devotional theme.

***

Joseph Moxon's description of printing is often criticised as idealising, but his chapter on 'Rules observed; and Remedies to the Inconveniences the Press-man may meet in a Train of Work' reads like a 13-page prose poem on error and contingency.

If he have taken too much *Inck* . . .
If he foresee the next Sheet will also be too *Black* . . .
If in doing this, the strength of the *Inck* have *Pull'd* the *Paper* to pieces . . .
If *Letters, Quadrats* or *Furniture Rise* . . .

---

[226] Exodus 19:5, Hebrews 12:19, KJV.

If any *Letters* are *Batter'd* ...
If *Bearers* Fail, that is, Squeeze thinner with long *Pulling* on ...
If *Register* be *Out*, which sometimes happens by the starting of the *Quoins* ...
If a few *Picks* are got into the *Form* ...
If he meets with naughty Sheets in his Work; as torn, or stain'd, &c. he Prints them not, but throws them under the *Paper-bench*.[227]

Like a proleptic reworking of Rudyard Kipling's 'If', Moxon's litany of potential problems constitutes, among other things, a powerful counter-blast to that narrative figuring the press as an efficient, modernising technology: less a march towards a stable, right product – the work of an 'advanced industry of mass production'[228] – printing appears a seemingly endless series of skirmishes with, and improvisations around, blunder. Moxon runs on and on:

If the *Hose* be worn ...
If the *Garter* be worn too wide ...
If the *Worms* of the *Nut* or *Spindle* be worn ...
If the *Toe* of the *Spindle* and its *Nut*, or either of them be worn irregularly ...[229]

When George Wither, as part of a sustained attack on the agents of book production, laments that the printer 'cares not how unworkmanlike it be parformed [sic], nor how many faults he lett goe to the Authors discredit, & the readers trouble', the typographical slip is a joke, presumably, perhaps by the compositor, and perhaps without Wither's knowledge.[230] But it is a joke that amplifies that sense of the printing press' capacity to get things wrong, and of the interpretative potential of those slips.

---

[227] Moxon, *Mechanick Exercises*, pp. 335–337; the chapter runs pp. 333–345.
[228] Peter W. M. Blayney, 'The Publication of Playbooks', in *A New History of Early English Drama*, ed. John D. Cox and David Scott Kastan (New York: Columbia University Press, 1997), pp. 383–422, 414.
[229] Joseph Moxon, *Mechanick exercises on the whole art of printing (1683–4)*, ed. by Herbert Davis and Harry Carter (New York: Dover Publications, 1978), p. 340.
[230] George Wither, *The Scholar's Purgatory* (1625), pp. 120–121. Quoted in modernised text in Dover Wilson, *Life in Shakespeare's England*, pp. 153–154.

CHAPTER 4

Printed Waste: 'Tatters Allegoricall'

John Aubrey is best known for his riveting series of biographical sketches – short vignettes that pulse on the page, of Geoffrey Chaucer, William Camden, John Colet, Thomas Hobbes and many others. But Aubrey also wrote his own short autobiography: or at least, he assembled a series of observations about his life and character, notes that flicker between first and third person, and that, in refusing to cohere either formally or in terms of the subjectivity they describe, suggest a sense of the self as a pile of scraps of paper. 'I was always enquiring of my grandfather of the Old time, the Rood-loft, etc'; 'his chief virtue gratitude'; 'If ever I had been good for any thing, 'twould have been a Painter'; 'I have been twice in danger of drowning'; 'having from his birth (till of late yeares) been laboring under a Crowd of ill Directions'.[1]

At the start of this autobiographical sketch, Aubrey added the instruction that he wished his *Life* 'to be interponed as a sheet of wast-paper only in the binding of a Booke.'[2] To be interponed means to be placed between, and in this phrase Aubrey is imagining his written life being used as waste to strengthen the physical construction of another book: to form a layer within the binding. In this chapter, I use the term 'waste' to describe papers that were once part of a published text, or a text intended for publication (usually, but not always, a book), or sheets that were once used in the book production process (such as proof sheets), which then, unwanted or superfluous in these roles, were employed to serve a different function in the physical composition of a new book. Aubrey's *Life*, according to this fate, would cease to be a text, and would become instead an entirely material thing, a useful resource for a bookbinder's workshop.

As Kate Bennett notes in her edition of *Brief Lives*, Aubrey may here be remembering the schoolbooks of his childhood, covered with parchment

---

[1] Aubrey, *Brief Lives* vol. I, pp. 429–443, pp. 431, 437, 442, 429.
[2] Aubrey, *Brief Lives*, vol. I, p. 429.

from manuscripts that were torn apart and scattered after the dissolution of the monasteries, just as, years later in Civil War Oxford, Aubrey watched soldiers scouring their guns with old manuscripts.[3] But Aubrey was writing in a culture in which the use of fragments of older manuscripts and printed texts to help constitute new books was common: he would have met with examples almost every reading day.

Once bound, new books in the sixteenth and seventeenth centuries carried fragments of old books – in the binding, in the paste boards, as end leaves – and this chapter is an exploration of this stark truth. I want to consider the mechanics of how this happened, and also the ways in which this practice affected the idea of the book in early modern England. In the spirit of a heuristic, I want to ask what can we, as literary critics, bibliographers and historians of the book, do with this kind of material? If a copy of Edward Lively's *A true chronologie of the times of the Persian monarchie, and after to the destruction of Ierusalem by the Romanes* (1597) carries parts of Philip Sidney's *Astrophel and Stella* (1591) as endpapers, then what are the consequences of this hybridity for our understanding of early modern literary-bibliographical culture? What is striking for a modern reader is just how legible and overt these 'interponed' fragments remain: to read this copy of Edward Lively's *Chronologie* means turning, unavoidably, at the start and the end, pages of Sidney's sonnets. Did readers look past such leaves, bleeding out the parts of texts they conveyed? Or did this everyday entwining of old and new encourage a sense of the printed book as something incorrigibly plural (to quote Louis MacNeice) compared to the neatly separate work typically produced by the modern bibliographical imagination?

Aubrey's prescription might be a straightforward statement of modesty: he was given to them, in a rather performative way, and described himself as a 'whetstone against which others sharpened their wits'.[4] But he was also profoundly aware of the bibliographical culture surrounding him – of books in their great physical richness – and a deeper sense of the practice of using waste in early modern binding might well suggest a subtler range of meanings to his comment. To bind one's *Life* in another book means not only assuming an obscured second place; it also means helping to instantiate another book, as if the waste were a hidden patron; it means placing one's text alongside another, in sociable company, with the possibility of dialogue and relationship;

---

[3] Aubrey, *Brief Lives*, vol. II, p. 1356; Ruth Scurr, *John Aubrey: My Own Life* (London: Random House, 2015), p. 71.

[4] Aubrey, *Brief Lives*, vol. I, p. 434. As Kate Bennett notes, Aubrey is borrowing lines from Horace's *Ars Poetica* (vol. 2, p. 1366).

it means having a sense of one's *Life* as sufficiently circulated to be categorised as waste, and therefore, paradoxically, it suggests cultural presence (like the almanacs or Bible pages used in bindings); and it means also, and crucially, being preserved. Waste within another book often endures. This chapter is an attempt to understand such possibilities. What did it mean, exactly, to ask that one's *Life* be interponed as waste in the binding of another book?

***

Early modern culture was preoccupied with the life story of paper: where it came from, where it might end up, and, sometimes, the moral lessons that such itineraries implied. Waste paper of various sorts loomed large in many authors' imaginations. We see this in *The Unfortunate Traveller* (1594) where, in the prefatory address to the 'Daper Monsieur Pages of the Court', Thomas Nashe narrates how

> Jack Wilton... hath bequeathed for waste-paper here amongst you certain pages of his misfortunes. In any case keep them preciously as a privy token of his good will towards you. If there be some better than other, he craves you would honour them in their death so much as to dry and kindle tobacco with them. For a need he permits you to wrap velvet pantofles in them also, so they be not woe-begone at the heels, or weather-beaten, like a black head with grey hairs, or mangy at the toes, like an ape about the mouth. But as you love good-fellowship and ames-ace [a dice game], rather turn them to stop mustard-pots than the grocers should have one patch of them to wrap mace in: a strong, hot, costly spice it is, which above all things he hates. To any use about meat and drink put them to and spare not, for they cannot do their country better service. Printers are mad whoresons; allow them some of them for napkins.[5]

Nashe is not talking directly about printed waste in the sense that I mean it – that is, pages from unwanted books, and leftovers from the printing process used in the production of later books – but rather, he is describing more generally a highly material literary world in which unwanted texts might soon serve one of many non-textual, bathetic functions. Jack's writing is offered to the readers as waste paper, as a 'privy token' (with a pun on the use of printed pages as toilet paper), as a pipe-lighter, as wrappers for expensive slippers ('velvet pantofles'), as stoppers for mustard pots, as wrappers for mace, or as napkins.[6] Versions of this role-call of fates appear in several literary works, including the 'Post-script to his Book-binder' that concludes Henry

---

[5] Thomas Nashe, *The Unfortunate Traveller and Other Works*, ed. J. B. Steane (London: Penguin, 1985), p. 253.
[6] In a variant on Nashe imagining his text wrapping slippers, 'Verses Made upon a paire of slippers sent for a New yeares guifte 1631' (Bod MS Ashmole 781, p. 165) puns on 'upon' to suggest verses both written about and over (or attached to) slippers.

Fitzgeffrey's *Satyres and Satyricall Epigrams* (1617). Fitzgeffrey, known to history for this single publication and for a life of financial debt, was almost certainly writing with the sound of Ben Jonson's third epigram, 'To my Bookseller', humming in his ear, as he imagines his text being 'eaten vnder *Pippin-pyes*',

> Or in th' *Apothicaryes* shop bee seene
> To wrap *Drugg's*: or to dry *Tobacco* in.
> First (might I chuse) I would be *bound* to wipe,
> Where he discharged last his *Glister-pipe*.[7]

This tradition of poems describing such bookish fates was informed by the real social life of paper: the antiquarian Anthony Wood 'asked for waste sheets at the Oxford printing press', and he wrote on two otherwise unrecorded parliamentary petitions, 'This I found in D[r] Lowers privy hous 24. May 1675 in Bow Street, London', and 'Tobacco wrapt up in this paper in the beginning of May 1693.'[8]

An awareness of the bathetic power of the recycled page appears too in John Dryden's 'Mac Flecknoe' (1682), his mock-heroic satire on misplaced literary and political ambition. Dryden describes the 'coronation' of Thomas Shadwell, heir to Richard Flecknoe (satirised previously by Andrew Marvell) as the supreme writer of dull, bad verse: 'All arguments, but most his Plays, / perswade, / That for anointed dullness he was made.' At this crowning moment, the streets of London are filled not with '*Persian* Carpets spread th' Imperial way,' but with discarded pages from torn-apart books:

> From dusty shops neglected Authors come,
> Martyrs of Pies, and Reliques of the Bum.
> Much *Heywood, Shirly, Ogleby* there lay,
> But loads of *Sh*– almost choakt the way.
> Bilk't *Stationers* for Yeomen stood prepar'd,
> And *H*– was Captain of the Guard.[9]

Dryden describes these waste pages as 'scatter'd Limbs of mangled Poets', and this is in part a literary wink to the knowing: a translation of a phrase from Horace's Satire 1.4, where Horace writes that in the work of a new poet endowed with divine judgement, the work will carry within itself the

---

[7] Henry Fitzgeffrey, *Satyres and Satyricall Epigrams* (1617), sig. G4. See also Alexander Brome, *Bumm-fodder, or, Waste-paper proper to wipe the nation's rump with or your own* (1660). Similar examples are mentioned in Chapter 2.
[8] Nicolas K. Kiessling (ed.), *Life of Anthony Wood in His Own Words* (Oxford: Bodleian Library, 2009), p. 159.
[9] James Kinsley (ed.), *The Poems of John Dryden* (Oxford: Clarendon Press, 1958), 4 vols, vol. I, pp. 265–271, 267, lines 100–105.

dismembered limbs of former authors.[10] But Dryden's coronation scene is not only intertextual: it is also highly material, a vignette saturated with the debased props of publishing. Waste papers, normally reserved for lining pies or wiping excrement, litter the floor, creating a kind of anti-canon of the discarded (dramatists Thomas Heywood and James Shirley; translator John Ogilby), while cheated ('Bilk't') publishers watch on, lining the roads. (H stands for Henry Herringman, Shadwell's publisher, and Dryden's, until he moved on to better things with Jacob Tonson the Elder in 1679.) The printed literary work, lauded one day, might quickly become waste paper, and Dryden seizes on this potential for paper to suddenly shift in terms of value and function in order to describe a scene of literary and moral debasement, and of a kind of authorship that is abject in the literal sense of having been thrown away.

Perhaps the most sustained reflection on the shape- and function-shifting qualities of paper comes in John Taylor's *The praise of hemp-seed* (1620), written to celebrate Taylor's 1619 adventure with his friend, vintner Roger Bird: for a bet they sailed down the Thames to Quinborough in a boat made from brown paper, kept half afloat by animal bladders filled with air. Taylor's verse on hempseed describes 'How when it is growne to Ragges, it is made into *Paper*', and 'How many liue by it',[11] and his rambling poem becomes an encomium to paper.

Taylor identifies two distinct, magical qualities that paper possesses. On the one hand, paper, as 'Th'Eternall Testament of our Weale', enables writers to endure. Poets, including Chaucer, 'Sedney', 'Spencer', Shakespeare, Dyer, Greene, 'Nash', and 'Daniell', whose lines otherwise 'had perish'd with their liues', 'in *Paper* they immortally / Do liue in spight of Death, and cannot die'.[12] (As ever, the seventeenth century's sense of its emerging literary canon is only somewhat similar to our sense of it; and it's worth noting that Shakespeare here is a writer for the very material page, not a dramatist for the stage.) One playful implication, fulfilled today, is that Taylor himself might endure, despite his defiantly liminal literary persona, because he, like Chaucer and Sidney, commits his lines to the page: 'And I in forme of *Paper* [a pun on the legal pleading *in forma pauperis*, that is, 'in the form of a pauper'] speake to you. / But *Paper* now's the subiect of my booke'.[13]

Paper, then, and permanence. But Taylor identifies paper's other power by noting its highly inconstant material life story, 'from whence *Paper* it's

---

[10] Christopher Yu, *Nothing to Admire: The Politics of Poetic Satire from Dryden to Merrill* (Oxford: Oxford University Press, 2003), p. 33.
[11] John Taylor's *The praise of hemp-seed* (1623), sig. A3.   [12] Taylor, *Praise*, pp. 25, 27.
[13] Taylor, *Praise*, p. 19.

beginning tooke: / How that from little *Hempe* and *Flaxen* seeds'.[14] Rather as Henry Vaughan, in his ghostly poem 'The Book' (1655), imagines the previous lives of the physical components of a book – the leather binding was, years before, a 'harmless beast' that 'Did live and feed'; the boards a 'tree ... [that] flourished, grew, and spread'; pages 'linen'[15] – Taylor writes that the pages carrying the words of Shakespeare and others were once ropes, or shirts, and that these items, in turn, were owned by people from wildly different strata of society. Taylor, the literary outlier, lingers lovingly over this fact. Paper muddles hierarchies, provides ironic juxtapositions of the once high and the once low, as today's poem is written on 'The Linnen of some Countesse, or some Queene ... / Mix'd with the rags of some Baud, Theefe, or Whore'. The lesson of such minglings is that 'earthy honour hath no certaine being. / For who can tell from whence these tatters springs? ... Thus are these tatters Allegoricall, / Tropes, tipes, and figures, of mans rise or fall.'[16]

Paper is thus for Taylor a source of a sort of rapturous reflection, which he calls 'Philosophy', precisely for this capacity to connect previously separated lives:

> May not a torne Shirt of a Lords or Kings
> Be pasht and beaten in the *Paper-mill*,
> And made *Pot-paper*, by the Workmans skill?
> May not the Linnin of a Tiburn slaue,
> More honour then a mighty Monarke haue?
> That though he dyed a Traytor most disloyall,
> His Shirt may be transform'd to *Paper royall*.
> And may not dirty Socks, from off the feet
> From thence be turnd to a *Crowne-paper* sheet?[17]

Taylor's philosophical musings, which seem a circling around a fanciful poetical conceit, were rooted in paper's material realities: Taylor was responding to the books and pages he saw around him, covering his desk, his shelves, the bookstalls he hovered around. We can see this sense of paper's life stages in the case of frisket sheets, used in the printing process. Medieval manuscripts were often sold to printers who broke them up and excised individual leaves to serve as protective masks, or friskets, to cover the non-printing areas of the forme and so to ensure that

[14] Taylor, *Praise*, p. 19.
[15] Henry Vaughan, *Silex Scintillans: Sacred Poems and Private Ejaculations* (1655), pp. 90–91.
[16] John Taylor, *The praise of hemp-seed* (1623), p. 20.
[17] Taylor is punning throughout on the names of paper-sizes.

only the desired (and thus exposed) type conveyed ink to page.[18] Once they had served their purpose, a bundle of used friskets, perhaps with other waste material, might be sold to a binder as waste. Extant frisket sheets recovered from bindings can retain marks that suggest this three-fold history: such sheets are, in the words of Elizabeth Upper,

> the palimpsests of functions: on some parchment fragments, the manuscript text and rubrications from their first life are covered by a glossy crust of printing ink from their second [as a frisket], which is covered with a thin layer of (browned) paste and residue from other binding material from their third.[19]

An awareness of the diachronic nature of paper defined the bibliographical culture in which printed waste played its part. The book might be only a momentary form assumed by leaves that have a much longer and more tumultuous life story.

***

Printed books frequently contained fragments of older texts in the boards (often constructed from pieces of paper pressed together), in the backing strips along the spine, in the hinges joining book to board, in pastedowns (leaves glued to the inside of the board over the top of the hinges and wood), or as flyleaves (extra leaves between the board and the text), or as free end leaves (conjugate with pastedowns).[20] Recycled texts were also sometimes used as wrappers for books, like the copy of Richard Stanyhurst's *The First Fovre Bookes of Virgils Æneis, Translated into English Heroicall Verse* (1583), which is contained in a wrapper made from a twelfth-century manuscript of the *Aeneid*.[21] And while wrappers are just outside the category of waste, they

---

[18] Elizabeth Upper, 'Red Frisket Sheets, ca. 1490–1700: The Earliest Artifacts of Color Printing in the West', in *Papers of the Bibliographical Society of America* 108:4 (2014), 477–522, 479. My thanks to Elizabeth Upper for correspondence on this subject.
[19] Upper, 'Red Frisket Sheets', 489. For an image of a used frisket sheet used in the binding of *Expositio hymnorum totius anni* (London, 1510), see https://exhibitions.lib.cam.ac.uk/tudorcolour/artifacts/frisket-sheet.
[20] Joseph A. Dane, *The Myth of Print Culture: Essays on Evidence, Textuality and Bibliographical Method* (Toronto: University of Toronto Press, 2003), p. 60. See also Joseph A. Dane, 'An Example of Netherlands Prototypography in the Huntington', in *Huntington Library Quarterly*, vol. 61, no. 3/4 (1998), 401–409.
[21] Bod Wood 106. The manuscript wrapper contains Latin text from Book 6, while the printed English text presents Books 1–4. A copy of William Godwin's *Damon and Delia* (1784) has the upper and lower outside boards covered with, respectively, an edition of Thomas Penrose's *A sketch of the lives and writings of Dante and Petrarch* and the anonymous Gothic novel *The Spectre* (1789). This example is notable for having demonstrably later waste: this must have been applied to the sheets at least five years after printing. Bod Vet. A5 f.4148.

are one more example of a culture of recycling old texts that is not an eccentric exception but a trait central to early modern book culture.[22]

Manuscripts were frequently used for these purposes, as is the case with a copy of Arthur Golding's translation of *The.xv. bookes of P. Ouidius Naso, entytuled Metamorphosis* (1657), now in the Huntington.[23] According to John Bale, and as mentioned in Chapter 2, at the Reformation, 'Lybrarye Bookes ... [were] sold to the Grossers and sope sellers, and some they sent over see to the Bokebynders, not in small nombre, but at tymes whole Shypps full, to the wonderynge of the foren Nacyons'.[24] This culture of manuscript waste has been meticulously catalogued by Neil Ker, with additional work by David Pearson, and so my focus here is largely on printed waste.[25] Much of the scholarship around such fragments has also, quite understandably, been preoccupied with questions of origin: with determining the lost source text that supplied the waste, or even in reconstructing that source from scattered fragments. The bibliographical scholarship animating such responses is often formidable, but this mode of proceeding is also a kind of impatience with the book open before us: such a method is more interested in the pre-waste life of fragments than in the nature of waste *qua* waste, or the relationship between host and waste. While I am certainly interested in where waste comes from, I would like in part to provide a corrective to this tendency by also considering waste *in situ*, in a relationship with its host.

In 1871, librarian and bibliographer Henry Bradshaw distinguished between binder's and printer's waste. By binder's waste, Bradshaw meant pages drawn

---

[22] For other non-waste examples of this culture of reuse, see Norfolk Record Office MC 175/1/1–4, where endpapers from a Bible are used for handwritten life-writing notes; Cheshire and Chester Archives and Local Studies Service EDC 1/26, a Consistory Court Book (1586–90) which uses a page from a service book with music as an endpaper; and East Sussex Record Office FRE/520/22IV, an account of rents received by Walter Everenden (1598 and 1609), which uses part of an illuminated medieval manuscript with text and music.

[23] HN 49035.

[24] *The Laborious Journey and Serche of Johan Leylande, for Englandes Antiquitees, geuen of hym as a newe yeares gyfte to Kynge Henry the viii in the xxxvii yeare of his Reygne, with declaracyons enlarged: by John Bale* (1549), sigs B1r-v. For English printed waste shipped abroad for use, see Margaret Lock, 'Reading the Endpapers: Five French Texts with Paper Bookbindings Using Printed Waste as Endpapers, and the Influence of Censorship on the Eighteenth-Century Book Trade', in *Papers of the Bibliographical Society of Canada* 48.2 (Autumn 2010), 257–298, esp. 267.

[25] Neil Ker and David Pearson, *Oxford Bookbinding 1500–1640: Including a Supplement to Neil Ker's Fragments of Medieval Manuscripts Used as Pastedowns in Oxford Bindings* (Oxford: Oxford Bibliographical Society, 2000). The Lost Manuscripts project at the University of Essex (www.lostmss.org.uk) is, at the time of this writing, engaged in a study of manuscript fragments contained within the 800 largely theological books in the library of Samuel Harsnett, Archbishop of York. The project's central methodology is to catalogue and conceptualise each fragment as both an individual entity in its own right, and as a part of a lost former whole.

from books that had been in circulation and which had then been discarded, often made from stronger vellum or paper. Waste from such a source might carry manuscript notes from readers and signs of consumption that recall John Taylor's fascination with the long history of paper, like the copy of *The workes of Geffray Chaucer* (1532) with end leaves from an edition of *Sermones Dominicales* (ca. 1500) covered in handwritten marginal annotations.[26] By printer's waste, Bradshaw meant sheets from the printer's office that never had a life in finished book form: cancelled pages, for example, or used frisket sheets, or pages carrying serious misprints, sometimes known as 'spoils', often unfolded since they never constituted a book.[27] This category might also include proof sheets, which are sometimes visible, complete with corrections, as waste – such as the proofs of two leaves from Francis Bacon's *Of the Advancement and Proficence of Learning* (1640) which once served as pastedowns (thus the visible glue marks around the edges) but are now end leaves in a copy of John Sharp's *Cursus theologicus* (1628) in Trinity College, Oxford.[28]

Printer's waste, as Joseph Dane has noted, thus constitutes an allusion to, rather than a fragment of, a book.[29] And although Bradshaw's binary is sometimes in practice difficult to maintain, principally since it is often hard to tell if waste falls into the category of binder's or printer's, it is at least a useful heuristic with which to work. The sale of waste paper was a regular part of the printer's business. In 1602, for example, the Stationers' Company Court received £3 10s for 'fourty reames of wast pap at xxjd the reame' – that is, about one penny for a quire of 25 sheets – while in 1663/4, £1211 was spent buying paper for printing of the English stock, and £8 was recouped from the sale of waste.[30]

Many scholars have found it hard to resist the urge to lament the practice of breaking apart old books and manuscripts to generate binding supports:

---

[26] Balliol College, Oxford 525 c 11.
[27] *Collected Papers of Henry Bradshaw* (Cambridge, UK: Cambridge University Press, 2012), p. 347. For a compositor's error resulting in a text being used as printed waste, see Oliver Pickering, 'Two Pynson Editions of the Life of St Katherine of Alexandria', in *The Library* 9:4 (2008), 471–478.
[28] Corrected proofs of leaves bb3r and cc3r from Francis Bacon, *Of the advancement and proficence of learning* (Oxford, '1640' [i.e., 1639]), now end leaves to John Sharp, *Cursus theologicus* (Aureliae-Allobrogum, 1628), Trinity College, Oxford H.1.13. Both proof leaves are unperfected and carry ink proof-corrections; a comparison with copies of the 1640 Bacon shows that these proof corrections were indeed implemented. Thanks to Paul Nash for informing me of this example.
[29] Dane, *Myth*, pp. 63, 65.
[30] Juliet Fleming, 'Damask Papers', in Andy Kesson and Emma Smith (eds), *The Elizabethan Top Ten: Defining Print Popularity in Early Modern England* (Farnham: Ashgate, 2013), pp. 179–191, 189–190. Fleming is drawing on Cyprian Blagden and William Jackson.

Strickland Gibson labelled Oxford binders who used fragments of books and manuscripts in this way 'miscreant[s]',[31] while Neil Ker, in his ground-breaking work, wrote that of 'handsome and legible' twelfth-century manuscripts '[i]t is both gratifying to find that the Oxford binders made little use of them before 1550 and shocking to find that they were still using them as late as 1590.'[32] Ker's book thus has a founding ambivalence, dedicated as it is to the meticulous cataloguing of a fragment practice that Ker largely laments. And yet the relationship between waste and preservation is entangled. Binders certainly 'played an active part in the destruction of books',[33] but one consequence of this culture of waste has been the preservation of fragments of texts otherwise lost. The list of valuable and sometimes unique works recovered from waste is long – the oldest fragment of an Anglo-Saxon minuscule codex preserved in England; a French translation of Galen from 1544;[34] a mid-ninth-century fragment of 47 lines of the Old Saxon epic poem *Heliand*[35] – and the prospect of discovery is evocatively conjured by William Blades, who in his *Life of Caxton* (1861) imagines bibliography (as many have) through the genre of romance as he describes searching the library of King Edward VI's Grammar School in St Albans:

> I pulled out one [book] which was lying flat upon the top of others. It was in a most deplorable state, covered thickly with a damp, sticky dust, and with a considerable portion of the back rotted away by wet. The white decay fell in lumps on the floor as the unappreciated volume was opened. It proved to be Geoffrey Chaucer's English translation of *Boecius de consolatione Philosophiæ*, printed by Caxton, in the original binding as issued from Caxton's workshop, and uncut! ... On dissecting the covers they were found to be composed entirely of waste sheets from Caxton's press, two or three being printed on one side only. The two covers yielded no less than fifty-six half-sheets of printed paper, proving the existence of three works from Caxton's press quite unknown before.[36]

This is certainly one way to respond to this culture of waste: to locate lost texts, and in a similar spirit, to study waste fragments as evidence of the early

---

[31] Strickland Gibson, 'Old Bindings as Literary Hunting-Grounds', in *The Academy* 1748 (4 November 1905), Illustrated Supplement, 1–4, 2.
[32] Neil F. Ker, *Fragments of Medieval Manuscripts Used as Pastedowns in Oxford Bindings with a Survey of Oxford Binding c. 1515–1620* (Oxford: Oxford Bibliographical Society, 2004 for 2000), p. ix.
[33] Gibson, 'Old Bindings', 2.
[34] Dorothy Schullian, 'Here the Frailest Leaves,' *Papers of the Bibliographical Society of America*, v. 47, no. 3 (1953), pp. 201–217, 202–203.
[35] For a description, see www.handschriftencensus.de/8335. Thanks to Falk Eisermann for alerting me to this latter example.
[36] William Blades, *Life of Caxton* (1861), ii.70, quoted in Edward Gordon Duff, *Early Printed Books* (Cambridge, UK: Cambridge University Press, 2011), p. 196.

history of printing. The antiquarian and one-man bibliographical tempest John Bagford (1650/1–1716) accumulated manuscript and printed fragments, some of them from waste, in an attempt to produce a never-completed 800-page history of what he called 'that most Universally Celebrated, as well as useful, *Art* of *Typography*', similar to Joseph Ames's *Typographical Antiquities* (1749).[37] Bagford, 'an eccentric and colourful man, fanatical in his pursuit of scraps of parchment and paper',[38] was a key figure within a network of late-seventeenth- and eighteenth-century fragment collectors that included Samuel Pepys, Thomas Tenison, Peter LeNeve, Thomas Hearne, Edmund Gibson and George Hickes. Bagford served as a supplier of fragments for this clientele, and himself drew on the services of bookseller Christopher Bateman, who 'alwayes gave me notice when he had any waste books to sell, & freely gave me Liberty to take out of them what I thought fit, as the blank leaves at the beginning of them, old pieces of MSS, Titles, Frontispieces, borders, Printers' devices, & by this civility hath very much added to my collection.'[39] The volumes that survive of Bagford's collections are large folios of hundreds of fragments, many of them title-pages, loosely thematised around topics such as handwriting, almanacs, printed ballads, with a particular interest in colophons and the identities and locations of printers.[40] Humfrey Wanley, cataloguer and keeper of the Harleian library (1672–1726), and an associate of this group, wrote a proposal for the Curators of the Bodleian, probably in 1698, in which he advocated removing manuscript waste from the bindings of printed books to produce a handbook of paleography, showing 'the several *Hands* of *England, Ireland, France, Italy, Holland, Germany, Spain, Greece*, &c. for many Ages together, and those in such Variety, as will exceed what may be found in any one Library ... [and] will also furnish him with other Observations, of the *different kinds of Parchment, Paper & Ink, different manners of Colouring & Illumination, Different ways of spelling*'. Wanley urged:

> He makes it his humble Request to Mr. Vice-Chancellor & the Curators, that they would be pleas'd to permit him to take off, from the books in the Bodleian Library, such useless Fragments of Parchment & Paper as he shall

---

[37] Milton McC. Gatch, '*Fragmenta Manuscripta* and *Varia* at Missouri and Cambridge', in *Transactions of the Cambridge Bibliographical Society* 9.5 (1990) 434–475, 450. BL MS Harley 5934 is a ca. 1707 subscription list for Bagford's project. For an outline of Bagford's collection, see A. W. Pollard, 'A Rough List of the Contents of the Bagford Collection', in *Transactions of the Bibliographical Society* 1st series, 7 (1902–1904), 143–159.

[38] McC. Gatch, '*Fragmenta Manuscripta*', 445.

[39] BL MS Harley 5910.iii, f. 120. Milton McC. Gatch, 'John Bagford as a Collector and Disseminator of Manuscript Fragments', in *The Library* 6th series, 7.2 (1985), 95–114, 107.

[40] See, for instance, BL MSS Harley 5960, Harley 5919, Harley 5937, C.40.m.9, C.40.m.10, C.40.m.11.

find necessary to his purpose, if it may be done without damage to the books. Each fragment being capable of becoming, in some sort, useful to him in a Collection, tho it be worthless when single.

Wanley's collection is not known to exist today, and was perhaps never assembled, but he promised that the collection thus produced would be deposited at the Bodleian, so that the 'Library will again have (but put into Order & rendered useful) the very same Fragments, which are now desired to be taken (or rather borrowed) out of it.'[41]

In the nineteenth and early twentieth centuries, interest in fragments in bindings produced what look to modern curatorial eyes like spectacularly insouciant moments of intervention, in character both learned and violent. This is the dynamic behind the production of nineteenth-century guard-books containing fragments excised from bindings.[42] In the 1880s at Corpus Christi College, Oxford, undergraduates Robert Proctor and J. G. Milne – 'doubtless in part due to the unusually happy relations between dons and undergraduates at that College' – spent 'wet Sunday afternoons' removing and identifying manuscript and printed binding waste from volumes in the library, usually in order to reconstitute previously scattered texts. The impulse towards the restoration of a prior bibliographical order proceeded through acts of dismembering that, remarkably, induced only 'a little alarm' in the college librarian.[43] At Corpus Christi, Proctor almost entirely reconstituted copies of Flavius Josephus, *De antiquitate Judaica. De bello Judaico* (Lubeck, 1475); Aristotle, *Opera* (Venice, 1482); and Aristotle, *De natura animalium libri nouem, De partibus animalium libri quattuor, De generatione animalium libri quinq[ue]* (Venice, 1492).[44] A triumphant final note in Proctor's hand in the 1482 Aristotle records that he has gathered '312 leaves out of 364'; of the 106 leaves of the 1492 Aristotle, only one is missing.[45] Proctor kept a record of the shelfmarks of the host

---

[41] Milton McC. Gatch, 'Humfrey Wanley's Proposal to the Curators of the Bodleian Library on the Usefulness of Manuscript Fragments from Bindings', in *Bodleian Library Record* 11 (1982–5), 94–98, 95. Wanley's proposal is BL Loan MS 29/259 misc. 29.

[42] For example, Queens College Oxford MSS 389, 389A, 389B; Bod Lat misc. b.18, compiled by the antiquary Philip Bliss; Bod Lat misc. b.17, from bindings in books of a library begun at Oxford by Hannibal Gammon ca. 1599–1619. For the latter two, see McC. Gatch, '*Fragmenta Manuscripta*', 437.

[43] A. W. Pollard (ed.), *Bibliographical Essays by Robert Proctor* (Chiswick Press: London, 1905), 'Memoir', p. ix; J. G. Milne, *The Early History of Corpus Christi College Oxford* (Oxford: Oxford University Press, 1946), p. 51.

[44] Respectively, CCC phi.C.4.4, phi.B.3.3 and phi.B.3.5. My thanks to Julie Blyth and Joanna Snelling at Corpus Christi College Library.

[45] Note also Proctor's fragment-gathering work in CCC WP.vi.10, an unbound but reconstructed copy of *D. Marcus Euangelista. Rodolphi Gualtheri Tigurini in Euangelium Iesu Christi secundum Marcum Homiliae CXXXIX* (Tiguiri, 1561); phi.F.3.4-5, 731 Proctor-recovered leaves out of 802 of

volumes from which the fragments were removed, but since the college's shelfmarks have changed it is often now difficult to identity the host text. It is clear, however, that the fragments were taken from dozens and dozens of separate volumes.

Proctor later worked at the British Museum but remained active as an extractor of scattered fragments. His private diary, dominated by his trinity of obsessions – his mother, the weather, and a squabbling British Museum work life – records his waste work. 'M[other]. better', he wrote on 19 March 1899; 'got up at 10. I spent all morning (9.30 to 1.30) soaking Claudin fragments, a desperate task'. Proctor was immersing printed leaves in water in order to separate out pieces used as waste. Three weeks later he wrote: 'A true April day, heavy showers of sleet & rain alternating with brilliant sunshine. Cold NW wind ... In aft. arranged the Grenoble fragments.'[46] These Grenoble fragments were recovered pieces of Guido Papa, *Decisiones Parlamenti Delphinalis* (Grenoble, 1490), now in the British Library – and turning the fragile, stained, rippled leaves today, one can detect the watery processes of their recovery on those windy days in 1899.[47] The same method was deployed by Dorothy Schullian, half a century later, to produce what is now known as the 'Bathtub Collection' at the National Library of Medicine in Bethesda, Maryland (formerly the Armed Forces Medical Library). 'Slowly and ploddingly,' Schullian wrote in 1953 of the library's bindings and covers, 'I have soaked them apart in my bathtub. My knees, I assure you, have suffered, but I have entered a bibliographer's paradise.'[48] By soaking bindings in water to loosen the paste and to separate the layers of leaves (the more moderate version is to damp apart leaves), then hanging leaves to dry, and finally placing them in labelled envelopes, Schullian recovered printed fragments of works by Menander, Terence, Cicero, Virgil, Ovid, Horace and Erasmus, alongside dozens of less canonical texts such as uncut sheets of playing cards.[49]

Proctor's reference to *Decisiones Parlamenti Delphinalis* as 'Grenoble' is consistent with his system of classifying incunabula by place that found

---

Opera Ioannis Chrysostomi (Venice, 1503); and WP.iii.49, 38 leaves of *Ortus Vocabulorum* (1516), a Latin-English language dictionary printed by Wynkyn de Worde.

[46] *A Critical Edition of the Private Diaries of Robert Proctor: The Life of a Librarian at the British Museum*, ed. J. H. Bowman (Lampeter: The Edwin Mellen Press, 2010), pp. 32, 35.

[47] BL IB.44405. The text is catalogued as a 'fragment, taken from a binding, consisting of quires h–k, two leaves apparently of quire r, quires t, v, leaves G 3–6, quire I, leaves N 1–7 (?) and quire T, together with duplicates of leaves t 2, 3, 6, 7. Most of the leaves are cropped and mutilated.'

[48] Schullian, 'Here the Frailest Leaves', 205.

[49] Schullian, 'Here the Frailest Leaves', 209, and www.nlm.nih.gov/exhibition/bathtub/.

expression in his *Index to the Early Printed Books in the British Museum: from the invention of printing to the year MD* (1898). The *Index* organised incunabula chronologically by country, town, press and then book, and its influence gave the lie to A. W. Pollard's pious posthumous assessment, after his friend disappeared on a solo walking trip in the Alps in 1903, that '[l]ike Browning's Grammarian Proctor had spent his life in the investigation of *minutiae* for which the world cares nothing.'[50]

Proctor valued printed waste for the potentially unique texts it might convey – at New College he found within bindings vellum fragments of a previously unknown Caxton, the *Donatus Melior* of Mancinellus[51] – and for the examples of early printing even single pieces of waste might provide: the Flavius Josephus of 1475, for instance, would have fascinated Proctor as one of the earliest books printed in Lubeck. The drawback with such approaches is that the waste text is separated from its original bibliographical context, which does damage both to the texts and to the bibliographical record of the book's history. Modern libraries and archives respond to waste with a less swashbuckling set of priorities. In stark contrast to Humfrey Wanley's proposal that regarded fragments in bindings as 'useless' until removed, current policy in major UK and North American institutions strongly favours leaving fragments of older texts *in situ*; recording the existence of printed or manuscript fragments in the binding field of the catalogue record of the host book; and, where possible, identifying and dating the fragment text(s).[52] For printed fragments, online full-text databases have made the previously daunting task of identifying the fragment often, but not always, possible. Such rigorously attentive policies are enacted, for example, at the Glasgow Incunabula Project at the University of Glasgow Library,[53] at the Beinecke Rare Book & Manuscript Library at Yale, and at Senate House Library, University of London, where a representative binding field record for a copy of Quintilian, *Institutiones Oratoriae* (Venice, 1480) with manuscript waste reads:

> ULL copy is bound in yellow paper over pasteboard, repaired. Manuscript waste used to line spine: fragments of two leaves of Italian lectionary, 1100–1150, containing parts of verses from Isaiah and Matthew (MS1020; see Watson, R. Descriptive list of fragments of medieval manuscripts in the University of London Library (1976), p 4, no. 58.)[54]

[50] Pollard, 'Memoir', p. xl.   [51] Pollard, 'Memoir', pp. xx–xxi.
[52] I am grateful for the generosity of librarians and archivists in replying in detail to my enquiries, chiefly via the SHARP and EXLIBRIS electronic forums.
[53] www.gla.ac.uk/services/incunabula/. Thanks to Robert MacLean.
[54] The full record for this copy of Quintilian, *Institutiones Oratoriae* (Venice, 1480) is at http://catalogue.ulrls.lon.ac.uk/record=b3073256-S1. Thanks to Karen Attar.

If one guiding principle for curatorial decisions is that the discoveries we make today should not prevent future discoveries of later scholars, then leaving fragments in place seems a sensible policy. As Eric White, Curator of Rare Books at Princeton University Library, put it, 'Guiding question: would we remove any other parts of an early book? For book history, the binding scraps may be as much a part of the story as the title page or the fold-out map'.[55]

Of course, particular cases put pressure on this commitment towards preservation. Curatorial policy at the Folger Shakespeare Library is to '[l]eave [inserted elements like waste] in place unless damage is actively occurring' – 'to keep anything relating to the history, readership, or use of materials with the materials themselves, making reasonable accommodation against damage.'[56] But that twin pull of preservation and conservation – the desire to keep materials *in situ*, but also to prevent decay – is a dialectic that animates a lot of curatorial discussion. Mirjam Foot prescribes a carefully balanced middle ground: 'I would not advocate the maxim that all action is bad. Too much action, however, certainly is, and so is the wrong kind of action.'[57] A principle of preservation gives way to a more complicated algorithm that incorporates the state of repair of both the host volume and the waste fragment, and the relative cultural significance of each.[58] A fragment of leaf B4 from *King Lear* (1619) – from the first attempt to collect Shakespeare into a composite volume, the 1619 'false folio' printed by William Jaggard for Thomas Pavier – was used as printed waste in the binding of *Officina Biblica noviter adaperta* (Leipzig, 1636) by the German divine Michael Walther, held at the Bodleian. The leaf, which conveys the transition from Act 1 Scene 3 to Act 1 Scene 4, was subsequently extracted from its host at an unknown date, repaired, and stored separately with its own shelf mark. The separation is expressive of the relative cultural value of even a fragment of a single leaf of Shakespeare's text, a sense of value compounded by the fact that the other printed waste in *Officina Biblica* was not removed: at the front, a fragment from a sheet from an unidentified Latin philosophical compendium, with running heads *De Politica* and *De Ethica*; at the back, an unfolded sheet from page 122 of Thomas Ridley's *A vievv of the civile and ecclesiasticall law* (Oxford, 1634).

The separation of *Lear* from its host reduces the possibility of attending to the Bodleian copy of Walther's *Officina Biblica* in its original bound form: of being sensitive to what Mirjam Foot calls 'the claims of history', by which she

---

[55] Via EXLIBRIS list-serv.
[56] http://folgerpedia.folger.edu/Things_in_books. Thanks to Meaghan Brown.
[57] Mirjam Foot, *Studies in the history of bookbinding* (Aldershot: Scholar Press, 1993), pp. 433–434.
[58] Thanks to Falk Eisermann for discussion of these issues.

means the physical form of the book as an archive of bibliographical information about its own composition.[59] While a note on the *Lear* box records some of the history ('Originally bound as printer's waste in the binding of MM4Th'), there is no record of its exact former position (front or back? boards, binding or end leaves?), suggesting amid the general bibliographical care that the relationship between fragment and host is not richly meaningful, or that any potential meaning is outweighed by the need to have the *Lear* leaf independently maintained.[60] In this instance, and often, an institution's response to printed waste – to remove or maintain? to catalogue or ignore? – is a useful indicator of the waste text's cultural standing at that moment.

When the owner of two 1550 black-letter ballad fragments wrote to the Bodleian in the late 1930s, asking if the library would be interested in acquiring them, the librarian's response focused on three key questions: Do the fragments present new texts? Do they offer valuable examples of early printing? And how can they be preserved for future readers, whose scholarly questions it is not possible to anticipate? The fragments, now in the Bodleian together with the correspondence that accompanied their transfer, were purchased by E. H. W. Meyerstein from a Bristol bookseller, Douglas Cleverdon, in the 1930s.[61] Cleverdon sold other fragments that 'came out of ... [the same] Berthelet binding' to the Huntington – that is, the binding of a book printed by Thomas Berthelet, formerly King's Printer for Henry VIII – including pieces of Zwingli's *Image of both pastours* (1550) and *The Book of Common Prayer* (1549).[62] The extant letters that passed back and forth against the background rumble of approaching war show the Bodleian's Mr Wright (that is, S. G. Wright, Assistant Secretary to the Librarian) wondering whether 'we might conceivably [already] have a complete copy'; describing the (failed) attempts 'to identify ... the printer'; worrying about the difficulty of recording these texts ('I wanted to be sure that it would not get pushed into some collection of miscellaneous fragments, uncatalogued and virtually lost'); and registering the need to assume that 'such fragments are likely in a public library to fall one day into hands that can make use of them, whether textually or bibliographically' – this latter commitment both a deferral of the question of what to do with waste and a vital curatorial principle.[63]

---

[59] Foot, *Studies*, p. 430.
[60] The *Lear* leaf is now Bod Vet. A2 e.504; the Walther is Bod MM 4 Th.
[61] Bod Don. d.80. The fragments come from STC 6795.
[62] Bod Don. d.80, letter from Cleverdon to Meyerstein, 23 January 1939.
[63] Bod Don. d.80, letters from Wright to Meyerstein, 20 October 1938; Wright to Meyersetin, 8 October 1938; Wright to Meyerstein, 16 October 1938.

***

The Appendix presents a small but representative sample of the large number of texts I have examined in libraries in the United Kingdom and North America in the form of a table of the details of 40 instances of host books carrying printed waste, arranged by chronological order of host publication. This conveys something of the variety I have encountered, but certain tendencies are apparent across this table, and across the larger body of waste cases I have studied.

There is often a small gap between the publication dates of host and waste: commonly, the waste text was published the same year, or between one and five years earlier. This wasn't always so: there might be a very large gap between host and waste, like the 180 years that separates a Lambeth Palace copy of George Hickes' *The Case of Infant Baptism* (1683) from the 1503 fragments of Justinian's *Institutes*;[64] and in many cases, the host text was published before the waste. If the waste was published after the host, then the publication date of the waste gives the earliest point at which the current binding could have taken place; if the host was published after the waste, then the host's date gives that earliest date.

Waste thus complicates or thickens the historicism of the text, since to read waste is to be aware of multiple temporalities. In *Untimely Matter in the Time of Shakespeare* (2009), Jonathan Gil Harris sets out a corrective to what he sees as the 'confining rubrics' of conventional historicism which assumes 'period purification and the sovereign moment-state' and instead argues that things are 'polytemporal'.[65] Taking his cue from the currently omnipresent Bruno Latour – '[s]ome of my genes are 500 million years old, others 3 million, others 100,000 years old, and my habits range in age from a few days to several thousand years'[66] – Harris argues that 'matter [can] ... collate diverse moments in time'.[67] In his discussion of the palimpsest (derived, as Harris notes, from the Greek *palimpsestos*, meaning 'scraped again'), Harris focuses on three particular models of temporal relations between older and newer: supersession (the later text obscures the earlier), explosion (the old text 'shatters the integrity' of the new), and conjunction ('the infinities of classical past and medieval present ... converse with each other').[68]

---

[64] Lambeth Palace Library G813.A2H5.
[65] Jonathan Gil Harris, *Untimely Matter in the Time of Shakespeare* (Philadelphia: University of Pennsylvania Press, 2009), p. 25.
[66] Brunto Latour, *We Have Never Been Modern* (Cambridge, MA: Harvard University Press, 1993), p. 75.
[67] Harris, *Untimely*, p. 4.   [68] Harris, *Untimely*, pp. 15–16.

Although Harris does not discuss printed waste, his three categories look helpful in accounting for some of the effects created between host and waste, although most instances of waste might be said to simultaneously embody more than one of these relationships. For example, one copy of *The Whole Booke of Psalmes* (Cambridge, MA, 1640), the first book printed in North America, contains an upside-down waste sheet on the inside board from the Sternhold-Hopkins psalmbook.[69] *The Whole Booke of Psalmes*, or The Bay Psalm Book, as it was known, has been understood by literary historians as a founding text of North American Congregationalism, a text used to distinguish the Massachusetts Bay community from, among other groups, those associated with the Church of England's Sternhold-Hopkins edition of the psalms. The use of Sternhold-Hopkins as waste in a text which seeks to define itself against Sternhold-Hopkins is thus powerfully suggestive, at once troubling this dynamic of separation (the Bay Psalm Book is made out of Sternhold-Hopkins) and seeming to enforce it (the Bay Psalm Book supercedes Sternhold-Hopkins). The book thus simultaneously suggests supersession, explosion, and conjunction, which serves to question the utility of Harris' trio of categories, or at least to suggest that they are all always in play.

The same host text might contain waste from more than one source: indeed, books can carry waste from dozens of separate works, like the copy of a folio Boethius, *De consolatione philosophiae* (Louvain, 1484), which used as printed waste three whole works and parts of nine others, mostly French verse, but also including leaves from a Book of Hours, a Breviary, and a Latin grammar, alongside considerable manuscript waste.[70] Waste in a single host might come from different periods: a copy of Horace's *Satires*, Book 2 from around 1700 contains printed waste from the incunable and post-incunable periods, before and after the main Horace text.[71] A 1513 volume by the Italian humanist Baptista Mantuanus has waste from one book by, and one book about, John Wycliffe.[72] This looks at first like a concerted selection of waste in terms of

---

[69] Matthew P. Brown, *The Pilgrim and the Bee: Reading Rituals and Book Culture in Early New England* (Philadelphia: University of Pennsylvania Press, 2007), pp. 37–38.

[70] L. A. Sheppard, 'Fragments from a Binding', in *The Library*, 4th series, 26.2-3 (1945), 172–175.

[71] *Q. Horatii Flacci Satt. 1. Ii. S. iii*, Bod Mar. 576. Thanks to Alan Coates for bringing this to my attention. The waste material comes from an index to an unidentified volume partly relating to papal history, and also from Martin Luther, *Simplex Et Pia Evangeliorum, Quae Dominicis Diebus, Et In Praecipuis Festis legi solent, explication* (Montanus et Neuber, 1545).

[72] Mantuanus Baptista, *Parthenice prima f. Baptiste Mantuani Carmellitæ* (n.p., 1513), with waste from *Two short treatises, against the orders of the begging friars, compiled by that famous doctour of the Church, and preacher of Gods word John Wickliffe* (Oxford: Joseph Barnes, 1608) and Thomas James, *An apologie for Iohn Wickliffe* (Oxford: Joseph Barnes, 1608), Christ Church College, Oxford D.2.1.18.

content – an artful composition – but the apparent connection between the Wycliffite subject matter of these two texts is almost certainly an epiphenomenon of the fact that both waste texts were printed by Joseph Barnes in 1608. The relationship between waste and host is meaningful, here – meaningful in the sense of being expressive of certain truths about these books' histories – but this is meaning on the level of geography and time, not theme: the two texts were to hand for a binder in Oxford, in or around 1608. While it is true that surveying printed waste suggests that 'anything is likely to turn up',[73] the content-level miscellaneity in fact expresses the movements, through space and time, of host and waste books.

A single text, or, in one instance I studied, a pair of texts, might be broken up to serve as waste in multiple volumes. Copies of two books from 1649 – Libert Froiodmont, *Philosophiæ Christianæ de anima libri quatuor* (Louvain, 1649) and Zacutus Lusitanus, *Zacuti Lusitani, medici, et philosophi praestantissimi* (Lyon, 1649) – contain cancel title leaves to two unpublished reissues: the planned second edition of Edward Symmons, *A loyall subjects beliefe, or, A theologicall discourse wherein is proved, that regall or monarchicall povver is not of humane, but of divine right* (Oxford, 1647), and *Divine truths discovered. Being the substance of all the most remarkeable discourses that hath beene published* (Oxford, 1647). These Royalist books were never published due to the fall of Oxford to Parliamentarian forces in June 1646.[74] The waste connection strongly suggests the same binder was responsible for both 1649 books. Among the Bodleian Library Records is the Binders Book for 1621–1624, which contains lists of piles of books sent from the Bodleian to a number of local binders, with their signatures confirming receipt: 'June 19 1621. Deliured to John Allam bookbinder'; 'Deliured to William Jhonson these bookes following to be bound the 19 of November 1621'; 'Reseaud by me William Webb these bookes aboue writen'.[75] The record for 17 February 1624 lists books 'Deliured to William Wildgoose', and among 'These bookes following to be bound' is the copy of Shakespeare's First Folio that is now in the Bodleian Library:

R1 William Cowper Works fol
R2 A Guide to Godlynesse by John Downham

---

[73] Ker and Pearson, *Oxford bookbinding*, p. 141.
[74] St Edmund Hall, Oxford 4° E 18(2); Trinity College Oxford, O.16.9-10. *Divine truths discovered* was perhaps intended for a reissue of Daniel Featley's *Sacra nemesis, the Levites scourge* (Oxford [i.e., London], 1644). Both publishing ventures never happened due to the fall of Oxford in 1646. My thanks to Paul Nash for this.
[75] Bod Library Records e.528, ff. 2, 4, 9.

156 Material Texts in Early Modern England

    R3 petr. de Arrubal Comment In 1am partem Thomæ
    R4 Martinus de Espilla diffinitiones rerum et verborum, quæ tractantur de Sacra Theologia
    R (Sermones et exhortations monasticæ Authore Laurentio de portel
    R5 (Francis sanchez In Ecclesiasten Comment
    R6 William Shakespeares comedies, histories
    R7 The Theater of honor and knighthood
    R8 Polyanthea noua Tom 2^d fol.[76]

Of these titles, four – Cowper (1623), Downame (1622), Sanchez (1619) and Shakespeare (1623) – carry printed waste from parts of a single copy of Cicero containing *De Officiis* and *Cato Major*, printed in Deventer by Richard Pafraet, between 1480 and 1485.[77] In retaining legible printed waste, the Wildgoose First Folio is rare: of the 232 extant copies of Shakespeare's book, only two others contain similar printed waste.[78] Most copies of the first folio were lavishly rebound, as an act of honour, between about 1775 and 1950, when any waste in the original binding would have been removed;[79] the particular history of the Bodleian's copy – sold to the Oxford bookseller Richard Davis in 1664 and then into the collection of Richard Turbutt of Ogston Hall, Derbyshire, where it remained until the Bodleian bought it back in 1906 – explains this lack of intervention. Wildgoose's distributed waste becomes a means of tracking a moment of binding: we know that these four volumes and the Cicero were in Wildgoose's workshop at the same time, and since we know which parts of the Cicero were used in which volumes, we can say with some

---

[76] Respectively, William Cowper, *Workes* (1623); John Downame, *A Guide to Godlynesse* (1622); Petrus de Arrubal, *Commentariorum, Ac Disputationum in Primam Partem [of the Summa Theologica] Diui Thomæ Tomus Primus* (1619); Martino de Espilla, *Diffinitiones rerum et verborum, quæ tractantur de sacra theologia, & de rebus moralibus: Vtilisimæ tàm omnibus concionatoribus, quàm in sacra pagina versatis, & etiam in moralibus studiosis* (1612); Laurentius de Portel, *Sermones et exhortationes monastic* (1617); Franciscus Sanchez, *In Ecclesiasten commentarium cum condordia Vulgatæ editionis, et Hebraici textus* (1619); William Shakespeare, *Comedies, histories, and tragedies* (1623); André Favyn, *The theater of honour and knight-hood. Or a compendious chronicle and historie of the whole Christian vvorld* (1623); *Polyanthea nova, hoc est, opus suavissimis floribus celebriorum sententiarum refertum: quod olim collegêre D. Nanus Mirabellius, B. Amantius & F. Tortius. Nunc verò ordine bono digestum, et auctum: studio & operà J. Langii* (1607).

[77] Respectively, Bod C 2.3 Th; Bod C 18. 11 Th (waste now removed); BB 12(1) Th; Arch. G c.7. For a digital facsimile of the Shakespeare text, including the waste, see http://shakespeare.bodleian.ox.ac.uk.

[78] Folger no. 41, which was bound by Roger Payne (1739–1797) and retains what is probably eighteenth-century waste; Newberry Library First Folio, in which the English black-letter waste is obscured and not identifiable. Thanks to Caroline Duroselle-Melish, Jill Gage and Eric Rasmussen for help with this. For a survey of all extant First Folios, see Eric Rasmussen and Anthony James West, *The Shakespeare First Folios: A Descriptive Catalogue* (Basingstoke: Palgrave, 2012).

[79] My thanks to Paul Nash for this point.

certainty that Wildgoose bound these books in the order of Sanchez, Cowper, Downame and Shakespeare.[80]

Ciceronian waste, then, was scattered across at least four volumes in a moment of binding in 1623. Other examples of the same book being used by a binder across several works comes via a number of books printed by Joseph Barnes (1549/50–1618), a key figure in the history of printed waste in Oxford. Barnes, a prosperous bookseller in the parish of St Mary's, Oxford, since at least 1573, and a wine merchant from 1575, was appointed Oxford's first university printer in 1584 with a rather meagre £100 loan. This followed a petition from individuals now unknown to the University's Chancellor, Robert Dudley, Earl of Leicester, seeking royal approval for the establishment of the office. These petitions lamented that Oxford 'surpasses all the universities of Europe in the grandeur of its colleges and the extent of their yearly revenues, and yet lags behind each and every one of them by its lack of press', and expressed hope that the office of university printer would ensure manuscript collections 'shamefully covered in dust' would be 'rescued from perpetual obscurity'.[81] In fact the history of Barnes' tenure as university printer is chequered, despite the general excellence of his work, not least due to the University's lack of financial support. Barnes died heavily in debt in 1618, despite having printed more than 260 titles before his retirement, and having become central to bibliographical culture in the city: Aubrey wrote that the fashion 'was, in those dayes [ca. 1605], to goe every satterday night (I thinke) to Joseph Barnes shop the bookseller ... where the Newes was brought from London'.[82] While there had been a few short-term efforts at establishing printing in Oxford, it was a remarkable fact that when Barnes became a bookseller in 1573, no book had been printed in the city for more than 50 years.[83] Barnes printed his first book as university printer in 1585 – a volume on Aristotelian moral philosophy by John Case[84] – and thereafter there was a steady supply of printed waste from Barnes' Oxford workshop. Oxford binders seeking waste had a rich

---

[80] Falconer Madan, G. M. R. Turbutt and Strickland Gibson, *The original Bodleian copy of the first folio of Shakespeare* (Clarendon Press: Oxford, 1905), pp. 12–13. More broadly, see Mirjam Foot, *Studies in the History of Bookbinding* (Aldershot: Scholar Press, 1993), pp. 432–438 ('Preserving Books and their History').

[81] Jason Peacey, '"Printers to the University" 1584–1658', in *The History of Oxford University Press*, vol. I, ed. Ian Gadd (Oxford: Oxford University Press, 2013), pp. 51–104, pp. 51–52.

[82] Aubrey, *Brief Lives*, vol. I, p. 182. See also Kate Bennett, 'John Aubrey, Joseph Barnes's Print-Shop and a Sham Newsletter', in *The Library* 21/1 (March 1999), 50–58.

[83] Ian Gadd, 'Barnes, Joseph (1549/50–1618)' 6th series, 21.1, in *Oxford Dictionary of National Biography* (Oxford University Press, Oct 2011; online edn, Jan. 2012).

[84] John Case, *Speculum moralium quaestionum in universam ethicen Aristotelis* (Oxford, 1585).

supply of pre-Reformation manuscripts, although this supply began to dwindle in the second half of the sixteenth century;[85] and college libraries could supply waste from older printed books. But Barnes' printed output represented another local source of waste, particularly valuable as expendable manuscript supplies declined, and, given the relatively small book making world of Oxford, a very high number of Oxford books feature waste drawn from Barnes-printed publications.

We see this in the case of *Microcosmos. The Discovery of the little world, with the government thereof*, first printed by Joseph Barnes in Oxford in 1603. This is a long poem of 6,000 lines about the passions, which feels, upon reading, considerably longer. Davies, often styled 'John Davies of Hereford' on title pages, enjoyed considerable renown as a writing master – 'the greatest master of the pen that England in her age beheld', according to Thomas Fuller[86] – but his poetry produced no great critical esteem, earned no money and was, in the words of Douglas Bush, 'slow, laborious, diffuse, and flat'.[87]

Fragments of *Mircocosmos* were used in at least five volumes bound in Oxford, as the table below shows.

Oxford College Library	Host text	Host place & date	Parts of *Microcosmos* used
Exeter	*Divi Caecilii Cypriani Episcopi Carthagiensis* [Works of Cyprian, Bishop of Carthage]	Rome, 1563	Nn sheet (upper board); Oo sheet (lower board)
Magdalen	Francisco Suarez, *Commentaria ac disputationes in primam partem divi Thomae, de deo uno & trino*	Moguntiæ, 1607	Kk sheet (upper board); Ll sheet (lower board)
New (i)	Luis Mercado, *Dn. Lud. Mercati, medici a cubiculo Philippi II. et III. Hispaniarum atque Indiarum Regum potentissimorum ... Opervm Tomvs II*	Frankfurt, 1608	A1v, A4r, A2r, and A3v (upper board); B2r, B3v, B1v and B4r (lower board)

[85] Neil Ker's *Fragments of Medieval Manuscripts* ends at 1620 because here manuscript waste dwindles as printed waste takes off.
[86] Thomas Fuller, *Worthies of England* (London, 1840), 2.79, quoted in P. J. Finkelpearl, 'Davies, John (1564/5–1618)', in *Oxford Dictionary of National Biography* (Oxford: Oxford University Press, 2004).
[87] J. N. D. Bush, *English Literature in the Earlier Seventeenth Century, 1600–1660* (Oxford: Oxford University Press, 1945), p. 86, quoted in Finkelpearl, 'Davies'.

(cont.)

Oxford College Library	Host text	Host place & date	Parts of *Microcosmos* used
New (ii)	Lud. Mercati, *medici a cubiculo Philippi II. et III. Hispaniarum atque Indiarum Regum potentissimorum . . . Opervm*	Frankfurt, 1608	sheets C and D; parts of 8 pages of the preface (2, 3, 6 and 7; 10, 11, 14 and 15)
Merton	Antonio Possevino, *Antonii Posseuini Mantuani, Societis Iesu Bibliotheca selecta de ratione studiorum: ad disciplinas, & ad salutem omnium gentium procurandam . . .*	Venice, 1603	P4, P1v, P3v, P2 (rear boards); sheet of Latin homilies (front boards)

Most of these books were printed shortly after *Microcosmos* was printed in 1603.[88] The binder used unfolded, unmarked sheets from *Microcosmos*: not proof sheets (which would contain pen markings), but probably not binder's waste, as Bradshaw understood it as former books, since the sheets were never folded – although unfolded sheets might have been sold, stored in a publisher's warehouse or a bookshop, perhaps for years.[89] Perhaps too many sheets were printed. Although I have not been able to confirm that these waste sheets came from the same copy of *Microcosmos*, the unique appearance of sheets in different hosts indicates that this may have been the case, suggesting a binder working through a copy of *Microcosmos*, just as William Wildgoose pulled apart his Cicero. The binder here performs a curious parody of reading: moving through the text, turning the leaves, evaluating the book, but evaluating it in terms of its material rather than its aesthetic properties (is this leaf or sheet large enough, tough enough?). The presence of Davies' poem in these different bibliographical contexts creates some sharp juxtapositions (Latin versus English vernacular; Catholic versus Protestant), but it is not content but place and time that unites hosts and waste: Davies' unwanted sheets were to hand at the moment when these volumes were to be bound.

Joseph Barnes is a crucial figure in the history of printed waste not only for his prominence as university printer, but also because his brother Roger was an

---

[88] There were also editions in 1605 and 1611.
[89] Such a case thus puts pressure on Bradshaw's distinction between printer's and binder's waste. Thanks to Paul Nash for discussion of this point.

Oxford-based bookbinder of considerable reputation, and waste seems to have passed from Joseph to Roger with particular frequency. According to Strickland Gibson, of the 18 binders employed by the Bodleian between 1613 and 1624, Roger Barnes' work was particularly accomplished, marked out by its standard of forwarding (sewing, trimming and attaching of boards, and fitting leather, to produce the functional but undecorated binding) and tooling (decorating a binding by impressing engraved tools into the surface, leaving a gold, colour or 'blind' impression), and for the quality of his leather.[90] The Bodleian Day Books often mention Roger Barnes, including on 10 August 1613: 'Delievered to Rog. Barnes ... Workes to be bound in 13. volumes in blacke leather & filleted about wth edges of gold'.[91]

We see this sibling relationship finding bibliographical expression in the ghostly history of *Great Brittaines Svnnes-set, bewailed with a shower of teares*, printed by Joseph Barnes in Oxford in 1613, and written by William Basse. Basse is best known today for his elegy 'On Shakespeare' in the First Folio, in which Basse advises Spenser and Beaumont to shift in their tomb to accommodate Shakespeare. *Great Brittaines Svnnes-set*, dedicated and addressed to Basse's patron Sir Richard Wenman, is an elegy for the death of Henry Frederick, Prince of Wales. Nineteen stanzas lament the loss of Henry in fairly orthodox terms, with a tortured syntax and a logic that speaks of the burden of writing grief from within convention (negative clauses and parentheses knot the verse). Like most elegies, Basse's poem also treads a fine line between mourning and, through the expression of that mourning, authorial self-promotion: the title page's mid-word line-break of '*shower*' reminds us of this problem by presenting '*bewailed with a show*'. The poem responds to the awkward challenge of integrating Charles, the new heir apparent as Prince of Wales, into a lament by sliding from 'mourning' to 'morning', with the final two stanzas of the total of 22 looking forward to a new era.[92]

Like Prince Henry, Basse's book exists only as a ghost of itself, in fragments recovered from the binding of books, many or all of which were the work of Joseph's brother Roger.[93] Today there is one whole copy, patched together from scattered parts;[94] at least six fragments which have been removed from (now unknown) bindings;[95] and two instances of parts of Basse's text still *in situ* as printed waste in texts

---

[90] Strickland Gibson, *Early Oxford Bindings* (Oxford: Oxford University Press, 1903), p. 13.
[91] Bodleian Library Records e.9, f. 3v.   [92] Stanza 20 is blank.   [93] Gibson, 'Old Bindings'.
[94] Bod Arch. A f.65.
[95] BL C.39.c.59; CUL 6000.e.103; Huntington 60329 and 131401:20; Merton, Oxford P.3:2; Harvard Typ 805.72.1945.

printed in 1609.⁹⁶ The history of these fragments – the volumes in which they originally served as waste; the dates when they were removed – is not recorded, but we do have some details of the pieces of Basse in Harvard. Basse's books collates A⁸ B⁴ (with B1 missigned 'A'); Harvard holds leaves A2–3, A6–8, and B1–4 – all the text minus the title page, dedication, and stanzas 5 through 8 – which have been bound into a 1872 facsimile of the reconstructed copy now in the Bodleian.⁹⁷ A handwritten note dated 1872 on the flyleaf by W. D. Macray, who worked at the Bodleian between 1845 and 1905, records that 'At the end of this copy I have inserted some fragments ... which I found in like manner [as flysheets or bindings] many years ago, in books sent to be rebound, and which I thus saved from destruction, but could never ascertain of what book they formed part.' Macray sees the use of Basse as waste as a material expression of the poor quality of the poetry: 'The turgid, forced bombast & affected conceits of the poem seem abundantly to justify the use to which the unsaleable copies appear to have been put by the old Oxford binders.'⁹⁸ Thus the decision to use this text as waste is in part a consequence of literary evaluation: not quite the literary evaluation of the binder – who almost certainly didn't read the poem, judge it bad, and so select this text as waste – but rather an earlier cultural evaluation of the text which led to the sheets becoming available to the binder as waste.

Often the texts used as waste are the texts we might expect: last year's almanac, used as endpapers in a copy of *The Booke of The Common Prayer* (1549); an Elizabethan proclamation about cloth manufacture, in the binding of John Cowell's *The interpreter: or Booke containing the significa-tion of words* (1607); a fragment of a corrected proof sheet, such as the outer forme of sheet L of Johannes Piscator's *Analysis Logica Evangelii secundum Johannem* (1595), used as end leaves in a copy of Cicero,⁹⁹ or of 'Lycidas', pasted on the inside back cover of *De literis et lingua Getarum sive*

---

⁹⁶ Christ Church, Oxford e.3.8, *Petri Berchorii Pictauiensis ordinis D. Benedicti Opera omnia totam S. Scripturae, morum, naturae historia[m] complectentia* (Antwerp, 1609); Lincoln College N.1.22. a sammelband of 10 texts, the second of which is printed by Joseph Barnes: John Glanville's *Articuli Christianæ fidei* (Oxford, 1613). *STC* and *Holdings of STC Books in Oxford Libraries* (1985) suggest further Basse copies (in Trinity, Oxford; Christ Church, Oxford; and Corpus Christi, Oxford), but these fragments cannot at present be located.

⁹⁷ W. H. Allnutt (ed.), *Great Brittaines sunnes-set, bewailed with a shower of teares* (Oxford: Oxford University Press, 1872).

⁹⁸ Harvard Typ 805.72.1945. The volume came to Harvard via Philip Hofer of the Department of Printing and Graphic Arts, who – an inscription on the inside front board notes – was given the book 'in honour of his LYLE [sic] LECTURES' in 1962. Thanks to John Overholt for help with the Harvard fragments.

⁹⁹ Bod 15/16 283. My thanks to Paul Nash and Sarah Wheale for bringing this to my attention.

Gothorum (1597).[100] Sometimes sheets were used as waste because they had errors. An endpaper in a work on runes from 1651 is a leaf from a Latin translation of Apollonius of Perga's work on conic sections, *Apollonii pergaei conicorum lib. V,* used because the etched illustration was accidentally printed upside down.[101] Fragments of the Bible were also commonly used as waste due to that text's near omnipresence: a copy of Francis Bacon's *The historie of the raigne of King Henry the Seuenth* (1622), for example, has hinge strengtheners made from a 1620 octavo edition of the King James Bible, Matthew 22, 23, 24, 27 and 28.[102]

All these texts in different ways had had their day at the moment when they shifted into the category of waste – even the 'Lycidas' proof, which for us today stands out as a buried jewel – rather as manuscript waste texts represent an archive of texts that had fallen out of fashion: handbooks of canon and civil law; Latin translations of and medieval commentaries on Aristotle, like the annotated sheets from the 1479 Oxford edition of Aristotle's *Nicomachean Ethics,* originally used as pastedowns, now detached as end-papers, in a copy of a multi-lingual work of textual criticism on the Gospels, from 1631.[103] But there are printed examples, too, that defy an easy sense of obsolescence. The most beguiling example is a recorded but missing text – so it may be a fantasy, or a deliberate bookseller's fiction. In the sale of George Thorn-Drury's library at Sotheby's on 15 June 1931, lot 1123 was a copy of John Donne's defence of suicide, *Biathanatos* (1644), once owned by the naturalist Robert Plot (1640–1696) who had signed the first leaf. The book featured an endpaper composed, according to this sales catalogue, of '[p]art of the leaf of verses facing the portrait of Shakespeare in the first folio.'[104] In other words, Ben Jonson's verse 'To the Reader' – 'This Figure, that thou here seest put, / It was for gentle Shakespeare cut' – had been taken from the First Folio to serve as waste in Donne's volume.[105]

---

[100] Lambeth Palace Library H5145.A2 (1549); Folger STC 5900 copy 1; CUL Adv.d.38.6.

[101] *[Runir], seu Danica literatura antiquissima, vulgò Gothica dicta* (Copenhagen, 1651), Trinity College Oxford, S.10.3. My thanks to Paul Nash for this and some of the following examples.

[102] St Edmund Hall, Oxford, AA 32. For similar examples, see *De interpretatione divinae scripturae epistolarum* (Heidelberg, 1605), Folger BR65.I8 D4 1605 Cage, with endpapers from 2 Maccabees; Lancelot Andrewes, *The copie of the sermon preached on Good-Friday before the Kings Maiestie* (1610?), Folger STC 598.2 copy 1, with a flyleaf made from a glossed commentary on the Book of Chronicles, Chapter 38.5.

[103] *Animadversiones sive Commentarius in quatuor Euangelia* (1631), Trinity College Oxford, K.3.8.

[104] *Catalogue of the Very Extensive and Well-Known Library . . . Formed by the late George Thorn-Drury* (London: Sotheby's, 1931), p. 131. My thanks to Henry Woudhuysen for alerting me to this.

[105] It is possible the catalogue means that a handwritten copy of these verses was used, not the printed original.

From the vantage point of our largely Bardolatrous culture, such an excising seems at least surprising, which in turn reminds us that attitudes to the importance of Shakespeare's material book have shifted dramatically over time. The book was bought in 1931 by the London booksellers Quaritch for stock at £8 10s, but no record survives for its subsequent ownership: it is presumably now in untracked private hands. We do know that the Sotheby's description was not quite right: a pencil note in the catalogue at Quaritch, presumably made by whoever viewed the book at the sale, records that the leaf in fact came from the third folio (1664), not the first, and comprises the heading and first six lines.[106] In the third folio, Jonson's poem is beneath, not facing, Shakespeare's portrait, so this suggests one possible (but still surprising) explanation: that Shakespeare's portrait was cut out to be mounted somewhere else (a not uncommon practice for author portraits),[107] leaving behind the Jonsonian tatters which served little purpose separated from the image.

If this case suggests a striking disjunction between our sense of value and the seeming estimation of the unknown bookbinder, there are nonetheless other comparable instances. Philip Sidney's texts were used as waste at the moment when we might expect their cultural stock to be at their absolute peak. A fragment of *The defence of poesie* (1595), for example, now boxed and catalogued as a separate item in the Bodleian library, may once have served as waste for the binding of a now unknown book.[108]

More strikingly still, and as briefly noted above, *A true chronologie of the times of the Persian monarchie, and after to the destruction of Ierusalem by the*

---

[106] My thanks to Katherine Thornbury at Quaritch, Ernest Sullivan, Josh Eckhardt, Daniel Starza Smith, Caroline Duroselle-Melish, Gabriel Heaton, Eric Rasmussen and John Overholt for advice. *American Book Prices Current* records that this copy of *Biathanatos* was not sold in America after 1975, and the major libraries with holdings from Thorn-Drury's library (the Bodleian and the Houghton) do not possess the book.

[107] A copy of Philip Sidney, *The Countesse of Pembrokes Arcadia* (1621), Huntington 45326, has an engraved portrait of Sidney pasted in on the front board.

[108] Bod J-J Sidney 78. The box is labelled 'SIR PHILIP SIDNEY. THE DEFENCE OF POESIE. 1595', although the unbound text only contains sigs B1–4 (the bottom thirds of B3 and B4 are torn away), E2–E3, and small pieces of text loose within the sheets. However, the use of the sheets as waste could have come some years or decades later, after Sidney's stock had fallen again. (Thanks to Paul Nash for discussion of this.) There are several examples of the converse structure, where non-Sidneian printed waste is used to support a Sidney text. See, for example, the printed collection of letters between Sidney and Hubert Languet, *Huberti Langueti, viri clarissimi Epistolæ politicæ et historicæ* (Frankfurt, 1633), All Souls, Oxford 12:SR.42.f.6, with unidentified printed Latin prose waste; *The Countesse of Pembrokes Arcadia . . . Now the ninth time published* (1638), Merton College, Oxford, 34.K.23, with fragments of printed waste showing Biblical family trees used as spine supports; *The Countesse of Pembrokes Arcadia . . . Now the sixt time published* (1627), All Souls, Oxford, 4.13, with unidentified printed Latin devotional waste featuring hand-coloured initials and rubrications; *A worke concerning the trunesse of Christian religion . . . the fourth time published* (1617), Bod 4° M 52 Th., with late fifteenth-/ early sixteenth-century printed Latin waste with a running head '*De testamētis*', that is, the fifth part of the Digests or Pandects, compendia of Roman law.

Romanes (1597), written by the Regius Professor of Hebrew at Cambridge University, Edward Lively, uses parts of leaves C2 and B2 (sonnets 39–44 and 19–24) from the second quarto of Sidney's *Astrophel and Stella* (1591) as, respectively, front and rear endpapers.[109] In each case, a single leaf has been cut from *Astrophel and Stella* and folded to produce four pages. On opening Lively's book, we first encounter the bottom half of Sidney's sig. C2, featuring all of sonnet number 41[110] ('Hauing this day, my horse, my hand, my Launce') and two lines of 42 ('O Eyes which do the Spheres of beautie moue'), the text sideways, left to right; then, across the next opening, sig. C2v, sideways right to left, featuring the rest of sonnet 42, all of sonnet 43 ('Faire eyes, sweet lips, deer hart, that foolish I'), and eight lines of 44 ('My words I know doe well set forth my minde'); then the top half of sig. C2, sideways left to right, with the last three lines of sonnet 39 and all of sonnet 40 ('As good to write, as for to lie and groane'), facing the title page of Lively's 1597 text (Figure 20).

Pages from *Astrophel and Stella* also end the volume: Lively's text concludes with a list of errata, prefaced by a brief address 'To the gentle Reader', written in the voice of the author, and characteristic of the kinds of address discussed in Chapter 3, and, opposite (Figure 21), the bottom half of Sidney's sig. B2, sideways left to right, conveying sonnet 31 ('Your words my freend right helthfull causticks blame'); then, all of sig. B2v, sideways right to left, with sonnets 22 ('In highest way of heauen the Sunne did ride'), 23 ('The curious wits, seeing dull pensiuenes'), and six lines of 24 ('Rich fooles there be, whose base and filthie hart'); and then, finally, sideways left to right, the top half of sig. B2, featuring the last six lines of sonnet 19, and 11 lines of sonnet 20 ('Fly, flye my friends, I haue my deathes wound, flye').

In addition to book-ending Lively's text, Sidney's sonnets also interrupt the book: at Lively's sig. Cc, next to 'A Chronologicall Table of the Greeke Olympiads', a single line from the fold of *Astrophel and Stella* sig. B2 tucks through at right angles to the main text, conveying the line (you need to look closely) 'But straight I saw motions of lightnings grace' (Figure 22).

That none of the 23 other extant copies of Lively's *Chronologie* in libraries in the UK, Ireland and North America I have checked contain Sidneian printed waste is not surprising: most likely this waste was inserted by a binder working across a series of different books, rather than on many copies of the same, just as William Wildgoose bound Shakespeare's First Folio alongside books by William Cowper, John Downame, Francisus

---

[109] Bod J-J Sidney 173.   [110] The 1591 text does not number the sonnets.

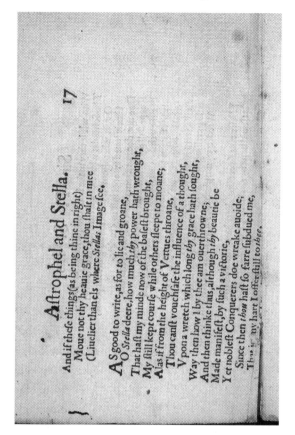

Figure 20 Printed waste from *Astrophel and Stella* (1591) facing the title page of Edward Lively's *A true chronologie of the times of the Persian monarchie* (1597). By permission of the Bodleian Library (J-J Sidney 173)

Sanchez and others.[111] Nonetheless, the use of *Astrophel and Stella* as printed waste probably seems to us surprising, given the cultural and

---

[111] Many copies of Lively's book have been rebound, often in the nineteenth century (the Houghton Library copy was, like most of Harry Elkins Widener's library, from which it comes, rebound in full nineteenth-century morocco), meaning that if there had been any waste paper it has now been removed, or is no longer visible under the re-backing. Some copies retain the original binding (for example, the copy in the Memorial Library, University of Wisconsin–Madison), but without waste. The copy in the Harry Ransom Center in Austin, Texas, contains manuscript waste, apparently from a letter to 'Daniell Hughes att Worcester'. Several copies are bound with other books: in Trinity College, Lively's book is bound with Robert Sanderson's *Episcopacy* (1661); in Marsh's Library, with *A True Description of the Mighty Kingdoms of Japan and Siam* (1671); in Lincoln Cathedral, with John More's *A Table From the Beginning of the World to this Day* (1593). My thanks to the librarians who helped me with this enquiry.

Figure 21 Sidney sonnet as waste, facing errata list in Lively, *A true chronologie*. By permission of the Bodleian Library (J-J Sidney 173)

literary significance we attach to a text that catalysed so many sonnet sequences of the 1590s: in the words of William Ringler, the publication of the two 1591 quartos of *Astrophel and Stella* transformed Sidney's reputation from a 'learned soldier and an accomplished courtier' to 'the foremost literary artist of his century.'[112] Our sense of value is probably compounded by the fact that the second quarto of *Astrophel and Stella* is today a scarce thing: alongside this fragment, the *English Short Title*

---

[112] W. A. Ringler, Jr., 'Sir Philip Sidney: The Myth and the Man', in *Sir Philip Sidney: 1586 and the Creation of a Legend*, ed. Jan van Dorsten, Dominic Baker-Smith and Arthur Kinney (Leiden: E.J. Brill, 1986), pp. 3–15, 11–12. Cited and discussed in Arthur F. Marotti, *Manuscript, Print, and the English Renaissance Lyric* (Cornell: Ithaca, 1995), p. 229.

Printed Waste: 'Tatters Allegoricall' 167

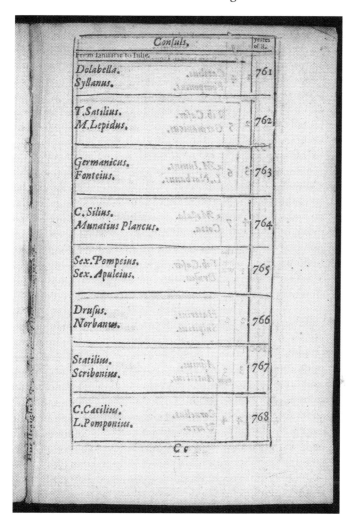

Figure 22 Lively sig. Cc, with binding support from sonnet. By permission of the Bodleian Library (J-J Sidney 173)

Catalogue records copies in the British Library (2); Cashel Cathedral Library, Ireland; and the Huntington, along with the eternally enigmatic 'Private collections'. The slightly earlier first quarto of *Astrophel and Stella*, printed by John Charlewood for Thomas Newman, was withdrawn at the order of William Cecil, Lord Burghley, in still unexplained circumstances: the Stationers' Register records only a payment of 15 shillings to

John Wolf 'when he ryd with an answere to my Lord Treasurer beinge with her majestie in progress for the taking in of bookes intituled Sir P: S: *Astrophell and stella.*'[113] The dedication to Francis Flower MP may have offended Cecil; textual errors perhaps angered the Sidney family. Our second quarto, printed by John Danter also for Newman, omitted the dedication and the bundle of sonnets by Samuel Daniel, Fulke Greville and others at the end of the volume; it also corrected much of the text, while maintaining the first quarto's ordering and omissions.[114] This was the book cut apart and used as waste for the binding of Lively's *Chronologie.*

Why use *Astrophel and Stella* as waste? The binder may have regarded Sidney's 1591 text as obsolete due to William Ponsonby's publication in 1598 of *The Countesse of Pembrokes Arcadia* in folio – 'a comprehensive, monumentalizing edition', in Arthur Marotti's words, which included *Astrophel and Stella.*[115] We shouldn't underestimate the degree to which, in the early modern period, a new edition was often seen to render obsolete an earlier edition, even if we today value that earlier edition as a vital text in its own right: this was true in the first century of print, when manuscripts were rendered superfluous by early printed editions,[116] and this was also the reason why the Bodleian library, on acquiring Shakespeare's Third Folio (1664), regarded their single copy of the First Folio as superfluous, selling it to the Oxford bookseller Richard Davis in 1664 in a packet of books for £24. (In 1906 the Bodleian bought it back from the magnificently named Turbutts of Ogston Hall for £3,000 with a mixture of fanfare and embarrassment.) Lively's text, printed in 1597, may well have been bound shortly after this publication, but the dismembering of a Philip Sidney volume at the time of his most intense popularity is still striking, even with a new edition just out, and raises certain paradoxes of print popularity.[117] The presence of Sidney's text as waste implies both a low cultural status (otherwise why tear up a copy?) and a high cultural status (copies were everywhere, so one torn up book wouldn't dent Sidney's presence). The popularity of a work – like Sidney's sonnets, or Erasmus' *Colloquia familiaria,* popular in many editions from 1518 and also deployed

---

[113] Edward Arber (ed.), *A Transcript of the Registers of the Company of Stationers of London 1554–1640* (London: privately printed, 1875), 5 vols, vol. I, p. 555.

[114] For textual details, see Francis X. Connor, *Literary Folios and Ideas of the Book in Early Modern England* (Basingstoke: Palgrave, 2014), pp. 23–60.

[115] Marotti, *Manuscript, Print,* p. 236.   [116] McC. Gatch, 'Fragmenta Manuscripta', 435.

[117] It is possible that these two sheets came from an imperfect copy, or one in which other sheets were damaged, which would have rendered the once-valuable book a pile of potential waste paper.

Printed Waste: 'Tatters Allegoricall' 169

as waste – might mean individual copies became expendable.[118] In a similar way, confronting the Sidneian end leaves troubles our sense of the literary canon, suggesting we might be fundamentally out of tune with Elizabethan taste; but those end leaves also confirm our sense of the 1590s, when Sidney's text was everywhere fluttering through the air. Reading the waste is like overhearing fragments of a passing literary conversation in the street in 1598 in which, reassuringly, the speakers' literary coordinates are our literary coordinates.

Is the presence of the Sidney sonnets in this copy of Lively's volume meaningful in a literary or aesthetic sense? The fact of their inclusion tells us something about a moment in binding history, and raises certain paradoxes about the popularity of Sidney's poems. But do the sonnets generate symbolic or aesthetic effects, particularly as they exist alongside Lively's *Chronologie*? If we follow D. F. McKenzie's insistence that 'forms effect meaning' – that it is 'quite impossible . . . to divorce the substance of the text on the one hand from the physical form of its presentation on the other', and that '[t]he book itself is an expressive means' – then what does this mean for printed waste?[119] How, and what, does waste signify, and does this particular instance of Sidneian waste invite or repay literary interpretation?

Although Lively's book, as a history of Persia and an attempt to establish a chronology of the world, is in many ways thematically distant from Sidney's, it is certainly possible to draw connections between waste and host at the level of the word – the kinds of connections that could be the start of a literary reading. The first three Sidney lines on the page facing Lively's title page – 'And if these things (as being thine in right) / Moue not thy heauie grace, thou shalt in mee / (Liuelier than els where *Stella* Image see' – produce a verbal and visual echo between Liuelier, the description of Stella's image in Sidney's text and Lively, the author.[120] If we linger on this, the Professor of Hebrew begins to be pulled inside the drama of the sonnet sequence, just as Stella and Astrophel become involved in Lively's Persian chronicle. Sidney uses 'liuely' four other times in his sequence, including 'Paint Woes blacke face so liuely to my sight' (158), but this opening alignment is the only capitalised instance, and is the instance that faces

---

[118] The Erasmus is used as waste in a single-volume collection of Thomas Browne, *Religio Medico*; Kenelm Digby, *Observations upon Religio Medici* (1644); and Kenelm Digby, *Observations on the 22. stanza in the 9th. canto of the 2d. book of Spencers Faery queen* (1644), Bod 8° A 7 Med. BS.
[119] D. F. McKenzie, 'The Book as an Expressive Form', in *Bibliography and the Sociology of Texts* (Cambridge, UK: Cambridge University Press, 1999), pp. 9–30, 12–13; D. F. McKenzie, 'Typography and Meaning: the Case of William Congreve', in *Making Meaning: Printers of the Mind and Other Essays* (Amherst: University of Massachusetts Press, 2002), pp. 199–236, 200.
[120] The second open bracket is an error of the 1591 text.

Lively's name: so the coincidence is at least noticeable.¹²¹ At the end of the book, the juxtaposition of Lively's errata list and the waste of Sidney's sonnet 21 may also suggest connections, as can be seen when the texts are laid out in parallel:

Gentle Reader, I am to desire thee to amend with thy pen these escapes, which in my absence, and through the Printers haste haue happened, which I haue here under set downe, being such as doe peruert the sence: as for other of lesse moment in the letters omitted, or changed in proper names, or otherwise, I remit to thy fauourable correction.	Your words, my friend, right healthfull caustics, blame My young mind marred, whom love doth windlass so That mine own writings like bad servants show, My wits, quick in vain thoughts, in virtue lame
Host errata list	Sidneian waste

Both passages address an unnamed reader in somewhat intimate terms, and provide a description of the way in which writing, under pressure, can reveal the wrong things. They are addresses about different kinds of mistake.

An eminently sensible response to these kinds of readings is to dismiss them: to object that these connections are coincidences, chance consequences of the book making process, and thus not expressive of any literary intent on the part of the agents of production.¹²² The presence of the single line 'But straight I saw motions of lightnings grace' as a shard emerging from the gutter at right angles to 'A Chronologicall Table of the Greeke Olympiads', is certainly affecting, but it is affecting in the way that any chance concatenation – like the juxtapositions created by switching randomly between radio stations – can be powerful. The two most persuasive critical voices arguing for the need to interpret material form do not do away with, but disperse, the category of intention. As I briefly described in the introduction, Jerome McGann argues that a 'double helix of perceptual codes', both bibliographical and linguistic, work to secure a literary work's effects, and in doing so, McGann makes a powerful case for the signifying capacity of the material text. But the examples McGann rehearses are

---

¹²¹ See also 'Effects of liuely heat' (sonnet 8); '*Morpheus*, the liuely sonne of deadly Sleepe' (32); and 'Prints his owne liuely forme in rudest braine' (98).
¹²² A question considered in Zachary Lesser, *Hamlet after Q1: An Uncanny History of the Shakespearean Text* (Philadelphia: University of Pennsylvania Press, 2014), p. 15, where Lesser discusses, and rejects, the symbolic power of the fact that, due to a missing final page, the copy of *Hamlet* (Q1) rediscovered in 1823 ended with the hanging catchword, 'Enter'. Such a feature is, Lesser writes, only an 'accidental by-product of the materiality' of book production.

overwhelmingly instances where the materiality of the text is to be taken on its (multiply-)intended, historicised terms: that is, material features such as the marginal glosses in 'The Rime of the Ancient Mariner' (1816), or the typeface and paper in William Morris' *The Story of the Glittering Plain* (1891), are to be read in terms of the intentions of the book makers.[123] D. F. McKenzie's sociology of texts functions similarly: the process of book production, now understood as not author-centric but involving a society of characters, results in texts whose material features signify in 'a complex structure of meanings which embraces every detail of its formal and physical presentation in a specific historical context'.[124] But McKenzie reads those material signs rather as he reads literary content, in terms of the meanings intended by the agents of making and, more broadly, by their historical moment. The shift is not from intention to anti-intention, but rather from intention as author-centric and singular, to intention as spread across several agents. The nature of the hermeneutic act hasn't fundamentally changed: bibliographical codes, like linguistic codes, have an interpretative urgency and liveliness that stems from a founding intent, however difficult that may be to recover.

All of which supports that notion that reading waste for symbolic meaning is to misunderstand the historicised textual object we are looking at. It may be the case that we are, today, inclined to notice such properties, and to feel them interpretatively rich, because of the rise since about 1960 of the artist's book, in which the physical form of the codex is manipulated in surprising ways, particularly through the carving of the book into a new form that relates to the contents (Brian Dettmer's *Life and Opinions of Tristram Shandy, Gentleman* (2014)), or the cutting or effacing of text to reveal new narratives (Jonathan Safran Foer's *Tree of Codes* (2010); Tom Phillips' *A Humument* (1966–2016)), or, more extravagantly, the converting of the physical book into a new form (Dieter Roth's *Literaturwurst* (1974)).[125] To eyes used to such objects, early modern printed waste can look strikingly like an earlier iteration of this carefully ludic materiality. But the waste effects in Lively's volume are not artistic, in the sense of being the product of skill or proficiency in creating aesthetic effects, and are therefore not responsive to literary criticism, because (this line of objection would argue) artistic effects require intention – even if criticism rightly recognises the difficulty of discerning that intention, or acknowledges the plurality of agents who might be its source (writers, printers,

---

[123] McGann, *Textual Condition*, p. 78. [124] McKenzie, 'Typography and Meaning', p. 223.
[125] For a useful survey, see Michael Hampton, *Unshelfmarked: Reconceiving the Artists' Book* (London: Uniform Books, 2015).

publishers, compositors and so on). There is of course a tradition of aleatoricism – of the use of chance in the creative process – as seen, for instance, in novels such as B. S. Johnson's *The Unfortunates* (1969), with sections to be shuffled in a random order, and in the cut-up techniques of the Dadaists of the 1920s. But these are profoundly intentionalist works where the author is deliberately exploring chance: chance is a variable playing out within the structures that the artist has created. If the literary critic's subject is the artfully made text, then the Sidneian–Lively hybrid does not conform to this category.

But there is a tension here. The example of *Astrophel and Stella* is intriguing or unsettling because in order to function as waste, Sidney's text is being asked to forget itself as text, and to become instead a merely material prop that does not signify in terms of literary content; its intended, culturally understood role in Lively's book is, exclusively, to help physically support and preserve *A true chronologie of the times of the Persian monarchie*. But that transformation from text to waste, that process of emptying out of signification, is only partially successful: there is a sort of refusal on the part of the Sidneian waste, as the poems remain legible, to conform entirely to its new role. McGann distinguished between a work's linguistic and its bibliographical codes – between what we might call content (whose chief authority is the author) and material form (whose chief authority 'normally falls to the publishing institution').[126] But printed waste complicates this opposition since waste *qua* bibliographical code had a prior life *qua* linguistic code. In instances where the waste text is still legible, and particularly in instances, like this one, where the waste text is legible and comes from a recognisable and culturally resonant text, that prior linguistic life persists, even as it is used as waste, and that remnant of a repressed symbolic meaning serves as a nagging call to interpret. The impression is of a kind of agency on the part of waste: a reluctance to die. This repression of a prior meaning that seems to return is the reason why the sudden encounter with printed waste is often uncanny. If Freud's account of the uncanny is a description of the response to the reviving of an experience that has been repressed from childhood, or that has been surmounted in man's development away from what Freud calls primitivism, printed waste is a textual-bibliographical analogue: a mix of the familiar and the strange as parts of known texts, cast aside, return in new formations.[127] As Susan Signe Morrison has noted, the etymological paradoxes of waste are such that the word signifies both that which is lacking purpose and that which is excessive: waste signifies both a poverty and an

---

[126] McGann, *Textual Condition*, pp. 66-67.
[127] Sigmund Freud, *The Uncanny*, translated by David McLintock (London: Penguin, 2003), p. 155.

excess, and this conflicting status lies behind that ambiguity about whether or not to read waste.¹²⁸ Is the Sidneian waste a literary text that has been drained of signification, or is it a waste text that stubbornly continues to signify? The felt pressure to read will vary according to where we, as readers, understand significance to lie: a literary critic is less likely to be drawn to a proclamation about the cloth trade than 'But straight I saw motions of lightnings grace'.

We might then think about printed waste as a prompt to possible readings that are raised but which need to be declined, in part out of respect for the historicised culture of the early modern book, a sense that we should read a 1597 book on its own terms, following its logic and expectations (by which poring over waste papers would be an odd thing to do), but also, more pragmatically, because those potential readings have to be declined in order for reading to proceed. As Pierre Bayard has argued, reading is always dependent on non-reading: we cannot read everything, so we select certain texts, and relegate others.¹²⁹ And while it is possible to find endless connections between texts – this is the theme of Tom Phillips' *A Humument*, and also the reason why any reading of Phillips' work can never be finished – such a state is paralysing, and intention – and its broader cultural equivalent, an historicised sense of what a book is, and how it works – are useful ways of filtering out the white noise of limitless signification. Printed waste thus prompts us to think about the pragmatics of reading: about what we do when we consume a book, where our reading stops, the limits we set, and where we look for significance.

More broadly, printed waste dramatises something important about the way writing always operates, in all periods, in relation to existing texts. Texts carry parts of other texts within themselves: new literary works necessarily contain fragments of older works, not in a material sense, but through a relationship of quotation, reference, critique, satire, emulation or influence. This was particularly so in an early modern culture in which writing so often grew out of a culture of commonplacing and, in the mid-seventeenth century, animadversion.¹³⁰ These older fragments may be concealed or foregrounded, but all works are in some sense patched together from older pieces, like Dryden's 'scatter'd Limbs of mangled

---

[128] Susan Signe Morrison, *The Literature of Waste* (Basingstoke: Palgrave, 2015), p. 8.
[129] Pierre Bayard, *How to Talk about Books You Haven't Read*, trans. Jeffrey Mehlman (London: Granta, 2007).
[130] Knight, *Bound to Read*, p. 94.

Poets'. Classical and early modern theorists of imitation drew on metaphors of digestion to describe the relationship between source and product: like bees, Seneca wrote, 'who flit about and cull the flowers that are suitable for producing honey, and then arrange and assort in their cells all that they have brought in ... [writers] ought to ... sift whatever we have gathered from a varied course of reading ... [and] so blend those several flavours into one delicious compound that, even though it betrays its origin, yet it nevertheless is clearly a different thing from that whence it came.'[131] Seneca posits a fine balance between revealing and concealing one's debt to a source – a text should somehow nod to its origins, but also be something new – but for Ben Jonson, good writing means 'the copy may be mistaken for the principal', and imperfect digestion of a source – which means a relationship of borrowing that is still visible – is like a bad meal: 'as a creature that swallows what it takes in crude, raw, or indigested.'[132] On these terms, legible printed waste, imperfectly integrated into the material form of the larger volume, has a host coughing and spluttering and, by materialising a relationship of borrowing, indebtedness and fragmentation that always occurs on the level of discourse, reminding us of the fiction of the autonomous work.

This final emphasis on the myth of the autonomous work – or, to put that another way, on the always-networked nature of writing – may well have been in Aubrey's mind as he scribbled the note that his *Life* should 'be interponed as a sheet of wast-paper only in the binding of a Booke.' As a metaphor, Aubrey's interponing suggests both modest effacement (obscurity besides another, bolder work) and permanence (the host text becoming an archive in which the waste persists); a sense of low cultural stock (the *Life* is unwanted) and also a sense of cultural presence (the *Life* is available for use). Figuring one's *Life* as waste suggests not only that the present moment is not one in which that *Life* can flourish, but also – because, as Aubrey knew, regimes of value change – that there may be a future when the *Life* finds its audience. But perhaps most of all for Aubrey, figuring one's *Life* as waste is an expression of a form of companionship, a commitment by Aubrey to enable other people's writing, to bring other books into being, to let other voices on different subjects speak.

---

[131] Seneca, *Epistulae morales*, no. 84, 3–6, in G. W. Pigman III, 'Versions of Imitation in the Renaissance', in *Renaissance Quarterly* 33.1 (Spring 1980), 1–32, 5.

[132] Ben Jonson, *Timber: or discoveries made upon men and matter*, in Brian Vickers, *English Renaissance Literary Criticism* (Oxford: Clarendon Press, 2003), p. 585. For early modern imitation, see Pigman III, 'Versions of Imitation'; Thomas M. Greene, *The Light in Troy: Imitation and Discovery in Renaissance Poetry* (New Haven: Yale University Press, 1982); and Knight, *Bound to Read*, pp. 90–94.

Conclusion

What was a book in early modern England? In *Material Texts in Early Modern England*, I hope to have combined the methods of book history and literary criticism to analyse the ways in which sixteenth- and seventeenth-century books were stranger, richer things than scholars have previously imagined. I have done this by attending to features of bibliographical culture that were real and significant but which have been under-examined by past critics: the paradoxical culture of knives and scissors in which books were cut up not in a spirit of censorship but as a form of careful reading; the link between books and book destruction in a culture which valued the transience of print; the centrality of error to print and the cultural and literary richness of mistakes; and the recycling of older, often lost printed texts in the bodies of new books, in the form of printed waste. In *Material Texts in Early Modern England*, I aim to recover these bibliographical cultures, and therefore modify our sense of what a book might be; and I explore the relationship between the book as material text and the book in the literary imagination. How did writers respond to the book as cut, burnt, error-filled, and recycled – writers including George Herbert, Henry Vaughan, Margaret Cavendish, John Taylor, Thomas Nashe, John Milton, Edmund Waller, Thomas Watson, 'Martin Marprelate', John Aubrey, John Dryden and Ben Jonson?

In doing so, in *Material Texts in Early Modern England* I continue a tradition of work that has developed since the 1999 publication of D. F. McKenzie's *Bibliography and the Sociology of Texts*, and which aims to put the study of the materiality of texts into lively dialogue with literary interpretation. Indeed, since attention to the material form has grown so pervasive among literary critics that there is a danger it will become naturalised as a seemingly inevitable and therefore under-interrogated set of interests and questions, it is worth offering a brief taxonomy of some of the central traits of this recent field of study, at least as I understand it, particularly as it contrasts with older traditions of bibliographical criticism:[1]

1. Most fundamentally, the study of material texts brings together separate but related disciplinary strands by combining, or at least by taking some of its bearings from, bibliography (the study of books as physical objects), the history of the book (the history of the creation, dissemination and reception of texts) and textual criticism (the analysis of different versions of a text as it was transmitted; an engagement with texts as things that exist in multiple forms).

2. Noting that the printed book was only one of many forms for conveying text in the early modern period, and that the history of the book has been both too print-centric and too bookish, scholars of material texts have, in the spirit of a corrective, explored manuscript culture and non-book forms (such as broadside ballads), and also, and in particular, the various kinds of bibliographical hybridity that characterised early modern textual culture: printed books with handwritten annotations;[2] multiple short texts bound together to produce large composite volumes, or *sammelbände*; texts patched together through a process of cutting up and reassembling, a kind of collage before that term was available.[3]

3. An investment in the transmission and dissemination of texts between different reading communities and across different media has led scholars to reconfigure the printed text (particularly the play book and the verse collection) as a collection of pieces-in-motion: less a stable whole than a collection of parts that might be crumbled and organised into new forms.[4] Prologues and epilogues might circulate separately from the rest of the text; a culture of commonplacing encouraged readers to excise sententious lines from printed literary works.

4. This interest in what we might call the social lives of texts has led critics to explore the reception of texts by examining signs of book use and creative misuse, including marginal annotations; and to attempt to

---

[1] For a comparable survey of past and recent work on material texts, see Brayman, Lander and Lesser (eds), *Book in History*, pp. 10–14.
[2] William Sherman, *Used Books: Marking Readers in Renaissance England* (Philadelphia: University of Pennsylvania Press, 2007).
[3] Juliet Fleming, William Sherman and Adam Smyth (eds), 'Renaissance Collage: Towards a New History of Reading', special edition of *Journal of Medieval and Early Modern Studies* 45.3 (2015).
[4] Tiffany Stern, *Documents of Performance in Early Modern England* (Cambridge UK: Cambridge University Press, 2009).

bring to critical prominence the multiple agencies involved in the production of literary texts: not only authors, but publishers, scribes, print shop workers (compositors, pressmen, correctors), binders and booksellers.[5]

5. Scholars have also, in recent years, shifted away from familiar and potentially Whiggish arguments about the modernity of print to emphasise links and continuities between medieval and early modern textual cultures.

6. Material texts scholarship is often concerned with the gap between the assumptions and discourses of modern bibliography, and early modern ways of imagining, producing and consuming texts: recent work often begins by noting the ways in which modern, often nineteenth-century archival or bibliographical categories serve to occlude or inhibit a more sympathetically historicised methodology. The coherence of the bound text, for example – that assumption that the single literary work should have a stable and autonomous material form – has been the subject of much critical investigation,[6] sustained in the present volume.

7. Perhaps most urgently of all, work on material texts aims to combine an attention to the material and the literary: to the text as linguistic structure, and the text as material thing.[7] It does this in many ways, but we might pick out three tendencies:

    (a) taking seriously the signifying potential of the materiality of texts: the degree to which aspects of a text such as format, typography, binding, even 'the very disposition of space itself, have an expressive function in conveying meaning'[8]

    (b) noting that early modern literature is awash with bibliographical metaphors ('this man's brow, like to a title-leaf, / Foretells the nature of a tragic volume' (Shakespeare, *Henry IV Part 2*, 1.1.60–1)), and thus reading literary works as texts frequently and self-reflexively engaged in describing, considering, contesting or ironising their material forms

---

[5] Bradin Cormack and Carla Mazzio, *Book Use, Book Theory 1500–1700* (Chicago: University of Chicago Library, 2005); Marta Straznicky, *Shakespeare's Stationers: Studies in Cultural Bibliography* (Philadelphia: University of Pennsylvania Press, 2012).
[6] Knight, *Bound to Read*.
[7] Leah Price, 'From The History of a Book to "The History of the Book"', in *Representations*, 108 (2009), 120–138, 120.
[8] McKenzie, *Bibliography*, p. 17.

(c) analysing the consequences of a literary work being conveyed with particular material traits:[9] thinking about the difference it makes that Edmund Spenser's *Faerie Queene* (1590) was printed in quarto; or that William Davenant's epic poem *Gondibert* (1651) appeared with cancelled and replacement pages; or that Margaret Cavendish added her own post-print handwritten corrections and paste-in slips to many of her books; or that some copies of John Milton's *Paradise Lost* (1667) open not with 'Of Man's first disobedience and the fruit / Of that forbidden tree', but an errata list of 13 printing mistakes ('for *lost* r.[ead] *last*') and the injunction that '[o]ther literal faults the Reader of himself may Correct'.

A final brief case study can illuminate these tendencies, and also show how much more work remains to be done.

The cry and reuenge of blood is an account of the murder by an individual named Norton of three members of the Leeson family. It was written by Thomas Cooper '[f]rom my house in White-crosse streete this 24. of August 1620', drawing on notes Cooper made during the trial at Bury assizes; it carries a dedication to Sir Henry Montague, Lord Chief Justice of England, and was printed by Nicholas Okes for John Wright, 'dwelling in Pie-corner', in 1620. The text is richly informed by the language of theatre, but it is also a clergyman's work of theodicy: Cooper describes the details of this murder in order to assert 'the Prouidence of God in permitting and ordering such horrible wickednesse ... For the confusion of the Atheist: And [for the] ... awakening of the secure and prophane Christians.'[10] This quarto text's title page has a large woodcut illustration of the crime (the murderer urged on by a satanic figure), and the work is designed to display 'the nature and haynousnesse of wilfull murther' which this particular case, 'a most lamentable history thereof, committed at Halsworth in High Suffolk', exemplifies.

The experience of ordering up the two copies of this text held at the Bodleian Library richly expresses the capacity of early modern print culture to confound modern bibliographical expectations. Requesting shelfmark Bodleian 4° G 29 Art brings to one's desk a limp vellum binding that, upon

---

[9] Roger Chartier, *The Author's Hand and the Printer's Mind*, translated by Lydia G. Cochrane (Cambridge, UK: Polity Press, 2014).

[10] Thomas Cooper, *The cry and reuenge of blood: Expressing the nature and haynousnesse of wilfull murther. Exemplified in a most lamentable history thereof, committed at Halsworth in High Suffolk, and lately conuicted at Bury assize, 1620* (1620), sig. B.

opening, encloses not one but six titles. This is a sammelband, an anthology of related texts, created by a reader who bought unbound texts with some governing thematic or generic consistency in mind, and gathered them into a single volume: a characteristic mode of textual organisation richly described by Jeffrey Todd Knight.[11] It is not hard to discern an organising logic behind most of this unique collection: Cooper's *The cry and reuenge of blood* is the final text in a corpus that includes *Newes from Perin in Cornwall of a most bloody and vn-exampled murther ... committed by a father on his owne sonne* (1618); *The triumphs of Gods revenege [sic] against the crying, and execrable sinne of murther* (1621); *A pittilesse mother. That ... murthered two of her owne children at Acton* (1616); and *A horrible creuel and bloudy murther, committed at Putney ... vpon the body of Edward Hall* (1614) – although the first text in the collection, *A booke of sundry draughtes, principaly serving for glasiers* (1615), doesn't immediately fit into this thematic order.

We were expecting one text, but we got six, and this raises questions about the relationship between Cooper's murder account and its other five partners in crime. The edges of Cooper's work dissolve, or at least they become a little more permeable, and the bibliographical form in our hand – the sammelband – inclines us, probably, to read intertextually, with a sense that a modern preoccupation with the autonomy of the literary work, of its excluding bibliographical and aesthetic perimeters, doesn't serve us well if we are reading this particular variety of book.

Ordering up Bodleian Vet. A2 f.405 brings to one's desk something stranger still. What appears is not a book at all, but a box: a leather-covered wooden box, with a separate lid, measuring about 13 by 9 cm, with slits in the leather suggesting it was once attached to a belt. This box's interior has been lined with portions of leaves F3v (the lid) and E3 (the main box) of Cooper's *The cry and reuenge of blood* (Figure 23): an instance of *découpage*, the decorating of an object with paper cut-outs, *avant la lettre*. (The *OED*'s first usage of *découpage* – from the French *découper*, to cut up or out – comes from a 1960 account of the decoration of seventeenth-century fans, suggesting the lively early modern presence of a practice with a twentieth-century name.) The date of the box isn't clear, but the printed waste suggests some time around 1620. The cataloguer's card that accompanies the box records, in the dead-pan register of bibliography, that this text-object was '[d]iscovered in the Rare Books Section F-Floor dump in 1995'.

---

[11] Knight, *Bound to Read*.

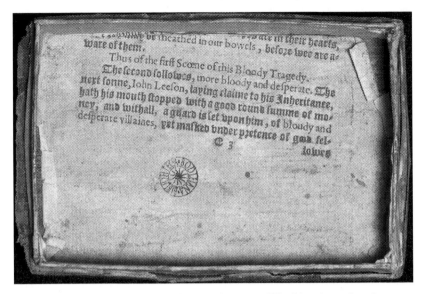

Figure 23 Thomas Cooper, *The cry and reuenge of blood* (1620), as a box. By permission of the Bodleian Library (Vet. A2 f.405)

Bodleian Vet. A2 f.405 is a box, but it is also a text, albeit a text in which the status of the printed words is not clear. Should we read the parts of the murder story we can see? Should we locate the larger whole from which these parts come? What is the relationship between text and box? Does the genre and subject matter of the text – a conflation of the devotional and the sensational – suggest something of the original purpose of the box, or is this a chance collision, expressive of nothing more than the waste paper to hand? Where is the rest of this copy of Cooper's text? How does one read a box?

Bodleian Vet. A2 f.405 is not a book, but it is one way in which Cooper's *The cry and reuenge of blood*, or at least parts of it (Figure 24), was conveyed into the world. It is thus a reminder of what we might call the regularly exceptional nature of early modern print culture, and a warning that bibliographical scholarship that doesn't observe this kind of diversity represents a failure of both archival rigour and of the imagination. We need to look beyond the book as that form is traditionally defined: to the cut-up-and-reordered gospels; the manuscript commonplace book containing fragments of print; the broadside pinned to the tavern wall; the printed waste composed from older texts; the coffer lined with a nativity

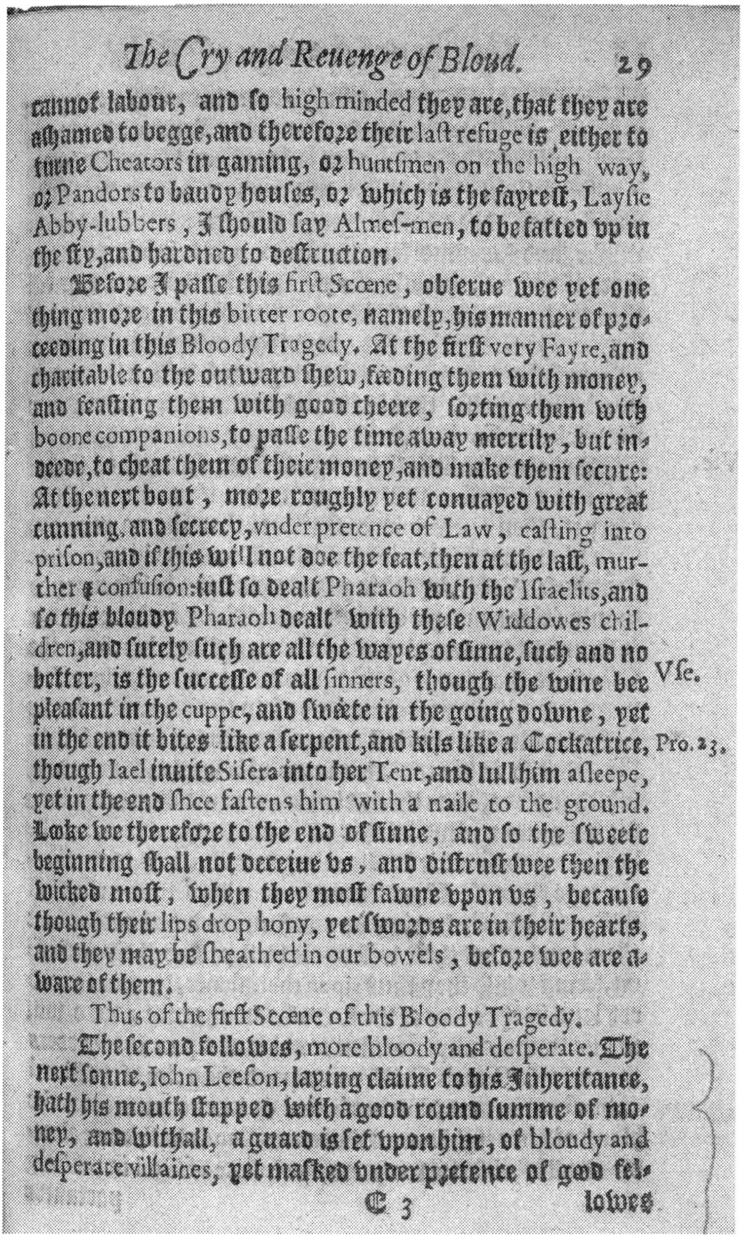

The Cry and Reuenge of Bloud. 29

cannot labour, and so high-minded they are, that they are ashamed to begge, and therefore their last refuge is, either to turne Cheators in gaming, or huntsmen on the high way, or Pandors to bawdy houses, or which is the fayrest, Lazie Abby-lubbers, I should say Almes-men, to be fatted vp in the sty, and hardned to destruction.

Before I passe this first Sceene, obserue wee yet one thing more in this bitter roote, namely, his manner of proceeding in this Bloody Tragedy. At the first very Fayre, and charitable to the outward shew, feeding them with money, and feasting them with good cheere, sorting them with boone companions, to passe the time away merrily, but in deede, to cheat them of their money, and make them secure: At the next bout, more roughly yet conuayed with great cunning, and secrecy, vnder pretence of Law, casting into prison, and if this will not doe the feat, then at the last, murther & confusion: iust so dealt Pharaoh with the Israelits, and so this bloudy Pharaoh dealt with these Widdowes children, and surely such are all the wayes of sinne, such and no better, is the successe of all sinners, though the wine bee pleasant in the cuppe, and sweete in the going downe, yet in the end it bites like a serpent, and kils like a Cockatrice, though Iael inuite Sisera into her Tent, and lull him asleepe, yet in the end shee fastens him with a naile to the ground. Looke wee therefore to the end of sinne, and so the sweete beginning shall not deceiue vs, and distrust wee then the wicked most, when they most fawne vpon vs, because though their lips drop hony, yet swords are in their hearts, and they may be sheathed in our bowels, before wee are aware of them. Vse.

Pro. 23.

Thus of the first Sceene of this Bloody Tragedy.

The second followes, more bloody and desperate. The next sonne, Iohn Leeson, laying claime to his Inheritance, hath his mouth stopped with a good round summe of money, and withall, a guard is set vpon him, of bloudy and desperate villaines, yet masked vnder pretence of good fellowes

E 3

Figure 24 Thomas Cooper, *The cry and reuenge of blood* (1620), sig. E3. By permission of the Folger Shakespeare Library (N867)

print;[12] the parcel wrapped in pages ('John Rawlinson ... *rescued* from the grocers, chandlers, etc., many rare documents');[13] the confiscated or unwanted sheets overprinted with patterns to produce damask papers, like the wallpaper discovered in Christ's College, Cambridge in 1911 made from an unwanted indulgence of Pope Julius II and a discarded poem on Henry VII's death;[14] the printed title page 'in cleft-sticks, advanced to make calls';[15] the engraving printed on ivory-laid paper to be cut out and worn as a headpiece, or the stag hunt etching designed to serve as a fan;[16] or, more extravagantly still, the printed birth girdle: a broadside amulet roll serving to safeguard women in childbirth, printed by Wynkyn de Worde in about 1520 and based on earlier manuscript models 'wrapped around a woman's body, with the strategic placement of particular prayers against her womb'.[17]

Material Texts in Early Modern England is an attempt to enrich our sense of the early modern book, and one of its happy conclusions is that sixteenth- and seventeenth-century print culture, in its teeming, strange fullness, awaits still further work.

---

[12] Suzanne Karr Schmidt, *Altered and Adorned: Using Renaissance Prints in Daily Life* (New Haven and London: Yale University Press, 2011), p. 58.
[13] Holbrook Jackson, *The Anatomy of Bibliomania* (Urbana and Chicago: The University of Illinois Press, 2001), pp. 130–131.
[14] Juliet Fleming, 'Damask Papers', in *The Elizabethan Top Ten: Defining Print Popularity in Early Modern England*, ed. Andy Kesson and Emma Smith (Farnham: Ashgate, 2013), pp. 179–191.
[15] Ben Jonson, Epigram III, 'To My Bookseller'.   [16] Schmidt, *Altered and Adorned*, pp. 51–54.
[17] Joseph J. Gwara and Mary Morse, 'A Birth Girdle Printed by Wynkyn de Worde', in *The Library*, 7th series, 13.1 (2012), 33–62, 37.

Appendix: Sample Instances of Printed Waste

Host[1]	Printed waste	Location
Bertrandus de Turre, *Sermones quadragesimales epistolares Bertrandi: Sermones epistolares de sanctis* (Strasburg: s.n., 1501–2)	Johannes Hamman, *Breviarium Saresberiense* (Venice: Johannes Hamman?, 1494)	Lambeth Palace Library H1756.(B3)
Mantuanus Baptista, *Parthenice prima f. Baptiste Mantuani Carmellitæ* (n.p., 1513)[2]	1. *Two short treatises, against the orders of the begging friars, compiled by that famous doctour of the Church, and preacher of Gods word John Wickliffe* (Oxford: Joseph Barnes, 1608) 2. Thomas James, *An apologie for Iohn Wickliffe* (Oxford: Joseph Barnes, 1608)	Christ Church College, Oxford D.2.1.18
The workes of Geffray [sic] *Chaucer newly printed with dyuers workes which were neuer in print before* (Thomas Godfray, 1532)	unidentified edition of *Sermones Dominicales* (German?, ca. 1500?)	Balliol College, Oxford, 525 c 11
Johann Brentz, *In Exodum Mosi Commentarius* (Halae Suevorum: Petri Brubachii, 1539)	Jaspar Laet, *Almanack and pronostication. of Iaspar Laet. Of the yare, of our Lord God. M.D.XLIIII* (s.n., 1544)	Lambeth Palace Library E1245.B7
William Tyndale, *Newe testament of the last translacion* (Thomas Petit, 1548)	Latin missal printed in red and black	Lincoln College Oxford, N.1.4 SR I

---

[1] Place of publication is London unless otherwise noted.
[2] Worldcat records a date of 1507, and a preliminary leaf is dated such, but the final colophon is dated 1513. Thanks for David Stumpp for helping with this.

(cont.)

Host	Printed waste	Location
The Booke of The Common Prayer (Edward Whitchurch, 1549)	Alphonsus Laet, *An Almanack and Pronosticacion* [sic] *for the yeare of oure Lorde M.D. and xlviii* ([S. Mierdman? for] Richard Jugge, 1548)	Lambeth Palace Library H5145.A2 (1549)
A Description of Mary's Wedding to the Dauphin (Edinburgh: J. Scot?, 1558)	David Lindsay, *Ane dialog betuix Experience and ane courteour off the miserabyll estait of the warld* (Edinburgh: J. Scot, 1559)	Lambeth Palace Library ZZ.1554.8
Divi Caecilii Cypriani Episcopi Carthagiensis [Works of Cyprian, Bishop of Carthage] (Rome: Manutius, 1563)	John Davies, *Microcosmos. The discovery of the little world* (Oxford: Joseph Barnes, 1603)	Exeter College, Oxford 9I 1563.2
Cicero, *Marcus Tullius Ciceroes three bookes of duties to Marcus his sonne, tourned out of Latine into English, by Nicolas Grimald* (Thomas Este, 1596)	Giovanni Boccaccio, *De casibus virorum illustrium*, book 5, unidentified edition	Folger STC 5286 copy 1
Edward Lively, *A true chronologie of the times of the Persian monarchie, and after to the destruction of Ierusalem by the Romanes* (Felix Kingston for Thomas Man, John Porter and Rafe Jackson, 1597)	Philip Sidney, *Astrophel and Stella* (John Danter for Thomas Newman, 1591)	Bod J-J Sidney 173
Shakespeare, *A pleasant conceited comedie called, Loues labors lost* (William White for Cutbert Burby, 1598)	Ships' bill of landing, eighteenth-century (partly legible text includes 'and are to be delivered in the like good Order and well-conditioned... the Danger of the Seas only excepted...')	Folger STC 22294 copy 3
Antonio Possevino, *Antonii Posseuini Mantuani, Societis Iesu Bibliotheca selecta de ratione studiorum: ad disciplinas, & ad salutem omnium gentium procurandam*	John Davies, *Microcosmos. The discovery of the little world* (Oxford: Joseph Barnes, 1603)	Merton College, Oxford 82.I.5

Appendix 185

(cont.)

Host	Printed waste	Location
(Venice: Altobellum Salicatium, 1603)		
Isidore of Pelusium, *De interpretatione divinae scripturae epistolarum* (Heidelberg: Ex officina Commeliniana, 1605)	King James Bible, II Maccabees	Folger BR65.I8 D4 1605 Cage
John Cowell, *The interpreter: or Booke containing the signification of words* (Cambridge: John Legate, 1607)	Elizabethan proclamation (1585?) concerning the cloth trade (legible text includes 'paine of forfeiture of all such Clothes made ouer and aboue the said length')	Folger STC 5900 copy 1
Francisco Suarez, *Commentaria ac disputationes in primam partem divi Thomae, de deo uno & trino* (Moguntiæ: Ex officina typographica Balthasari Lippij, sumptibus Hermanni Mylij Birckmanni, 1607)	John Davies, *Microcosmos. The discovery of the little world* (Oxford: Joseph Barnes, 1603)	Magdalen College, Oxford i.5.6
Petri Berchorii Pictauiensis ordinis D. Benedicti Opera omnia totam S. Scripturae, morum, naturae historia[m] complectentia (Antwerp: Ioannem Keerbergium, 1609)	William Basse, *Great Brittaines Svnnes-set, bewailed with a shower of teares* (Oxford: Joseph Barnes, 1613)	Christ Church College, Oxford e.3.8
John Boys, *An exposition of al the principall Scriptures vsed in our English liturgie* (Felix Kingston for Martin Clerk, 1609), bound with nine other texts	William Basse, *Great Brittaines Svnnes-set, bewailed with a shower of teares* (Oxford: Joseph Barnes, 1613)	Lincoln College, Oxford N.1.22
Lancelot Andrewes, *The copie of the sermon preached on Good-Friday before the Kings Maiestie* (Robert Barker, 1610)	Glossed commentary on the Book of Chronicles, Chapter 38.5	Folger STC 598.2 copy 1

186   *Appendix*

(cont.)

Host	Printed waste	Location
John Donne, *Pseudo-martyr* (William Stansby for Walter Burre, 1610)	1. Latin catalogue of books 2. Latin table relating to climate	St John's College, Oxford N.4.34
Sancti Ephraem Syri, Patris et scriptoris ecclesiae antiquissimi et dignissimi (Cologne: Arnoldum Quentelium, 1616)	Thomas James, *Catalogus librorum Bibliothecae, quam Thomas Bodleius in academia Oxoniensi instituit* (Oxford: Joseph Barnes, 1605)	All Souls College, Oxford SR.73.h.3
Philippe de Mornay, trans. Philip Sidney and Arthur Golding, *A worke concerning the trunesse of Christian religion: against, atheists, epicures, paynims, Iewes, mahumetists, and other infidels* (George Purslowe, 1617)	Latin prose text, running title *De testamētis* [i.e., 'of testaments', the fifth part of the Digests or Pandects of Roman law], late c15/early c16	Bod 4° M 52 Th
Franciscus Sanchez, *In Ecclesiasten commentarium* (Barcelona: s.n., 1619)	Cicero, *De Officiis* from *De Officiis, Cato Major* (Deventer: Richard Paffraet, ca. 1480–5)	Bod BB 12(1) Th
Petrus de Arrubal, *Commentariorum, Ac Disputationum in Primam Partem Diui Thomæ Tomus Primus* (Madrid: s.n., 1619)	John Mayer, *The English catechisme explained* (Augustus Mathewes for John Marriot, 1623)	Bod A.20.17.Th
Francis Bacon, *The historie of the raigne of King Henry the Seuenth* (William Stansby for Matthew Lownes, and William Barret, 1622)	*King James Bible* (1620), octavo, Matthew 22, 23, 24, 27, 28	St Edmund Hall, Oxford AA 32
John Downame, *A Guide to Godlynesse* (F. Kingston for E. Weuer and W. Bladen, 1622)	Cicero, *De Officiis, Cato Major* (Deventer: Richard Paffraet, ca. 1480–5)	Bod C 18. 11 Th; waste now removed
William Shakespeare, *Comedies, histories, & tragedies* (Isaac Jaggard and Edward Blount, 1623)	Illegible English black-letter prose	Newberry Library Vault Case Oversize YS 01
William Shakespeare, *Comedies, histories, & tragedies* (Isaac Jaggard and Edward Blount, 1623)	Illegible English ledger, c18?	Folger First Folio number 41

(cont.)

Host	Printed waste	Location
William Shakespeare, *Comedies, histories, & tragedies* (Isaac Jaggard and Edward Blount, 1623)	Cicero, *Cato Major* from *De Officiis, Cato Major* (Deventer: Richard Paffraet, ca. 1480–5)	Bod Arch. G c.7
William Cowper, *Workes* (John Budge, 1623)	Cicero, *De Officiis* from *De Officiis, Cato Major* (Deventer: Richard Paffraet, ca. 1480–5)	Bod C 2.3 Th
Philip Sidney, *The Countesse of Pembrokes Arcadia* (William Stansby, Humphrey Lownes and Robert Young for Simon Waterson, 1627)	Latin religious text, hand rubricated	All Souls College, Oxford, pp. 4, 13
John Taylor, *All the vvorkes of Iohn Taylor the water-poet: Beeing sixty and three in number* (John Beale, Elizabeth Allde, Bernard Alsop and Thomas Fawcet for James Boler, 1630)	Hugh Plat, *The Garden of Eden, or, An accurate description of all flowers and fruits now growing in England* (William Leake, 1653)	St John's College, Oxford Phi.2.46
John Donne, *Poems, by J. D.: VVith elegies on the authors death* (Miles Flesher for John Marriot, 1633), bound with Phineas Fletcher, *The Purple Island, or The Isle of Man* (Cambridge: Thomas Buck and Roger Daniel, 1633)	William Ames, *De conscientia et ejus jure vel casibus* (many editions from 1630, printed in Amsterdam and Oxford)	All Souls College, Oxford pp. 16.13(1)
Michael Walther, *Officina Biblica noviter adaperta* (Lepizig: Gregorius Ritzsch for Johannis Hallervordt, 1636)	1. William Shakespeare, *King Lear* (William Jaggard for Thomas Pavier, 1619) 2. unidentified Latin philosophical compendium (running heads *De Politica* and *De Ethica*) 3. Thomas Ridley, *A view of the civile and ecclesiasticall law* (Oxford: William Turner, 1634)	Bod MM4Th; *Lear* now removed as Bod. Vet. A2 e.504

(cont.)

Host	Printed waste	Location
Philip Sidney, *The Countesse of Pembrokes Arcadia* (Robert Young and Thomas Harper for J. Waterson, R. Young and T. Downes, 1638)	Biblical genealogies	Merton College, Oxford 34.K.23
Thomas Browne, *A true and full coppy of . . . Religio medici* (Andrew Crooke, 1645), bound with Kenelm Digby, *Observations on the 22. stanza in the 9th. canto of the 2d. book of Spencers Faery queen* (Daniel Frere, 1644)	Erasmus, *Colloquia familiaria* (many editions)	Bod 8° A 7 Med. BS
John Donne, *Biathanatos* (Humphrey Moseley, 1648)	Edmund Calamy, *The noble-mans patterne of true and reall thankfulnesse presented in a sermon preached before the Right Honourable House of Lords* (G. M. for Christopher Meredith, 1643)	Queen's College, Oxford UU. b.4552
Libert Froiodmont, *Philosophiæ Christianæ de anima libri quatuor* (Louvain: Hieronymi Nempaei, 1649)	1. Edward Symmons, *A loyall subjects beliefe, or, A theologicall discourse wherein is proved, that regall or monarchicall povver is not of humane, but of divine right* (Oxford: William Webb, 1647) 2. *Divine truths discovered. Being the substance of all the most remarkeable discourses that hath beene published* (Oxford: s.n., 1647)	St Edmund Hall, Oxford 4° E 18(2)
Robert Sanderson, *Fourteen sermons heretofore preached* (Roger Norton for Henry Seile, 1657)	*A Discourse presented to those who seeke the reformation of the Church of England wherein is shewed that the new church discipline is daungerous both to religion, and also to the whole state* (W. W. and J. B., 1642)	Merton College Oxford, 92. I.20(1)

(cont.)

Host	Printed waste	Location
George Hickes, *The Case of Infant-Baptism* (Thomas Basset, Benjamin Tooke and F. Gardiner, 1683)	Justinian's Institutes (Ulrich Gering and Berthold Rembolt: Paris, 1503)	Lambeth Palace Library G813. A2H5
R. B., *The Divine Banquet: or Sacramental Devotions. Consisting of Morning and Evening Prayers, Contemplations and Hymns* (N. Crouch, 1711)	printed form (including printed text 'Day of [blank] is appointed for hearing Appeals, within this …')	Bod Vet. A4 f.2337

Bibliography

Primary Works

Manuscripts

Bodleian Library

  Ashmole 781
  Library Records e.9
  Wood 106

British Library

  Add. MS 4900
  Add. MS 37719
  C.23.e.4
  C.40.m.9
  C.40.m.10
  C.40.m.11
  Harley 5919, 5934, 5937, 5960

Folger Shakespeare Library

  Folger V.a. 391
  Folger V.a. 395
  Folger V.a. 515

Print[1]

The Academy of Pleasure (1656)
Allott, Robert. *England's Parnassus* (1600)
Andrewes, Lancelot. *Scala coeli: Nineteen sermons concerning prayer* (1611)

---

[1] Place of publication is London unless otherwise stated.

Bibliography

A Manual of the Private Devotions and Meditations of The Right Reverend Father in God Lancelot Andrews (1648)

The Arminian Nunnery (1641)

Aubrey, John. *Brief Lives with an Apparatus for the Lives of Our English Mathematical Writers*, ed. Kate Bennett (Oxford: Oxford University Press, 2015), 2 vols

Bale, John. *The Laborious Journey and Serche of Johan Leylande, for Englandes Antiquitees, Geuen of Hym as a Newe Yeares Gyfte to Kynge Henry the viii in the xxxvii Yeare of His Reygne, with Declaracyons Enlarged: By John Bale* (1549)

Bell, Thomas. *The Catholique Triumph Conteyning, a Reply to the Pretensed Answere of B.C. (a masked Iesuite)* (1610)

Bellings, Richard. *A Sixth Booke to the Countesse of Pembrokes Arcadia* (Dublin, 1624)

Blake, Stephen. *The Compleat Gardeners Practice* (1664)

Blount, Thomas. *Animadversions upon Sr. Richard Baker's Chronicle* (1672)

de Bonnefons, Nicolas. *The French Gardiner Instructing How to Cultivate All Sorts of Fruit-trees and Herbs for the Garden* (1658)

Boorde, Andrew. *The First Book of the Introduction of Knowledge* (1562)

Briggs, Henry. *Tabulæ logarithmicæ, or Two tables of logarithms* (1663)

Brinsley, John. *Ludus Literarius: Or, The Grammar Schoole* (1612)

Browne, Thomas. *Hydriotaphia, Urne-Buriall* (1658)

Bullein, William. *Bulleins Bulwarke of Defence Against All Sicknesse, Soarenesse, and Vvoundes That Doe Dayly Assaulte Mankind* (1579)

Burton, Robert. *The Anatomy of Melancholy* (1621)

The Card of Courtship (1653)

Cary, Lucius, Lord Falkland. 'An Eclogue on the Death of Ben Jonson, between Melybaus and Hylas', in *Jonsonus Virbius, or, The Memorie of Ben: Johnson* (1638), pp. 1–9

Catalogue of the Pepys Library at Magdalene College, Cambridge, gen. ed. Robert Latham, vol. III 'Prints and Drawings', part I 'General', compiled by A. W. Aspital (Cambridge: D.S. Brewer, 1980)

Cavendish, Margaret. *Orations* (1662)
 Philosophical and Physical Opinions (1663)
 CCXI Sociable Letters (1664)
 The life of ... William Cavendish (1667)
 The Description of a New World Called the Blazing-World (1668)
 Grounds of Natural Philosophy (1668)
 Plays Never before Printed (1668)

Cervantes Saavedra, Miguel de. *The Ingenious Hidalgo Don Quixote de la Mancha*, trans. by John Rutherford (London: Penguin, 2000)

Chambers, Robert. *Palestina* (1600)

Chapman, George. *The Poems of George Chapman*, ed. Phyllis Brooks Bartlett (Oxford: Oxford University Press, 1941)

Chester, John. *An Orthographie, Conteyning the Due Order and Reason, Howe to Write or Paint Thimage of Mannes Voice* (1569)

Clapham, Henoch. *An Abstract of Fayth Grounded on Moses, and Applyed to the Common Creede; Plainely and Briefly* (1606)

Cooper, Thomas. *The Cry and Reuenge of Blood: Expressing the Nature and Haynousnesse of Wilfull Murther* (1620)

Croft, Robert. *The Plea, Case, and Humble Proposals of the Truly-loyal and Suffering Officers* (1663)

Dekker, Thomas. *Satiromastix*, in *The Dramatic Works of Thomas Dekker*, 4 vols, vol. I, ed. Fredson Bowers (Cambridge, UK: Cambridge University Press, 1953)

The Wonderfull Yeare (1603)

The Diall of Princes (1557)

Dickinson, Emily. *The Gorgeous Nothings: Emily Dickinson's Envelope Poems*, ed. Marta Werner and Jen Bervin (New York: New Directions, 2013)

Donne, John. *A Sermon Vpon the XV. Verse of the XX. Chapter of the Booke of Judges* (1622)

Complete Poetry and Selected Prose, ed. John Hayward (New York: Nonesuch Press, 1929)

The Courtier's Library, or Catalogus Librorum Aulicorum incomparabilium et non vendibilium, ed. and trans. by Evelyn Mary Simpson (London: Nonesuch Press, 1930)

Douglas, Keith. *Complete Poems* (London: Faber and Faber, 2011)

Dryden, John. *The Poems of John Dryden*, ed. James Kinsley (Oxford: Clarendon Press, 1958), 4 vols

Englands Helicon (1614)

F., J. *A Sermon Preached at Ashby De-La-Zouch in the countie of Leicester: At the Funerall of the Truly Noble and Vertuous Lady Elizabeth Stanley one of the Daughters and Coheirs of the Right Honourable Ferdinand Late Earle of Derby* (1635).

Ferrar, John. *Materials for the Life of Nicholas Ferrar*, ed. Lynette R. Muir and John A. White (Leeds: Leeds Philosophical and Literary Society, 1996)

Finlay, Ian Hamilton. *Selections* (Berkeley: University of California Press, 2012)

Fitzgeffrey, Henry. *Satyres and Satyricall Epigrams* (1617)

Florio, John. *Florio His Firste Fruites Which Yeelde Familiar Speech, Merie Prouerbes, Wittie Sentences, and Golden Sayings* (1578)

Ford, Emanuel. *Parismus, Part 2* (1599)

Gil, Alexander. *Logonomia Anglica* (1619)

Goodman, Godfrey. *The Fall of Man* (1618)

Greene, Robert. *The Defence of Conny Catching* (1592)

Hakewill, George. *Apologie of the Power and Prouidence of God in the Gouernment of the World* (Oxford, 1627)

Herbert, George. *Herbert's Remains, or Sundry Pieces of That Sweet Singer, Mr. George Herbert, Containing A Priest to the Temple, or the Countrey Parson, Jacula Prudentum, &c.* (1652)

The Works of George Herbert, ed. F. E. Hutchinson (Oxford: Clarendon Press, 1941)

The English Poems of George Herbert, ed. Helen Wilcox (Cambridge, UK: Cambridge University Press, 2011)

Herrick, Robert. *The Complete Poetry of Robert Herrick*, ed. Tom Cain and Ruth Connolly, 2 vols (Oxford: Oxford University Press, 2013)

Heywood, Jasper. *The Seconde Tragedie of Seneca Entituled Thyestes* (1560)

Heywood, Thomas. *An Apologie for Actors* (1612)
  The Exemplary Lives and Memorable Acts of Nine the Most Worthy Women in the Vvorld Three Iewes. Three Gentiles. Three Christians (1640)

Hill, Geoffrey. *Broken Hierarchies: Poems 1952–2012* (Oxford: Oxford University Press, 2015)

Jonson, Ben. *The Cambridge Edition of the Works of Ben Jonson*, gen. ed. David Bevington, Martin Butler and Ian Donaldson (Cambridge, UK: Cambridge University Press, 2012), 7 vols

Josselin, Ralph. *The Family Life of Ralph Josselin: A Seventeenth-Century Clergyman*, ed. Alan Macfarlane (Cambridge, UK: Cambridge University Press, 1970)

Lavater, Ludwig. *Of ghostes and Spirites Walking by Nyght and of Strange Noyses, Crackes, and Sundry Forewarnynges* (1572)

Leutbrewer, Christophe. *Nouuelle method pour se disposer aisément à vne bonne & entiere confession de plusieurs années, en moins de deux heures; & rendre vn compte exact de toutes les fautes que l'on peut auoir commises, mesme durant toute sa vie, pourueû que l'on obserue soigneusement ce qui y est prescript* (Paris, 1658)
  Excellent et Facile Methode Pour se preparer à une Confession generale de toute sa vie (Brussels, 1721)

Lichfield, Richard. *The Trimming of Thomas Nashe* (1597)

Ludham, John. *The Practis of Preaching* (1577)

Mackenzie, George. *Aretina, or, The Serious Romance* (1660)

Marlowe, Christopher. *Doctor Faustus*, ed. David Scott Kastan (New York and London: W.W. Norton and Company, 2005)

Marprelate, Martin. *The Martin Marprelate Tracts: A Modernized and Annotated Edition*, ed. Joseph Black (Cambridge, UK: Cambridge University Press, 2008)

Mather, Samuel. *The Figures or Types of the Old Testament* (1685)

Mercator, Gerhard. *A Geographicke Description of the Regions, Countries and Kingdomes of the World* (1633)

Milles, Thomas. *The Misterie of Iniquitie* (1611)

Milton, John. *Areopagitica. A Speech of Mr. John Milton for the Liberty of Unlicenc'd Printing, To the Parlament of England* (1644)
  Paradise Regain'd (1671)
  The Major Works, ed. Stephen Orgel and Jonathan Goldberg (Oxford: Oxford University Press, 2003)

Morley, Thomas. *First Booke of Ayres* (1600)

Moxon, Joseph. *Mechanick Exercises on the Whole Art of Printing (1683–4)*, ed. Herbert Davis and Harry Carter (New York: Dover Publications, 1978)

Munday, Anthony. *A Discouerie of Edmund Campion, and His Confederates, Their Most Horrible and Traiterous Practises, Against Her Maiesties Most Royall Person* (1582)

The Mysteries of Love and Eloquence (1658)

Nashe, Thomas. *Lenten Stuffe* (1599)

   The Unfortunate Traveller and Other Works, ed. J. B. Steane (Penguin: London, 1985)

Oberndorf, Johann. *The Anatomyes of the True Physition, and Counterfeit Mountebanke* (1602)

Parker, George. *Parker's Ephemeris for the Year of Our Lord 1710* (1710)

Peacham, Henry. *The Garden of Eloquence* (1577)

Penn, William. *The Great Case of Liberty of Conscience* (1670)

Perkins, William. *A Discourse of Conscience: Wherein Is Set Downe the Nature, Properties, and Differences Thereof: As Also the Way to Get and Keepe Good Conscience* (Cambridge, 1596)

Pond, Edward. *An Almanack for the Year of Our Lord God 1696* (Cambridge, 1696)

Proctor, Robert. *A Critical Edition of the Private Diaries of Robert Proctor: The Life of a Librarian at the British Museum*, ed. J. H. Bowman (Lampeter: The Edwin Mellen Press, 2010)

Rabelais, François. *Gargantua and Pantagruel*, ed. and translated by M. A. Screech (London: Penguin, 2006)

Rainbowe, Edward. *A Sermon Preached at the Funeral of the Right Honorable Anne, Countess of Pembroke, Dorset, and Montgomery* (1677)

Record, Robert. *The Ground of Artes Teaching the Worke and Practise of Arithmetike* (1552)

Richardson, Jonathan. *Explanatory Notes and Remarks on Milton's Paradise Lost* (1734)

Rider, Cardanus. *British Merlin* (1680)

Scot, Reginald. *A Perfite Platforme of a Hoppe Garden* (1574)

A Sermon Preached at the Funeral of Mr. John Bigg (1691)

Shakespeare, William. *Sonnets*, ed. Katherine Duncan-Jones (London: Arden, 2010)

Shakespeare, William. *Arden Shakespeare Complete Works*, ed. Ann Thompson, David Scott Kastan and Richard Proudfoot (London: Bloomsbury Publishing, 2014)

Sorocold, Thomas. *Supplications of Saints: A Booke of Prayers* (1612)

Spenser, Edmund. *The Faerie Queene*, ed. A. C. Hamilton (Harlow: Pearson, 2007)

Storer, Thomas. *The Life and Death of Thomas Wolsey Cardinall Diuided into Three Parts: His Aspiring, Triumph, and Death* (1599)

Strode, William. *Concerning Death and the Resurrection, Preached in St. Maries, at Oxford* (1644)

Taylor, John. *Sir Gregory Nonsence His Newes from no Place* (1622)

   The Praise of Hemp-seed (1623)

   All the Workes (1630)

Mad Verse, Sad Verse, Glad Verse and Bad Verse (1644)
Taylor, Thomas. *The Beawties of Beth-el* (1609)
Tomkis, Thomas. *Lingua: or, The Combate of the Tongue, and the Fiue Sences for Superioritie. A Pleasant Comoedie* (1657)
Turbeville, George. *The Booke of Faulconrie or Hauking* (1575)
Urquhart, Thomas. *Ekskybalauron: or, The Discovery of a Most Exquisite Jewel* (1652)
Vaughan, Henry. *Silex Scintillans: Sacred Poems and Private Ejaculations* (1655)
Waller, Edmund. *The Poems of Edmund Waller*, ed. George Thorn-Drury (London: Routledge, 1893), 2 vols
Walton, Izaak. *The Lives of Dr. John Donne, Sir Henry Wotton, Mr. Richard Hooker, Mr. George Herbert* (1670)
Watson, Thomas. *The hekatompathia or Passionate centurie of loue* (1582)
Wharton, George. *Calendarium Carolinum* (1664)
White, John. *Briefe and Easie Almanack for This Yeare* (1650)
Wither, George. *The Scholar's Purgatory* (1625)
Wits Recreations (1640)
Wolferston, Francis. *The Three Books of Publius Ovidius Naso, De Arte Amandi* (1661)
Wood, Anthony. *Life of Anthony Wood in His Own Words*, ed. Nicholas K. Kiessling (Oxford: Bodleian Library, 2009)

Secondary Works

Allsopp, Niall. '"Lett none our Lombard author rudely blame for's righteous paine": An Annotated Copy of Sir William Davenant's *Gondibert* (1651)', in *The Library* 16.1 (2015), 24–50
Arber, Edward (ed.). *A Transcript of the Registers of the Company of Stationers of London 1554–1640* (London: privately printed, 1875), 5 vols
Asals, Heather. *Equivocal Predication: George Herbert's Way to God* (Buffalo, NY: University of Toronto Press, 1981)
Bahr, Arthur, and Alexandra Gillespie. 'Medieval English Manuscripts: Form, Aesthetics, and the Literary Text', in *The Chaucer Review* 47.4 (2013), 346–360
Barber, Tabitha, and Stacy Boldrick (eds). *Art Under Attack: Histories of British Iconoclasm* (London: Tate Publishing, 2013)
Bayard, Pierre. *How to Talk About Books You Haven't Read*, trans. Jeffrey Mehlman (London: Granta, 2007)
Bennett, Kate. 'John Aubrey, Joseph Barnes's Print-Shop and a Sham Newsletter', in *The Library* 6th series, 21.1 (March 1999), 50–58
  'John Aubrey and the Circulation of Edmund Waller's "of a Tree Cut in Paper"' in *Notes and Queries* 49 (2002), 344–345
Binns, James. 'STC Latin Books: Evidence for Printing-House Practice', in *The Library* 5th series, 32.1 (1977), 1–27
  'STC Latin Books: Further Evidence for Printing-House Practice', in *The Library* 6th series, 1.4 (1979), 347–354

Blades, William. *The Enemies of Books* (Cambridge, UK: Cambridge University Press, 1888, 2015)

Blair, Ann. 'Reading Strategies for Coping with Information Overload ca. 1550–1700,' in *Journal of History of Ideas* 64 (2003), 11–28

'Errata Lists and the Reader as Corrector', in *Agent of Change: Print Culture Studies after Elizabeth L. Eisenstein*, ed. Sabrina Alcorn Baron, Eric N. Lindquist and Eleanor F. Shevlin (Amherst: University of Massachusetts Press, 2007), pp. 21–40

Too Much to Know: Managing Scholarly Information Before the Modern Age (New Haven: Yale University Press, 2010)

Blake, Erin C., and Stuart Sillars (eds). *Extending the Book: The Art of Extra-Illustration* (Seattle: University of Washington Press, 2010)

Bland, Mark. 'Ben Jonson and the Legacies of the Past', in *Huntington Library Quarterly* 67 (2004), 371–400

Blayney, Peter W. M. 'The Publication of Playbooks', in *A New History of Early English Drama*, ed. John D. Cox and David Scott Kastan (New York: Columbia University Press, 1997), pp. 383–422

The Stationers' Company and the Printers of London, 1501–1557 (Cambridge, UK: Cambridge University Press, 2013), 2 vols

Bloom, Harold. *A Map of Misreading* (Oxford: Oxford University Press, 2003)

Boffey, Julia. *Manuscript and Print in London c. 1475–1530* (London: British Library, 2012)

Bolton, Claire M. *The Fifteenth-Century Printing Practices of Johann Zainer, Ulm, 1473–1478* (Oxford: Oxford Bibliographical Society, 2016)

Bonnard, G. A. 'Two Remarks on the Text of Milton's *Areopagitica*', in *Review of English Studies* 4.16 (1928), 434–438

Bosanquet, Eustace F. *English Printed Almanacks and Prognostications: A Bibliographical History to the Year 1600* (London: Chiswick Press, 1917)

Bowers, Fredson. 'Dryden as Laureate: The Cancel Leaf in "King Arthur"', in *Times Literary Supplement* 2671 (10 April 1953), 244

Bradshaw, Henry. *Collected Papers of Henry Bradshaw* (Cambridge, UK: Cambridge University Press, 2012)

Brown, Bill. 'Thing Theory', in *Critical Inquiry*, vol. 28, no. 1 (Autumn, 2001), 1–22

Brown, Matthew P. *The Pilgrim and the Bee: Reading Rituals and Book Culture in Early New England* (Philadelphia: University of Pennsylvania Press, 2007)

Brown, Piers. '"Hac ex consilio meo via progredieris": Courtly Reading and Secretarial Mediation in Donne's *The Courtier's Library*', in *Renaissance Quarterly* 61.3 (Fall 2008), 833–866

Burrow, Colin. 'Rancorous Old Sod', in *London Review of Books* 36.4 (20 February 2014), 11–13

Butler, George F. 'Milton's "sage and serious Poet Spencer": Error and Imitation in *The Faerie Queene* and *Areopagitica*', in *Texas Studies in Literature and Language*, 49.2 (Summer 2007), 101–124

Calè, Luisa. 'Dickens Extra-Illustrated: Heads and Scenes in Monthly Parts (The Case of "Nicholas Nickleby")', in *The Yearbook of English Studies*, 40 (2010), 8–32

Candy, Hugh C. H. 'Milton Autographs Established', in *The Library*, 4th series, 13.2 (1932), 192–200

Catalogue of the Very Extensive and Well-Known Library . . . Formed by the late George Thorn-Drury (London: Sotheby's, 1931)

Cauchi, Simon. 'The 'Setting Foorth' of Harington's Ariosto', in *Studies in Bibliography* 36 (1983), 137–168

de Certeau, Michel. *The Practice of Everyday Life*, trans. by Steven Rendall (Berkeley: University of California Press, 1984)

Chapman, R. W. *Cancels* (London and New York: Constable & Co. / Richard R. Smith Inc., 1930)

Charles, Amy. 'Herbert and the Ferrars: Spiritual Edification', in *Like Season'd Timber: New Essays on George Herbert*, ed. Edmund Miller and Robert DiYanni (New York: Peter Lang, 1987), pp. 1–18

Chartier, Roger. *The Author's Hand and the Printer's Mind*, trans. by Lydia G. Cochrane (Cambridge, UK: Polity Press, 2014)

Cloud, Random. 'FIAT fLUX', in *Crisis in Editing: Texts of the English Renaissance*, ed. Randall M. Leod (New York: AMS, 1994), pp. 61–172

'Enter Reader,' in *The Editorial Gaze: Mediating Texts in Literature and the Arts*, ed. Paul Eggert and Margaret Sankey (New York, 1998), pp. 3–50

Connor, Francis X. *Literary Folios and Ideas of the Book in Early Modern England* (Basingstoke: Palgrave, 2014)

Considine, John. 'Cutting and Pasting Slips: Early Modern Compilation and Information Management', in Fleming, Juliet, William Sherman and Adam Smyth (eds). *The Journal of Medieval and Early Modern Studies* 45.3 (September 2015, special edition on 'Renaissance Collage: Towards a New History of Reading'), 487–504

Cormack, Bradin, and Carla Mazzio, *Book Use, Book Theory 1500–1700* (Chicago: University of Chicago Library, 2005)

Cressy, David. 'Book Burning in Tudor and Stuart England', in *The Sixteenth Century Journal* 36.2 (Summer 2005), 359–374

Cummings, Brian. 'Iconoclasm and Bibliophobia in the English Reformations, 1521–1558', in *Images, Idolatry, and Iconoclasm in Late Medieval England: Textuality and the Visual Image*, ed. Jeremy Dimmick, James Simpson and Nicholette Zeeman (Oxford: Oxford University Press, 2002), pp. 185–206

Dane, Joseph A. 'An Example of Netherlands Prototypography in the Huntington', in *Huntington Library Quarterly*, vol. 61, no. 3/4 (1998), 401–409

The Myth of Print Culture: Essays on Evidence, Textuality and Bibliographical Method (Toronto: University of Toronto Press, 2003)

Darbishire, Helen. 'Pen-and-Ink Corrections in Books of the Seventeenth Century', in *The Review of English Studies* 7.25 (January 1931), 72–73

Davis, Herbert. 'Note on a Cancel in *The Alchemist* 1612', in *The Library*, 5th series, 13.4 (1958), 278–280
Deng, Stephen. *Coinage and State Formation in Early Modern English Literature* (Basingstoke: Palgrave, 2011)
Derrida, Jacques. 'Structure, Sign, and Play in the Discourse of the Human Sciences', in *Writing and Difference* (1967; London: Routledge Classics, 2002), 351–370
  Of Grammatology, trans. by Gayatri Chakravorty Spivak (Baltimore: Johns Hopkins University Press, 1974, 2013)
Dietz, Feike. 'Gedrukte boeken, met de pen gelezen. Sporen van leesinterpretaties in de religieuze manuscriptcultuur', in *De Zeventiende Eeuw*, 2 (2010), 152–171
Dobranski, Stephen. *Readers and Authorship in Early Modern England* (Cambridge, UK: Cambridge University Press, 2005)
Donaldson, Ian. 'Jonson, Shakespeare, and the Destruction of the Book', in *Jonson's Magic Houses: Essays in Interpretation* (Oxford: Clarendon Press, 1997), pp. 198–216
Dover Wilson, J. 'The Missing Title of Thomas Lodge's Reply to Gosson's "School of Abuse"', in *The Modern Language Review* 3.2 (1908), 166–168
Duff, Edward Gordon. *Early Printed Books* (Cambridge, UK: Cambridge University Press, 2011)
Dutton, Richard. 'The Birth of the Author', in *Elizabethan Theater: Essays in Honor of S. Schoenbaum*, ed. R. B. Parker and S. P. Zitner (Newark and London: University of Delaware Press, 1996), 71–92
Dyck, Paul. '"So Rare A Use": Hands and Minds on the Gospels at Little Gidding', in *George Herbert Journal* 27 (2006), pp. 67–81
  '"A New Kind of Printing": Cutting and Pasting a Book for a King at Little Gidding', in *The Library*, 7th series, 9.3 (2008), 306–333
Eisenstein, Elizabeth L. *The Printing Revolution in Early Modern Europe* (Cambridge, UK: Cambridge University Press, 1983)
Elsky, Martin. 'George Herbert's Hieroglyphic Poems and the Materiality of Language: A New Approach to Renaissance Hieroglyphics', in *ELH* 50 (1983), 245–260
Erler, Mary C. 'Pasted-in Embellishments in English Manuscripts and Printed Books, c. 1480–1533', in *The Library*, 6th series, 14.3 (1992), 185–206
Erne, Lukas. *Shakespeare as Literary Dramatist* (Cambridge, UK: Cambridge University Press, 2003)
  Shakespeare and the Book Trade (Cambridge, UK: Cambridge University Press, 2013)
Felski, Rita. *The Limits of Critique* (Chicago: University of Chicago Press, 2015)
Finkelpearl, P. J. 'Davies, John (1564/5–1618)', in *Oxford Dictionary of National Biography* (Oxford: Oxford University Press, 2004; online edn, May 2006)
Fish, Stanley. *Self-Consuming Artifacts: The Experience of Seventeenth-Century Literature* (Berkeley: University of California Press, 1972)

Fitzmaurice, James. 'Margaret Cavendish on Her Own Writing: Evidence from Revision and Handmade Correction', in *Papers of the Bibliographical Society of America*, 85 (September 1991), 297–307
Fleming, Juliet. *Graffiti and the Writing Arts of Early Modern England* (London: Reaktion, 2001)
  'Afterword,' *Huntington Library Quarterly* 73 (2010), 543–552
  'Damask Papers', in *The Elizabethan Top Ten: Defining Print Popularity in Early Modern England*, ed. Andy Kesson and Emma Smith (Farnham: Ashgate, 2013), pp. 179–191
Fleming, Juliet, William Sherman and Adam Smyth (eds). *The Journal of Medieval and Early Modern Studies* 45.3 (September 2015, special edition on 'Renaissance Collage: Towards a New History of Reading')
Foot, Mirjam. *Studies in the History of Bookbinding* (Aldershot: Scholar Press, 1993)
Foxon, D. F. 'The Varieties of Early Proof: Cartwright's *Royal slave*, 1639, 1640', in *The Library* 5th series, 25.2 (1970), 151–154
Freud, Sigmund. *The Psychopathology of Everyday Life* (London: Penguin, 2002)
  The Uncanny, trans. by David McLintock (London: Penguin, 2003)
Fulton, Thomas. *Historical Milton: Manuscript, Print and Political Culture in Revolutionary England* (Amherst: University of Massachusetts Press, 2010)
Gadd, Ian. 'Barnes, Joseph (1549/50–1618)', in *Oxford Dictionary of National Biography* (Oxford: Oxford University Press, Oct 2011; online edn, Jan. 2012)
Gants, David. 'The 1616 Folio (F1): Textual Essay', in *Cambridge Edition of the Works of Ben Jonson Online*, http://universitypublishingonline.org/cambridge/benjonson/k/essays/F1_textual_essay
Garvey, Ellen Gruber. *Writing with Scissors: American Scrapbooks from the Civil War to the Harlem Renaissance* (Oxford: Oxford University Press, 2013)
Gaskell, Philip. *A New Introduction to Bibliography* (Oxford: Clarendon Press, 1972)
Gatch, Milton McC. 'Humfrey Wanley's Proposal to the Curators of the Bodleian Library on the Usefulness of Manuscript Fragments from Bindings', in *Bodleian Library Record* 11 (1982–5), 94–98
  'John Bagford as a Collector and Disseminator of Manuscript Fragments', in *The Library* 6th series, 7.2 (1985), 95–114
  '*Fragmenta Manuscripta* and *Varia* at Missouri and Cambridge', in *Transactions of the Cambridge Bibliographical Society* 9.5 (1990) 434–475
Gerrard, Brian. 'A new taxonomy of post-impression corrections', in *An Index of Civilisation: Studies of Printing and Publishing in Honour of Keith Maslen*, ed. R. Harvey, W. Kirsop and B. J. McMullin (Melbourne: Monash University, 1993), pp. 45–54
Gibson, Strickland. *Early Oxford Bindings* (Oxford: Oxford University Press, 1903)
  'Old Bindings as Literary Hunting-Grounds', in *The Academy* 1748 (4 November 1905), Illustrated Supplement, 1–4
Gordon, Andrew. *Writing Early Modern London* (Basingstoke: Palgrave, 2013)
Grafton, Anthony. *Bring Out Your Dead: The Past as Revelation* (Cambridge, MA: Harvard University Press, 2002)

The Culture of Correction in Renaissance Europe (London: British Library, 2011)

Gwara, Joseph J., and Mary Morse. 'A Birth Girdle Printed by Wynkyn de Worde', in *The Library*, 7th series, 13.1 (2012), 33–62

Hackel, Heidi Brayman. *Reading Material in Early Modern England: Print, Gender and Literacy* (Cambridge, UK: Cambridge University Press, 2005)

Hampton, Michael. *Unshelfmarked: Reconceiving the Artists' Book* (Uniform Books: London, 2015)

Harris, Jonathan Gil. *Untimely Matter in the Time of Shakespeare* (Philadelphia: University of Pennsylvania Press, 2009)

Henderson, George. 'Bible Illustration in the Age of Laud', in *Transactions of the Cambridge Bibliographical Society* 8 (1982), 173–204

Hessayon, Ariel. 'Incendiary texts: book burning in England, c.1640 – c.1660', in *Cromohs*, 12 (2007): 1–25, www.cromohs.unifi.it/12_2007/hessayon_incend texts.html

Hobson, Geoffrey. *Bindings in Cambridge Libraries* (Cambridge, UK: Cambridge University Press, 1929)

Jackson, Holbrook. *The Anatomy of Bibliomania* (Urbana and Chicago: The University of Illinois Press, 2001)

Jardine, Lisa. *Erasmus, Man of Letters: The Construction of Charisma in Print*, rev. edn (Princeton: Princeton University Press, 2015)

Jardine, Lisa, and Anthony Grafton. '"Studied for Action": How Gabriel Harvey Read His Livy', in *Past and Present* 129 (1990), 30–78

Jenkins, Harold. *The Life and Work of Henry Chettle* (London: Sidgwick & Jackson, 1934)

Johnston, G. B. 'Notes on Jonson's "Execration Upon Vulcan"', in *MLN* 46.3 (1931), 150–153

Jowett, John. 'Johannes Factotum: Henry Chettle and *Greene's Groatsworth of Wit*', in *The Papers of the Bibliographical Society of America* 87 (1993), 453–486

'Henry Chettle: "Your old Compositor"', in *Text* 15 (2003), 141–161

Kearney, James. *The Incarnate Text: Imagining the Book in Reformation England* (Philadelphia: University of Pennsylvania, 2009)

Ker, Neil F. *Fragments of Medieval Manuscripts Used as Pastedowns in Oxford Bindings with a Survey of Oxford Binding c. 1515–1620* (Oxford: Oxford Bibliographical Society, 2004 for 2000)

Ker, Neil, and David Pearson. *Oxford Bookbinding 1500–1640: Including a Supplement to Neil Ker's Fragments of Medieval Manuscripts Used as Pastedowns in Oxford Bindings* (Oxford: Oxford Bibliographical Society, 2000)

Kesson, Andy, and Emma Smith (eds). *The Elizabethan Top Ten: Defining Print Popularity in Early Modern England* (Farnham: Ashgate, 2013)

Kiséry, András, and Allison Deutermann. 'The Matter of Form: Book History, Formalist Criticism, and Francis Bacon's Aphorisms', in *The Book in History, The Book as History: New Intersections of the Material Text. Essays in Honor of*

David Scott Kastan, ed. Heidi Brayman, Jesse M. Lander and Zachary Lesser (New Haven and London: Yale University Press, 2016), pp. 29–63

Knight, Jeffrey Todd. *Bound to Read: Compilations, Collections, and the Making of Renaissance Literature* (Philadelphia: University of Pennsylvania Press, 2013)

Knowles, James. 'Hastings, Elizabeth, countess of Huntingdon (*bap.* 1587, *d.* 1633)', in *Oxford Dictionary of National Biography* (Oxford: Oxford University Press, 2004; online edn, May 2006)

Knuth, Rebecca. *Libricide: The Regime-Sponsored Destruction of Books and Libraries in the Twentieth Century* (Westport, CT: Praeger, 2003)

Latour, Brunto. *We Have Never Been Modern* (Cambridge, MA: Harvard University Press, 1993)

Lavin, Irving. 'Divine Inspiration in Caravaggio's Two St. Matthews', in *The Art Bulletin* 56.1 (March 1974), 59–81

Lerer, Seth. *Error and the Academic Self: The Scholarly Imagination, Medieval to Modern* (New York: Columbia University Press, 2002)

Lesser, Zachary. *Renaissance Drama and the Politics of Publication: Readings in the English Book Trade* (Cambridge, UK: Cambridge University Press, 2004)

  Hamlet after Q1: An Uncanny History of the Shakespearean Text (Philadelphia: University of Pennsylvania Press, 2014)

Lewalski, Barbara K. *The Life of John Milton: A Critical Biography* (Oxford: Blackwell, 2000)

Lock, Margaret. 'Reading the Endpapers: Five French Texts with Paper Bookbindings Using Printed Waste as Endpapers, and the Influence of Censorship on the Eighteenth-Century Book Trade', in *Papers of the Bibliographical Society of Canada* 48.2 (Autumn 2010), 257–298

Loewenstein, Joseph. 'Personal Material: Jonson and book burning', in *Re-presenting Ben Jonson: Text, History, Performance*, ed. Martin Butler (Basingstoke: Macmillan, 1999), 93–113

Loxley, James. 'My Gossip's Foot Voyage: A Recently Discovered Manuscript Sheds New Light on Ben Jonson's Walk to Edinburgh', in *Times Literary Supplement*, no. 5554, 11 September 2009, 13–15

Loxley, James, Anna Groundwater and Julie Sanders. *Ben Jonson's Walk to Scotland: An Annotated Edition of the 'Foot Voyage'* (Cambridge, UK: Cambridge University Press, 2015)

Madan, Falconer, G. M. R. Turbutt and Strickland Gibson. *The Original Bodleian Copy of the First Folio of Shakespeare* (Oxford: Clarendon Press, 1905)

Marotti, Arthur. *Manuscript, Print and English Renaissance Lyric* (Ithaca: Cornell University Press, 1995)

Masten, Jeffrey. 'Material Cavendish: Paper, Performance, "Social Virginity"', in *Modern Language Quarterly* 65.1 (2004), 49–68

May, Steven W., and Arthur F. Marotti. *Ink, Stink Bait, Revenge, and Queen Elizabeth: A Yorkshire Yeoman's Household Book* (Ithaca: Cornell University Press, 2014)

McGann, Jerome J. *The Textual Condition* (Princeton: Princeton University Press, 1991)

McKenzie, D. F. *Bibliography and the Sociology of Texts* (Cambridge, UK: Cambridge University Press, 1999)

'Typography and Meaning: The Case of William Congreve', in *Making Meaning: 'Printers of the Mind' and Other Essays*, ed. Peter D. McDonald and Michael F. Suarez, S.J. (Amherst: University of Massachusetts Press, 2002), pp. 198–236

McKitterick, David. *A History of Cambridge University Press* (Cambridge, UK: Cambridge University Press, 1992), 3 vols

Print, Manuscript and the Search for Order 1450–1830 (Cambridge, UK: Cambridge University Press, 2003)

McPherson, David. 'Ben Jonson's Library and Marginalia: An Annotated Catalogue', in *Studies in Philology*, vol. 71, no. 5, Texts and Studies (December 1974)

Milne, J. G. *The Early History of Corpus Christi College Oxford* (Oxford: Oxford University Press, 1946)

Morgan, Paul. 'Frances Wolfreston and "Hor Bouks": A Seventeenth-Century Woman Book-Collector', in *The Library*, 6th series, 12.1 (1989), 197–219

Morrison, Susan Signe. *The Literature of Waste* (Baskingstoke: Palgrave, 2015)

Myers, Anne M. 'Restoring "The Church-porch": George Herbert's Architectural Style', in *English Literary Renaissance*, 40 (2010), 427–457

Nevitt, Marcus. 'Ben Jonson and the Serial Publication of News', in *Media History* 11 (2005), 53–68

Nicholl, Charles. *A Cup of News: The Life of Thomas Nashe* (London: Routledge, 1984)

Nuttall, A. D. *A New Mimesis: Shakespeare and the Representation of Reality* (New Haven: Yale University Press, 2007)

Panayotova, Stella. 'Cuttings from an Unknown Copy of the *Magna Glossatura* in a Wycliffite Bible (British Library, Arundel MS. 104)', in *British Library Journal* 25 (1999), 85–100

Peacey, Jason. '"Printers to the University" 1584-1658', in *The History of Oxford University Press*, vol. I, ed. Ian Gadd (Oxford: Oxford University Press, 2013), 51–104

Peltz, Lucy. 'Facing the Text: The Amateur and Commercial Histories of Extra-Illustration, c. 1770-1840', in *Owners, Annotators and the Signs of Reading*, eds Robin Myers, Michael Harris and Giles Mandelbrote (New Castle, DE: Oak Knoll, 2005), 91–135

Pickering, Oliver. 'Two Pynson Editions of the Life of St Katherine of Alexandria', in *The Library* 9.1 (2008), 471–478

Pigman III, G. W. 'Versions of Imitation in the Renaissance', in *Renaissance Quarterly* 33.1 (Spring 1980), 1–32

Pollard, A. W. 'A Rough List of the Contents of the Bagford Collection', in *Transactions of the Bibliographical Society* 1st series, 7 (1902–4), 143–159

(ed.). *Bibliographical Essays by Robert Proctor* (London: Chiswick Press, 1905)

Poole, William. 'The Vices of Style', in *Renaissance Figures of Speech*, ed. Sylvia Adamson, Gavin Alexander and Katrin Ettenhuber (Cambridge, UK: Cambridge University Press, 2007), pp. 236–251
   'The Evolution of George Hakewill's *Apologie or Declaration of the Power and Providence of God*, 1627–1637: Academic Contexts, and Some New Angles from Manuscripts', in *The Electronic British Library Journal* (2010), article 10
   'John Reinolds, Dead Poet (1614), or, What Did Fellows Own When They Died in College?', in *New College Notes* 5 (2014), www.new.ox.ac.uk/new-college-notes
Prescott, Anne Lake. *Imagining Rabelais in Renaissance England* (New Haven: Yale University Press, 1998)
Price, Leah. 'Reading Matter', in *PMLA* 121.1, Special Topic: 'The History of the Book and the Idea of Literature' (January 2006), 9–16
   'From the History of a Book to "The History of the Book"', in *Representations* 108 (2009), 120–138
   How to Do Things with Books in Victorian Britain (Princeton: Princeton University Press, 2012)
Rajan, Balachandra. *Milton and the Climates of Reading: Essays*, ed. Elizabeth Sauer (Toronto: University of Toronto Press, 2006)
Ransome, David R. 'Ferrar, John (c. 1588–1657)', in *ODNB* (2004), www.oxforddnb.com./view/article/60958
Ransome, Joyce. 'Monotessaron: The Harmonies of Little Gidding,' in *The Seventeenth Century* 20 (2005), 22–52
   'George Herbert, Nicholas Ferrar, and the "Pious Works" of Little Gidding', in *George Herbert Journal*, 31 (2007–2008), 1–19
Rasmussen, Eric, and Anthony James West. *The Shakespeare First Folios: A Descriptive Catalogue* (Basingstoke: Palgrave, 2012)
Riggs, David. *Ben Jonson: A Life* (Cambridge, MA: Harvard University Press, 1989)
Ringler, Jr., W. A. 'Sir Philip Sidney: The Myth and the Man', in *Sir Philip Sidney: 1586 and the Creation of a Legend*, ed. Jan van Dorsten, Dominic Baker-Smith and Arthur Kinney (Leiden: E.J. Brill, 1986), pp. 3–15
Roberts, Dunstan. 'The Expurgation of Traditional Prayer Books (c. 1535–1600)', in *Reformation* 15 (2010), 23–49
Roberts, Helen I. 'St Augustine in "St. Jerome's Study": Carpaccio's Painting and Its Legendary Source', in *The Art Bulletin*, 41.4 (December 1959), 283–297
Roberts, R. J. 'John Dee's Corrections to His "Art of Navigation"', in *The Book Collector* 24 (1975), 70–75
Schmidt, Suzanne Karr. *Altered and Adorned: Using Renaissance Prints in Daily Life* (New Haven and London: Yale University Press, 2011)
Schullian, Dorothy. 'Here the Frailest Leaves', in *Papers of the Bibliographical Society of America*, vol. 47, no. 3 (1953), 201–217
Scott-Baumann, Elizabeth. *Forms of Engagement: Women, Poetry, and Culture 1640–1680* (Cambridge, UK: Cambridge University Press, 2013)
Scott-Warren, Jason. 'Reading Graffiti in the Early Modern Book', in *Huntington Library Quarterly* 73 (2010), 363–381

Scurr, Ruth. *John Aubrey: My Own Life* (London: Random House, 2015)
Shaddy, Robert A. 'Grangerizing: "One of the Unfortunate Stages of Bibliomania"', in *The Book Collector*, vol. 49, no. 4 (Winter 2000), 535–546
Sharpe, Kevin. *Sir Robert Cotton, 1586–1631: History and Politics in Early Modern England* (Oxford: Oxford University Press, 1979)
Shawcross, John T. 'Establishment of a Text of Milton's Poems Through a Study of *Lycidas*', in *Papers of the Bibliographical Society of America* 56 (1962), 317–331
Sheppard, L. A. 'Fragments from a Binding', in *The Library*, 4th series, 26.2-3 (1945), 172–175
Sherman, William H. *Used Books: Marking Readers in Renaissance England* (Philadelphia: University of Pennsylvania Press, 2007)
Sherman, William H., and Heather Wolfe. 'The Department of Hybrid Books: Thomas Milles between Manuscript and Print', in Juliet Fleming, William Sherman and Adam Smyth (eds), *The Journal of Medieval and Early Modern Studies* 45.3 (September 2015, special edition on 'Renaissance Collage: Towards a New History of Reading'), 457–486
Simpson, Percy. *Proof-Reading in the Sixteenth, Seventeenth and Eighteenth Centuries* (Oxford: Oxford University Press, 1935; second edn 1970)
Smith, Nigel. *Is Milton Better than Shakespeare?* (Cambridge, MA: Harvard University Press, 2008)
Smyth, Adam. '"Rend and teare in peeces": Textual Fragmentation in Seventeenth-Century England', in *The Seventeenth Century* 19 (2004), 36–52
  'Not to Be Read Without Shuddering', in *London Review of Books* 36.4 (20 February 2014), 31–32
Smyth, Adam, and Michelle O'Callaghan. 'Tavern and Library: Working with Ben Jonson', in *Authors at Work: the Creative Environment*, ed. Ceri Sullivan and Graeme Harper (Suffolk: Boydell and Brewer, 2009), 155–171
Spraggon, Julie. *Puritan Iconoclasm During the English Civil War* (Woodbridge: Boydell and Brewer, 2003)
Spufford, Margaret. *Small Books and Pleasant Histories: Popular Fiction and Its Readership in Seventeenth-Century England* (Cambridge, UK: Cambridge University Press, 1981)
Stallybrass, Peter. '"Little Jobs": Broadsides and the Printing Revolution', in *Agent of Change: Print Culture Studies After Elizabeth L. Eisenstein*, ed. Sabrina Alcorn Baron, Eric N. Lindquist and Eleanor F. Shevlin (Amherst: University of Massachusetts Press, 2007), pp. 315–341
Stallybrass, Peter, Roger Chartier, John Franklin Mowery and Heather Wolfe. 'Hamlet's Tables and the Technologies of Writing in Renaissance England', in *Shakespeare Quarterly* 55.4 (Winter 2004), 379–419
Steinberg, S. H. *Five Hundred Years of Printing* (London: Faber and Faber, 1959)
Stern, Tiffany. *Documents of Performance in Early Modern England* (Cambridge, UK: Cambridge University Press, 2009)
Stewart, Stanley. *The Enclosed Garden: The Tradition and the Image in Seventeenth-Century Poetry* (Madison: University of Wisconsin Press, 1966)

Straznicky, Marta. *Shakespeare's Stationers: Studies in Cultural Bibliography* (Philadelphia: University of Pennsylvania Press, 2012)
Stubbings, F. H. 'A Cambridge Pocket-Diary, 1587–92', in *Transactions of the Cambridge Bibliographical Society*, v (1971), 191–202
Summit, Jennifer. *Memory's Library: Medieval Books in Early Modern England* (Chicago and London: University of Chicago Press, 2008)
te Hesseon, Anke. 'News, Paper, Scissors: Clippings in the Sciences and Arts around 1920', in *Things That Talk: Object Lessons from Art and Science*, ed. Lorraine Daston (New York: Zone Books, 2008), pp. 297–327
Thomas, Keith. 'Diary', in *London Review of Books* 32.11 (10 June 2010), 36–37
Tillotson, G., and A. 'Pen-and-ink corrections in mid-seventeenth-century books', in *The Library*, 4th series, 14.1 (1933–4), 59–72
Timpanaro, Sebastiano. *The Freudian Slip: Psychoanalysis and Textual Criticism* (London: Verso, 1985)
Upper, Elizabeth. 'Red Frisket Sheets, ca. 1490–1700: The Earliest Artifacts of Color Printing in the West', in *Papers of the Bibliographical Society of America* 108:4 (2014), 477–522, 479
Vickers, Brian. *English Renaissance Literary Criticism* (Oxford: Clarendon Press, 2003)
Wakelin, Daniel. *Scribal Correction and Literary Craft: English Manuscripts 1375–1510* (Cambridge, UK: Cambridge University Press, 2014)
Ward, James. *Adventures in Stationery: A Journey Through Your Pencil Case* (London: Profile Books, 2014)
Watt, Tessa. *Cheap Print and Popular Piety, 1550–1640* (Cambridge, UK: Cambridge University Press, 1994)
Williams, Jr., Philip. 'The "Second Issue" of Shakespeare's *Troilus and Cressida*, 1609', in *Studies in Bibliography* 2 (1949–50), 25–33
Wolfe, Heather, and Georgina Ziegler. 'A newly uncovered presentation copy by Margaret Cavendish', in *The Collation* (26 January 2012), http://collation.folger.edu/2012/01/a-newly-uncovered-presentation-copy-by-margaret-cavendish
Woodward, D. H. 'The Manuscript Corrections and Printed Variants in the First Edition of *Gondibert* (1651)', in *The Library*, 5th series, 20.4 (1965), 298–309
Wood, E. R. 'Cancels and Corrections in *A discovery of errors*, 1622', in *The Library*, 5th series, 13.2 (1958), 124–127
Woudhuysen, Henry. 'Writing-Tables and Table-Books', in *The Electronic British Library Journal* (2004), article 3
Yu, Christopher. *Nothing to Admire: The Politics of Poetic Satire from Dryden to Merrill* (Oxford: Oxford University Press, 2003)
Zurcher, Andrew. 'Getting It Back to Front in 1590: Spenser's Dedications, Nashe's Insinuations, and Ralegh's Equivocations', in *Studies in the Literary Imagination* 38:2 (2005), 173–198.

Index

A manual for A justice of peace his Vade-mecum, 23
A sermon preached at the funeral of Mr. John Bigg, 23
Aeneid, 143
almanacs, 23, 24, 37, 56, 78
Ames, Joseph
  Typographical Antiquities, 147
Andrewes, Lancelot, 37
Aphorismes, or, Certaine Selected Points of the Doctrine of the Jesuits, 25
Apollonius of Perga, 162
Aristotle
  De natura animalium libri nouem, De partibus animalium libri quattuor, De generatione animalium libri quinq[ue], 148
  Nicomachean Ethics, 162
  Opera, 148
Asals, Heather, 47
Aubrey, John, 60, 70, 157, 175
  Life, 9, 137–139, 174
authorship, 60, 91
  and printing, 15, 92–95

Bacon, Francis
  Of the Advancement and Proficence of Learning, 145
  The historie of the raigne of King Henry the Seuenth, 162
Bagford, John, 147
Bahr, Arthur, 12
Baldwin, William, 15
  A Mirror for Magistrates, 102
  Marvelous History Entitled Beware the Cat, 102
Bale, John, 71, 144
Barnes, Joseph, 157–162
Basse, Roger, 160
Basse, William, 160
Bateman, Christopher, 147
Bayard, Pierre, 173
Beale, John, 101

Beinecke Rare Book & Manuscript Library, 150
Bennett, Kate, 137
Berthelet, Thomas, 152
Biblical Harmonies, 39, 47, *See* Gospel Harmonies
Bishops Ban, 58
Blades, William
  Life of Caxton, 146
Blair, Ann, 24, 99
Bloom, Harold, 112
Blount, Thomas, 93
Bodleian Library, 10, 18, 40, 61, 105, 147, 148, 151, 152, 155, 156, 160, 161, 163, 168, 178
Bodley, Thomas, 73, *See* Bodleian Library
Boethius
  De consolatione philosophiae, 154
Boffey, Julia, 25
Bolton, Claire, 87
book burning, 55–74
  and religion, 58
  as punishment, 59
book destruction, 8, 36, 57, 58, 175, *See* cutting; book burning
  as preservation, 68
  as productive, 71
  as recycling, 73
Book of Common Prayer, 24, 56, 58, 116, 119, 161
book, concept of the, 37, 47–49, 68
botches, 106
Bradshaw, Henry, 144
Breton, Nicholas, 67
bricolage. See Derrida Jacques
Briggs, Henry
  Tabulæ logarithmicæ, or Two tables of logarithms, 26
Brinsley, John
  Ludus Literarius: or, The Grammar Schoole, 73
British Library, 149, 167
broadside ballads, 56, 176

Brooke, Ralph
  A Catalogue and Succession of the Kings, Princes, Dukes, Marquesses, Earles, and Viscounts of this Realme of England, 117
Brown, Bill, 87
Bucer, Martin, 58
Buck, Thomas, 19
Bull, Digby
  A letter of a Protestant clergy-man to the reverend clergy of the Church of England, and to all other good Protestants, 119
Bullein, William
  Bulwarke of Defense, 114
Burton, Robert, 24, 73
  The Anatomy of Melancholy, 20

cancel pages. *See* errata
Canterbury Cathedral
  The Presentation in the Temple (stained glass window), 35
Cardinal Wolsey, 58
Carravagio
  Saint Matthew and the Angel, 51
  The Inspiration of St Matthew, 52
Cary, Lucius, 74
castigata. *See* errata
Cavendish, Margaret, 9, 116, 125–128, 175, 178
Cecil, William, Cecil, Lord Burghley, 167
censorship, 57, 59, 60
Cervantes, Miguel de
  Don Quixote, 67
Chambers, Robert
  Palestina, 81
Chapman and Hall, 13
Chapman, George, 66
  The Whole Works of Homer, Prince of Poets, 64
Chapman, R.W., 130, 132
Charles I, 31, 47, 51
Chartier, Roger, 14
Chester, John
  An Orthographie, 88
  The Practis of Preaching, 96
Chettle, Henry, 15, 91
  Kind-Harts Dreame, 102
China, 57
Cicero, 156, 161
Cleverdon, Douglas, 152
Clifford, Lady Anne, 49
Cloud, Random, 49
Collett, Anna and Mary, 18, 51
Collett, Susanna, 18
Comenius, Johann
  Orbis sensualium pictus, 74

commonplace book, 24, 26, 63, 115, 180, *See* commonplacing
commonplacing, 37
commonplacing. *See* commonplace book
confession coupée, 40
Congreve, William, 13
Constable, Henry
  Diana: The praises of his mistres, in certaine sweete sonnets, 123
Cooper, Thomas
  An admonition to the people of England: wherein are answered . . . the slaunderous untruethes, reprochfully vttered by Martin the libeller, 118
Cornwallis, William, 56
Corpus Christi College, Cambridge, 72
corrections. *See* errata
Coryate, Thomas
  Crudities Hastily gobbled up in five Moneths trauells, 94
Cotgrave, John, 73
Cotton, Robert, 72
Cowell, John
  The interpreter: or Booke containing the signification of words, 161
Cowley, Abraham, 20
Cressy, David, 59
Cummings, Brian, 57
cutting, 8, 17–54
  as textual production, 38, 51
  cut-and-paste, 34, 36, 38
  découpage, 179

Dada, 172
Dane, Joseph, 145
Danter, John, 101
Davenant, William
  Gondibert, 104, 178
Davies, John
  Microcosmos, 158–159
De literis et lingua Getarum sive Gothorum, 162
de Worde, Wynkyn, 182
découpage. *See* cutting
Dee, John
  General and Rare Memorials, 117
Dekker, Thomas
  Satiromastix, 69
  The Wonderfull Yeare, 22
Derrida, Jacques, 6
  bricolage, 6
  Of Grammatology, 113
Dettmer, Brian, 171
Deutermann, Allison, 13
Dickens, Charles, 11
  Pickwick Papers, 13
Dickinson, Emily, 11

Digges, Leonard, 55
Döblin, Alfred
   Berlin Alexanderplatz, 21
Donaldson, Ian, 60
Donne, John, 9, 12, 65, 112, 129
   Biathantos, 162
   Catalogus librorum aulicorum incomparabilium et non vendibilium, 64
   The Courtier's Library of Rare Books Not for Sale, 64
Douglas, Keith
   'Stars', 1
Drake, Richard
   A manual of private devotion, 37
Drummond, William, 72
Dryden, John, 10, 173, 175
   MacFlecknoe, 140–141
   The Hind and Panther, 85
Dudley, Robert, Earl of Leicester, 157
Dyck, Paul, 31

Edward VI, 25
Eisenstein, Elizabeth, 84
Eliot, T.S., 29
Elton, Edward
   God's Holy Mind, 59
endpapers, 56, 144
Englands Helicon, 121
Erasmus
   Colloquia familiaria, 168
Erler, Mary, 25
errata
   cancel pages, 78, 129–136
   cancels, 116, 117, 132
   castigata, 77, 80
   corrections, 104
   errata lists, 80–85, 103
   paste-in slips, 9, 78, 85, 117, 118, 122, 127
   tegens, 116
errata lists. *See* errata

Fabyan, Robert
   Great Chronicle of London, 25
   New Chronicles and Great Chronicle, 25
Fagius, Paul, 58
Ferne, John
   The Blazon of Gentrie: Deuided into Two Parts. The First Named The Glorie of Generositie. The Second, Lacyes Nobilitie, 121
Ferrar, John, 30
Ferrar, Nicholas, 8, 29
Fish, Stanley, 43
Fitzgeffrey, Henry
   Satyres and Satyricall Epigrams, 140
Flecknoe, Richard, 140

Fleming, Juliet, 20, 24, 114
Fletcher, Joseph, 129, 135
Florio, John, 93
Folger Library, 23, 56, 116, 126, 151
Foot, Miriam, 151
Foxe, John
   Actes and Monuments, 58
   Book of Martyrs, 68
Freud, Sigmund
   and error, 80
   The Psychopathology of Everyday Life, 79
   The Uncanny, 172
frisket, 2, 142, 145
Froiodmont, Libert, 155

Galen, 146
Gaskell, Philip, 2
Gerrard, Brian, 116, 130
Gibson, John, 40
Gibson, Sir John, 26
Gil, Alexander
   Logonomia Anglica, 89
Gillespie, Alexandra, 12
glue, 23, 24, 36, 114–115
Goodman, Godfrey
   The Fall of Man, 78, 91
Gospel Harmonies. *See* Biblical Harmonies
Gosson, Stephen
   Playes confuted in fiue actions: prouing that they are not to be suffred in a Christian common weale, 118
   Schoole of Abuse, 118
Grafton, Anthony, 105
Granger, James
   Bibliographical History of England, 21
   Grangerizing, 21
Grangerizing. *See* Granger, James
Greene, Robert
   The defence of conny catching, 112
Gruber Garvey, Ellen, 21

Hakewill, George
   Apologie of the Power and Prouidence of God in the Government of the World, 82
Hamilton Finlay, Ian
   'Errata of Ovid', 83
Harmonies. *See* Gospel Harmonies, Biblical Harmonies
Harris, Jonathan Gil, 153
Harvey, Gabriel, 102
Hasting, Elizabeth, Countess of Huntingdon, 129–130
Hayward, John
   The First Part of the Life and Raigne of King Henrie IIII, 58

Index

Heather Wolfe, 127
Heliand, 146
Henry VII, 36, 182
Henry VIII, 25, 152
Herbert, George, 8, 28, 29, 41, 175
  'Paradise', 17
  'Superliminare', 49
  'The Church Porch', 49
  'Time', 19
  'Altar', 49
  'Confession', 50
  'Easter wings', 46
  'Good Friday', 50
  'The Altar', 46
  'The Flower', 47
  'The Forerunners', 43
  'The H. Scriptures II', 31
  A Priest to the Temple, 31
  The Country Parson, 31
  The Temple, 19, 49, 51
Herrick, Robert, 9, 132
  Hesperides, 75–76
Heydon, John
  A new method of Rosie Crucian physic, 82
Heywood, Jasper
  Hercules Furens, 104
  Seconde Tragedie of Seneca entituled Thyestes, 103
  Troas, 103
Heywood, Thomas, 22, 141
  An Apologie for Actors, 87
Hickes, George
  The Case of Infant Baptism, 153
Hill, Geoffrey, 101
  Triumph of Love, 83
Hobson, Geoffrey, 50
Holy Communion, 47
Horace, 69, 140
  Ars Poetica, 63
  Satires, 154
Huntington Library, 22, 167

iconoclasm, 35
inventio, 41

Jacobus of Voragine, 53
Jaggard, William, 87, 151
James I, 58
Jardine, Lisa, 37, 105
Johnson, B.S.
  The Unfortunates, 172
Jonson, Ben, 26, 67, 69, 101, 174, 175
  'An Execration upon Vulcan', 9, 61
  'To my Bookseller', 140
  Alchemist, 131
  and printing, 92
  Eastward Ho, 61
  Every Man in His Humour, 67
  Sejanus His Fall, 59
  The Isle of Dogs, 61
  The Staple of News, 63
  The Works of Claudian, 61
  Volpone, 69
  Workes, 9, 55
Josephus, Flavius
  De antiquitate Judaica. De bello Judaico, 148
Josselin, Ralph, 58
Jude the Obscure, 36
Justinian
  Institutes, 153

Ker, Neil, 144, 146
Kiséry, András, 13
Knight, Jeffrey Todd, 179
Knox, John, 118
Koran, 67

Latour, Bruno, 153
Leland, John
  The Laborious Journey and Serche . . . for Englandes Antiquitees, 71
Lerer, Seth, 99
Lesser, Zachary, 132
Leutbrewer, Christophe, 40
Lévi-Strauss, Claude, 6
Lichfield, Richard
  The Trimming of Thomas Nashe, 22
Little Gidding, 8, 29, 44, 46, 50, 53, 69
Lively, Edward, 10, 164
  A true chronologie of the times of the Persian monarchie, and after to the destruction of Ierusalem by the Romanes, 10, 138, 164
Loewenstein, Joseph, 61
Lombard, Peter, 24
Loxley, James, 63
Ludham, John
  The Practis of Preaching, 95
Lusitanus, Zacutus, 155
Luther, Martin, 58

Machyn, Henry
  'Book of Remembrance', 58
Macray, W.D., 161
manuscript, 144
  as a source of printing error, 90
  cultures of, 12, 25, 176
  relationship to print, 80, 95, 109, 118
Marlowe, Christopher
  Doctor Faustus, 68
Marotti, Arthur, 168

Marprelate, Martin, 2, 118, 175
  The Protestatyon of Martin Marprelat, 102
Masten, Jeffery, 120
Mather, Samuel
  The figures or types of the Old Testament, 85
Matthew, gospel of, 47, 51, 76, 120, 162
McGann, Jerome, 10, 11, 12, 13, 170, 172
McKenzie, D.F., 11, 13, 14, 125, 169, 171, 175
McKitterick, David, 80, 89
Milles, Thomas
  The Misterie of Iniquity, 126
Milton, John, 9, 68, 105, 175
  'Lycidas', 161, 162
  Areopagitica, 68, 111–114
  Lycidas, 106–111
  Paradise Lost, 178
  Paradise Regain'd, 85
Montaigne, 106
More, Thomas, 99
Morley, Thomas, 123
Morris, William, 171
  The Story of the Glittering Plain, 11, 171
Morrison, Susan Signe, 172
Mowery, John Franklin, 14
Moxon, Joseph, 135
  Mechanick exercises on the whole art of printing, 88
Munday, Anthony, 15, 102
  A Discovery of Edmund Campion, 82

Nashe, Thomas, 15, 22, 101, 175
  Lenten Stuffe, 103
  The Unfortunate Traveller, 139

Obendorf, Johann
  The anatomyes of the true physition, and counterfeit mounte-banke, 82
Officina Biblica noviter adaperta, 151
Ovid, 96, 149

palimpsest, 114, 153
Papa, Guido
  Decisiones Parlamenti Delphinalis, 149
Parker, Matthew, Archbishop of Canterbury, 72
paste-in slips. *See* errata
Peacham, Henry
  Garden of Eloquence, 94
Penn, William, 93
  The Great Case of Liberty of Conscience Once More Briefly Debated and Defended, 85
Petrarchan, 43, 80, 101, 123, 124, 125
Phillips, Tom
  A Humument, 171, 173
Pollard, A.W., 150

Pond, Edward, 24
Prescott, Anne Lake, 65
Price, Daniel
  The Spring, 20
Price, Leah, 13, 56
  How to Do Things with Books in Victorian Britain, 11
printing error, 5, 9, 77, *See* errata
printing process, 3–5, 15
Proctor, Robert, 148, 149
  Index to the Early Printed Books in the British Museum: from the invention of printing to the year MD, 150
Protestantism, 37, 39, 40, 99, 118–119
Prynne, William
  Histro-Mastix, 59

Queen Elizabeth, 58
Quintilian
  Institutiones Oratoriae, 150

Rabelais
  Pantagruel, 65
Ralegh, Walter, 122
recycling, 10, 55–56
Reformation, 57
Reinolds, John, 127
Ridley, Thomas
  A vievv of the civile and ecclesiasticall law, 151
Riggs, David, 66
Roberts, Helen I., 37
Roth, Dieter, 171

Sabinus, 59
Safran Foer, Jonathan, 171
sammelband, 15, 72, 161, 176, 179
Scot, Reginald
  A perfite platforme of a hoppe garden, 92
Seneca, 104, 174
Shadwell, Thomas, 140
Shakespeare, William, 70
  A Comedy of Errors, 20
  and authorship, 92
  First Folio, 9, 55, 60, 69, 155, 156, 160, 162, 164, 168
  Hamlet, 15, 70
  Henry IV Part 2, 14, 177
  King Lear, 70, 151
  Macbeth, 70
  Richard II, 20
  Romeo and Juliet, 102
  Sonnets, 50
  Titus Andronicus, 101
  Troilus and Cressida, 131

Sharp, John
  Cursus theologicus, 145
Shelton, Thomas, 67
Sherman, William, 24, 127
Sidney, Philip, 10, 50, 121, 123, 141, 163, 169
  Astrophel and Stella, 10, 138, 164, 165, 172
Skelton, John
  The Tunnyng of Elynour Rummyng, 56
Smythe, Sir John
  Instructions, obseruations, and orders mylitarie Requisite, 91
Sommers, Thomas, 59
sonnet, 101, 123, 169
Sorocold, Thomas
  Supplications of Saints: A booke of prayers, 88
Spenser, Edmund, 9, 111, 113, 121, 160
  The Faerie Queene, 9, 72, 112, 178
Spufford, Margaret, 56
Stallybrass, Peter, 14, 95
Stanyhurst, Richard
  The First Fovre Bookes of Virgils Æneis, Translated into English Heroicall Verse, 143
Stewart, Stanley, 31
Strode, William, 16
Summit, Jennifer, 71
Symmons, Edward, 155

Taylor, John, 10, 22, 56, 91, 145, 175
  Sir Gregory Nonsence His Newes from no place, 99–101
  The praise of hemp-seed, 141–143
te Hesson, Anke, 21
tegens. *See* errata
'The Rime of the Ancient Mariner', 11
The Academy of Pleasure, 23
The Card of Courtship, 46
The Compleat Gardeners Practice, 18
The Countesse of Pembrokes Arcadia, 168
The cry and reuenge of blood, 178
The grounde of artes teaching the perfect vvorke and practise of arithmetike, 94
The Mysteries of Love and Eloquence, 80, 98
The Whole Booke of Psalmes, 154
Thorn-Drury, George, 162
Tomkins, Thomas
  Lingua: or, The combate of the tongue, and the fiue sences for superioritie, 73
Tonson, Jacob, 13, 141
Treasure Island, 36

Triplett, Robert
  Writing Tables with a Kalender for xxiii. Yeeres, 15
Turbeville, George
  The Booke of Faulconrie or Hauking, 89
Turbutt, Richard, 156, 168
Tusser, Thomas, 23
Tyndale, William, 58, 99

Upper, Elizabeth, 143
Urquhart, Sir Thomas
  Ekskybalauron: or, The discovery of a most exquisite jewel, 88

Vaughan, Henry, 10, 142, 175
Vincent, Augustine
  A Discovery of Errors in the first edition of the Catalogue of Nobility published by Raphe Brooke, York Herald, 117
Virgil
  Poetaster, 69

Waller, Edmund
  'Of a Tree Cut in Paper', 38
Walton, Izaak, 29
  Lives, 104
  The life of Mr. Rich. Hooker, 96
Wanley, Humfrey, 147, 150
Watson, Thomas
  The hekatompathia or Passionate centurie of loue, 101
Watts, John, 13
weasels, 134
White, Eric, 151
White, John, 23
Wilcox, Helen, 47
Wildgoose, William, 155–157
Wits Recreations. *See Recreations for Ingenious Head-peeces*
Wodenoth, Arthur, 30
Wolfe, Heather, 14
Wolfe, John, 102
Wolfreston, Frances, 96, 121
Wolsey, Thomas, 77
Wood, Anthony, 140
Wycliffe, John, 154

Zainer, Johann, 87
Zwingli, 152

Printed in the United States
By Bookmasters